Boys
ADRIFT

REVISED AND UPDATED EDITION

Boys
ADRIFT

The Five Factors Driving the Growing Epidemic of
Unmotivated Boys and Underachieving Young Men

Leonard Sax, MD, PhD

BASIC BOOKS
NEW YORK

Book design by Linda Mark

Boys adrift : five factors driving the growing epidemic of unmotivated
boys and underachieving young men / Leonard Sax.
    p. cm.
  Includes bibliographical references.
  ISBN-13: 978-0-465-07209-5
  ISBN-10: 0-465-07209-7
  1. Boys—Education. 2. Young men—Education. 3. Motivation in
education. 4. Sex differences in education. I. Title.
LC1390.S29 2007
371.823—dc22
2007012761

ISBN: 978-0-465-04082-7 (2016 paperback)
ISBN: 978-0-465-04081-0 (2016 e-book)

10 9 8 7 6 5 4 3 2

For my daughter,
Sarah
And for my wife,
Katie

Contents

A Word of Caution

In this book, I discuss psychiatric conditions such as Attention-Deficit Hyperactivity Disorder (ADHD), as well as some of the medications used to treat such conditions. The discussion here is intended to provide general guidance and background information. Nothing stated here should be taken as a guide to specific treatment of any individual. In particular, you should never change a medication or discontinue any medication without consulting your physician.

Leonard Sax, MD, PhD

I

The Riddle

I DIDN'T KNOW WHAT TO SAY.

I'd just finished speaking to a parents' group in Calgary, Alberta. The talk—about the subtleties of difference between how girls and boys learn, how they play, and how they are motivated—had gone well. I have been doing these talks for parents' groups, and for schools, since 2001. I'm pretty comfortable with the format.

The presentation is the easy part. The questions afterward are more difficult.

"Dr. Sax, my son Billy is very bright," one father said.[1] "We've had him tested, twice, and both times his overall IQ has been in the 130 range. But he just has no motivation to learn."

"What do you mean?" I asked.

"I mean that he doesn't do his homework and he won't study for tests. He doesn't seem to care whether he gets an A or a C or an F."

"How old is he?" I asked.

"Sixth grade."

"Umm. What does he like to do in his spare time?" I asked.

"Actually Billy loves to read. Science fiction mostly. He just refuses to read the books the school assigns. I don't know why he seems to hate school so much. It's a good school."

"Which school does he attend?" I asked.

Dad named a local private school that I knew was regarded as one of the best in the city. Class sizes at that school are small. The teachers are well trained and highly regarded.

Stall for time. "Have you spoken with anyone at the school?" I asked.

He nodded. "The school counselor thinks Billy might have ADD, but I just don't buy that. How could he have ADD? He's read Isaac Asimov's entire Foundation trilogy twice. He can quote whole passages from *The Lord of the Rings*; he's even memorized some of the poems in Elvish. That just doesn't sound to me like a boy who has ADD. Billy loves to read. He just doesn't like *school*."

I paused. I wanted to say that I couldn't give any specific advice without meeting Billy myself and doing my own evaluation, an evaluation that would probably take at least an hour. That was the truth—but I knew it would sound like a cop-out, since I was flying out early the next morning to return home. There would be no time to meet with Billy on this trip.

While I hesitated, a woman spoke up: "My son's in a similar predicament, but he's younger. Second grade. Outside of school my Jason is as sweet as an angel. But he's been sent to the principal's office several times now for hitting other kids. Each time, he says he was just playing. He's never actually hurt anybody, but the teachers say they have to refer any child who hits another child.

Referral to a specialist is mandatory after three episodes. So now they're saying that I have to have Jason evaluated."

I wanted to point out that Jason's predicament wasn't in any way similar to Billy's situation. Billy hasn't been hitting anybody, but he seems to lack the motivation to succeed at school. Jason's problems seem to be behavioral, not motivational. But I knew better than to say that.

I just didn't know what to say. So I turned the tables. I asked the parents a question of my own: "How many of you are in a similar situation: You have a son who's having problems with school, or some kind of issues with school, but it's not clear why?"

About half the parents raised their hands.

"I'd like to hear from you, then. What do you think is going on? Do you have any thoughts as to why your son is having a problem?"

"School has become too academic," one father said immediately. "Kindergarten isn't kindergarten anymore. My son, and my daughter last year, came home with homework their first week of kindergarten. Can you imagine assigning homework to kids in kindergarten? Five-year-old kids with an hour of homework to do. It's crazy. No wonder kids hate school."

Several parents nodded. *But why would that affect boys more than girls?* I wanted to ask. Another father said, "The schools have become feminized. The only man at my son's elementary school is the janitor. The teachers all want the students to sit still and be quiet. For some boys, that's not easy."

"It's not the teachers who are to blame," a woman said firmly. "It's the kids. I'm sorry, I don't mean to give offense, but kids today are lazy. The boys especially. They'd rather just sit at home and play video games. They wouldn't go to school at all if it were up to them. I know a boy across the street who doesn't do anything except play video games. He doesn't do homework. He doesn't help around the house. He doesn't play sports. It's just video games, video games, video games."

More nods.

"When I was their age, we had to walk to school, three miles each way, no matter the weather," an older man said. "We didn't have any of these school buses you see nowadays. We had to walk. Even in the snow. And I'll tell you one thing. When you've walked three miles in the snow to get to school, you make darn sure you learn something. You don't want that long walk to be for nothing. I think it motivates you. Nowadays the kids get chauffeured everywhere. No wonder they don't have any motivation. They don't have to work for anything."

No one made any reply. After a moment, a young woman said, "I read somewhere that plastic might have something to do with it."

"How do you mean?" I asked.

"Something about plastic. And hormones in beef. Toxins. They mess up children's brains. That's why so many boys are having problems."

That sounds a little far-fetched, I wanted to say. But I've learned that it's best to humor the people with the wackiest ideas—while still expressing courteous skepticism, so that the sane people won't think you've completely lost your marbles. "But why would those toxins affect boys differently from girls?" I asked politely. "Aren't girls and boys equally exposed?"

"I don't know. It just does," the woman said.

I have now spoken at more than 400 venues around the United States, Australia, Canada, England, Germany, Italy, Mexico, New

Zealand, Scotland, Spain, and Switzerland. Scenes similar to the one described above have been repeated many times. I've engaged in ongoing correspondence with parents and teachers who are struggling to encourage boys to work up to their potential. And of course I've seen many such boys as a family physician, first in Maryland and more recently in Pennsylvania.

I've heard any number of explanations for why so many boys are having trouble connecting with school. Some parents blame the school. In some cases, Mom believes it's because the boy's father walked out when her son was little, so he's never had a strong male role model. Others blame video games or "society" or plastics or Hollywood. One parent even blamed Hillary Clinton. Another blamed the American involvement in Iraq.

"What's the connection between Iraq and your son's problems in school?" I asked that parent.

"Our country is spending so much money on Iraq, when we ought to be spending money on the schools," she replied.

But how would spending more money on public schools help *your son?* I wondered. *Your son attends a private school.*

But I didn't ask that question. I wasn't interested in having an argument. I was interested in finding some answers.

I'm a family physician. For 18 years I lived and worked in the same suburb of Washington, DC, where we had more than 7,000 patients in our practice. I saw hundreds of families where the girls are the smart, driven ones, while their brothers are laid-back and unmotivated. The opposite pattern—with the boy being the intense, successful child while his sister is relaxed and unconcerned about her future—is rare. Since relocating to Pennsylvania, I have observed the same pattern in the Philadelphia suburbs.

It's not just Maryland or Pennsylvania, either. As you and I re-view what's known about this problem, we will see that the prob-lem of boys disengaging from school and from the American dream is widespread. It affects every variety of community: urban, suburban, and rural; white, black, Asian, and Hispanic; affluent, middle-income, and low-income.

The end result of this spreading malaise is becoming increas-ingly familiar. Emily (or Maria or Destiny) goes to college, she earns her degree, she gets a job. She has a life. Justin (or Carlos or Damian) may go to college for a year, or two, or six, and he may or may not get a degree, but he doesn't get as far. If he goes to college he's likely to have a great time there, in part because there are now roughly three girls at college for every two boys. At some universities, there are now two young women for every young man. But the young women at college are more likely to be study-ing while the young men are goofing off.[2] That boy just doesn't seem to have the drive that his sister has. I know one family where the daughter graduated in four years with a double major, in Chinese language and in international business. Immediately upon graduation she had multiple job offers in the $100,000 range. Her brother attended the same university and graduated in six years with a degree in anthropology. He's working part-time at Starbucks and living at home with his parents.

But here's what's really strange, and new, about this picture: that young man isn't bothered by his situation. His parents are. His girlfriend, if she hasn't left him yet, is at least having second thoughts about him. But he seems to be oblivious to their con-cerns as he surfs the Net on the computer his parents have pro-vided, or plays video games on the flat-screen television his parents bought for him.

But haven't boys always been that way?

During the question-and-answer section of another one of my talks focusing specifically on boys, one father objected: "Dr. Sax, I'm not hearing anything new here. Haven't boys always regarded school as a boring waste of time? Wasn't that pretty much Tom Sawyer's attitude? What's changed?"

He's got a point. There's a long tradition of iconic American boys who disdain school, from Tom Sawyer to Ferris Bueller. But while those boys weren't heavily invested in school, they were still highly motivated to succeed—on their own terms, pursuing their own schemes. Tom Sawyer is determined to outwit Injun Joe, to go exploring with Huck Finn, and to win the affection of Becky Thatcher. Ferris Bueller disdains school because he has other more important and engaging missions to accomplish in the real world—which for him is any world outside of school.

What's troubling about so many of the boys I see in the office, or the boys I hear about from parents and teachers, is that they don't have much passion for any real-world activity. Some of the boys are seriously engaged in video games, but as we'll see in chapter 3, the video games these boys play seldom connect with the real world—unless you want to race cars or fly combat aircraft. The boys I'm most concerned about don't disdain school because they have other real-world activities they care about more. They disdain school because they disdain everything unless they can manipulate it on a screen. Nothing in the real world really excites them.

Even more disturbing is the fact that so many of these boys seem to regard their laid-back, couldn't-care-less attitude as being somehow quintessentially male. "You need to care about what grade you get. It's important," one mother told her son.

"Girls care about getting good grades. Geeks care about grades. *Normal* guys do *not* care about grades," her 14-year-old son informed her in a matter-of-fact tone. That's just the way it is—for that boy. For many boys, not caring about anything has become the mark of true guydom. This attitude is something new, as we'll see in more detail beginning in the next chapter.

The hostility I'm seeing toward school among so many boys— no longer confined to black and Latino boys in low-income neighborhoods, but now including white boys in affluent suburbs—is also new. If you're my age or older, you can remember when the Beach Boys had a major hit with their song "Be True to Your School": *"Be true to your school / just like you would to your girl."* That song describes a boy who is proud to wear a sweater emblazoned with the name of the school, a boy who insists that allegiance to one's school should be on a par with the enthusiasm a boy has for his girlfriend. There is no trace of irony in the song. If you're my age or older, you remember Sam Cooke singing *"Don't know much about history . . . but maybe by being an A-student, baby / I could win your love for me,"* in his song "Wonderful World." That was a #1 hit song in the United States, five decades ago. It's hard to imagine any popular male vocalist singing such a line today, except as a joke. Can you imagine Akon or Eminem or Justin Bieber singing, without irony and in all seriousness, about wanting to earn an A in geometry, in order to impress a girl? I can't.

These changes may be insignificant by themselves, but they are symptomatic of something deeper. As we'll see in the next chapter, a growing proportion of boys are disengaging from school. More and more of them will tell you that school is a bore, a waste of time they endure each day until the final bell rings. As far as that boy is concerned, his real life—the life he cares about—only begins each day when the final bell rings, allowing him finally to leave school and do something he really cares about. "What he really cares about" may be playing video games, hanging out with his friends, or doing drugs and alcohol. It may be anything at all—except for school or anything connected with school.

"But you need to care about your schoolwork, or you won't get into a good college," his mom says.

"I hate school," her son answers. "It's like prison. I'm just doing my time till they let me out. Then I'm done. Why would I want to sign up for four more years?"

The university is where the gender gap in motivation really shows up. Men are the minority at college, and they have been for three decades now. Women are now more likely to attend college than their brothers are; and, once enrolled, women are now more likely than their brothers to earn a degree.[3] Among those pursuing advanced degrees in American universities, women now outnumber men by 59 percent to 41 percent.[4]

Over the past five decades, college campuses have undergone a sex change: they've changed from majority male to majority female. Here are the numbers for the male proportion of students enrolled in four-year colleges and universities in the United States, from 1970 to 2014:

1970: 57.7 percent of undergraduate students were male
1980: 47.7 percent were male
1990: 45.0 percent were male
2000: 43.9 percent were male
2010: 43.3 percent were male
2014: 43.1 percent were male[5]

Let's be clear. Successful young women are not the problem. Unsuccessful young men are the problem. The fact that more women are attending college and graduating from college is good news. Our question is: Why can't their brothers keep up with them? Why didn't we level out at 50 percent and stay there? Why are men now in the minority?

Colleges and universities now are scrambling to recruit qualified males. One mother told me that when it was time for her son to apply to college, she had some concerns. Her recollection of her own college experiences 30 years ago led her to worry that admission offices would discriminate against her son, because, after all, he is a white male. "Instead," she said in her e-mail to me, "I found that males today are on the receiving end of a kind of affirmative action for any boy who tests well. This gets them into college, but doesn't teach them how to cope with the bigger choices they will eventually have to face."

Young men attending four-year colleges and universities today are now significantly less likely than their female peers to earn high honors or to graduate. Forty years ago, the opposite was true: in that era, young men were more likely than young women to graduate.[6] Today, Justin is significantly less likely than his sister Emily to go to college, less likely to do well at college, less likely to graduate from college, and less likely to earn a graduate degree.[7] This is not primarily an issue of race or class. We're talking about brothers and sisters from the same family. They have the same parents, the same resources.

Not all boys have been infected by this weird new virus of apathy. Some are still as driven and intense as their sisters. They still want the same independence, financial and otherwise, for which we expect young people to strive. Because we still see some of these successful young men around us, it's easy to miss the reality that more young men than ever before are falling by the wayside on the road to the American dream. The end result: frantic parents wondering why their son can't, or won't, get a life. He's adrift, floating wherever the currents in the sea of his life may carry him—which may be no place at all.

Why does one young man succeed, while another young man from the same neighborhood—or even the same household—drifts along, unconcerned?

Where is he headed?

Is there anything you can do about it?

Those will be the central questions that you and I will explore together.

I HAVE BEEN RESEARCHING THIS ISSUE FOR THE PAST 15 YEARS. IN 2001, I wrote an academic paper on this topic for a journal published by the American Psychological Association.[8] In 2005, I published my first book, *Why Gender Matters*. That book was in part a progress report on my research on this question; I also addressed some of the ways in which American society has become toxic to *girls*, a topic that I explored at greater length in my third book, *Girls on the Edge*.

In addition to being a board-certified family physician, I have the advantage of being a PhD psychologist with a background in scholarly research. So I've been able to investigate what I'm seeing, quantitatively and systematically. I've talked with parents and with their sons in large cities like New York, Chicago, Toronto, and Los Angeles, as well as in smaller cities like Daytona Beach and San Antonio and Cleveland and Calgary and Memphis. I've visited schools in affluent suburbs like Chappaqua, New York, and Lake Forest, Illinois, and Potomac, Maryland, as well as in low-income neighborhoods in North Philadelphia and South Dallas and Columbus, Ohio; and also in diverse rural communities, such as Camden, Alabama; Yakutat, Alaska; and Devils Lake, North Dakota.

The first edition of this book was published in 2007. In the years since, I have heard hundreds of additional stories from parents, teachers, friends, and researchers who are concerned about this issue, as well as from the boys themselves. You will find some of those stories in these pages. And I have systematically updated and expanded the scholarly references.

I think I have figured out what's going on. I have identified five factors that are driving this phenomenon. I'm also finally in a position to share some strategies to improve the odds, to decrease the likelihood that your son will succumb to this epidemic of apathy—as well as practical tips for helping your son find his way back if he's already disengaged.

More Than Just School

This book begins with an evaluation of how the theory and practice of education have changed over the past 40 years, and how those changes have caused a growing proportion of boys to disengage from school. That's the first factor, which I take up in chapter 2. But this book is about much more than boys disengaging from school. In chapter 5, for example, we will consider evidence that some characteristics of modern life—toxins found in the food we eat and the water we drink—may have the net effect of emasculating boys. We will see that the average young man today has a sperm count much lower than what his grandfather had at the same age. Likewise, a young boy today has bones that are significantly more brittle than a boy of the same age 30 years ago. The explanations for the drop in sperm counts and for the decline in bone density are linked, as we will see. We will find that the mother who said something about "plastics" may not be so wacky, after all.

In chapter 3, we will explore in detail the controversy surrounding video games. We will try to understand why many boys are at risk of becoming addicted to video games, and why girls are at lower risk. I will share evidence-based guidelines to help you decide which video games are OK for your son to play, and which are not; and also, how much time is OK to spend playing video games, and how much is too much.

In chapter 4, I talk at length about the growing tendency to prescribe medications such as Adderall, Ritalin, Concerta, Metadate, Focalin, Vyvanse, and other stimulants to children, particularly boys. We will explore research suggesting that these medications may have adverse consequences that your doctor may not know about—adverse consequences not for cognitive function, but for motivation. The most serious cost of taking these medications may be a loss of drive.

In chapter 6, we will begin to calculate the consequences of these four factors—not only in terms of academic achievement, but also in outcomes that are harder to quantify: outcomes such as pursuing a real-world goal or sustaining a romantic relationship. Chapter 7 introduces a fifth factor, which I call "the revenge of the forsaken gods." In the closing chapter, chapter 8, I try to pull all five factors together and consider specific strategies that parents, educators, counselors, and others involved in the lives of boys and young men might usefully deploy. I also recommend some relevant strategies at various points throughout each chapter.

P LEASE DON'T MISUNDERSTAND ME. WHEN I TALK ABOUT THE problems I'm seeing in the boys whom I encounter in the office, I'm not saying that girls don't have problems. Girls have problems too. I know roughly as many parents who are concerned about their daughters as I know parents who are concerned about their sons. But the problems are different.

- "I told my 11-year-old daughter that under no circumstances would her father and I allow her to buy those low-rise jeans. I just couldn't believe that any store would even have such an item on sale for girls her age. But she said we were totally clueless. When her father and I held our ground, she started shouting 'You're ruining my life! Why do you hate me?!' How are we supposed to handle that?"
- "My Samantha has never had any problems making friends. But something happened at the start of 8th grade. She says that her best friend—or the girl she thought was her best friend— totally betrayed her and started saying things about her that aren't true. Cruel things. And now she's the odd girl out. I hear her crying at night into her pillow and it breaks my heart, it really does. But I don't know what to do. She doesn't want me to interfere."

- "Caitlyn is always talking about how she wants to be a size two or a size zero. She looks beautiful just the way she is: five feet four, 120 pounds, size four or size six depending on the label. Everybody says what a pretty girl she is. Still she's always talking about how fat she is and how she needs to lose weight. I'm worried she's at risk for an eating disorder."

These are serious problems, as difficult and as consequential as the boys' issues I will address throughout the book. I explored those problems at length in my third book, *Girls on the Edge*. But the problems the girls face are different from the boys'. The girls' problems are no less important. Just different.

This book is about boys—and the five factors driving their growing apathy and lack of motivation.

2

The First Factor

Changes at School

Your son is 5 years old. He's smart. He's friendly. But at your first conference with his kindergarten teacher, she tells you that your son is fidgety and has trouble sitting still. "He's not doing as well as he could be. And it's very distracting to the other children," she says. She suggests that you may want to have him tested for ADHD, Attention-Deficit Hyperactivity Disorder. "There was a boy in my class just like your son, last year," she says reassuringly. "He was bright, just like your son, but he had trouble doing what was expected of him. We all knew he could do better. He was such a smart boy. Just like your son. The pediatrician suggested Adderall. I'll tell you something, going on Adderall made a world of difference for that boy. It was like night and day. He became a really excellent student."

"But I don't think my son needs to be on medication," you say. "And—he's only 5 years old."

"Well, we could just put him in the play group," the teacher says. "Those are the kids who aren't ready to learn to read and write. Every child is different, we understand that. In the play group, he could run around, and jump up and down, without distracting the other children."

"The play group?" you say. "But I thought the play group was for slow learners. My son is not a slow learner."

"I agree," the teacher says. "That's why I think you should have him tested."

THREE DECADES AGO, A PASTOR NAMED ROBERT FULGHUM PUBLISHED a slim book of essays entitled *All I Really Need to Know I Learned in Kindergarten*. Pastor Fulghum's book stayed on the *New York Times* best-seller list for nearly two years, selling over 15 million copies. The title essay emphasized the key lesson he himself had learned in kindergarten, namely, to "live a balanced life," by which he meant that every day one should

Learn some and think some and draw and paint and sing and dance and play and work every day some.

Sounds nice.

Pastor Fulghum was drawing on recollections of his own kindergarten experience in 1942–1943 along with the kindergarten experiences of his four children in the 1960s and early 1970s. But even while the pastor's book was selling millions, celebrating the kindergarten he and his children had known, kindergarten was changing. Pastor Fulghum had written about how children in kindergarten actually could "draw and paint and sing and dance and play." But that's no longer true. Today, most kids don't "draw and paint and sing and dance and play" in kindergarten. They learn to read and write. As the superintendent of my own school district proudly wrote, the 21st-century kindergarten needs to be "rigorous" and "academic."[1] Traditional kindergarten activities such as finger painting and duck-duck-goose have been largely eliminated in most public schools and in many private schools across North America, replaced by a relentless focus on learning to read and write. "Kindergarten" isn't kindergarten anymore, as that parent in Calgary correctly observed in the opening of chapter 1. Kindergarten has become 1st grade. Today, the kindergarten curriculum at most North American schools, both public and private, looks very much like the 1st-grade curriculum in the 1970s. It's all about learning to read and write.

Why Is That a Problem?

In the past decade, a flood of research has demonstrated large sex differences in how the brains of girls and boys develop. There are big sex differences in how genes are expressed in a girl's brain compared with a boy's brain, even before birth.[2] Gray matter develops earlier and faster in girls, with the result that the gray matter in the brain of the average adolescent girl is about 2 years more mature than that of the same-age boy.[3] Increasing testosterone levels are associated with increased thickness of the visual cortex in boys' brains, but with decreased thickness of the visual cortex in girls' brains.[4] The different regions of the brain develop in a different sequence and tempo in girls compared with boys: in some regions of the brain, such as the parietal gray matter—the region of the brain most involved with integrating information from different sensory modalities—girls and boys develop along similar trajectories, but the pace of the girls' development is roughly 2 years ahead of the boys'. In other regions, such as temporal gray matter—the region of the brain most involved with spatial perception and object recognition—girls and boys develop along similar trajectories, but the pace of the boys' development is slightly faster than the girls'. In yet other regions, such as occipital gray matter—visual cortex—the trajectories of brain development are remarkably different, with no overlap between girls and boys. In this region of the brain, girls between 6 and 10 years of age show rapid development, while boys in the same age group do not. After 14 years of age, this area begins to diminish slightly in girls—the amount of brain tissue in this region actually shrinks in girls over 14—while in boys over 14 this area is growing at a rapid pace.[5]

It's important to remember that brain maturation is often associated with a pruning, or reduction, in the size of brain regions. The fact that one region of the brain is shrinking in teenage girls while the same region is growing in teenage boys doesn't mean that boys are smarter than girls, or that girls are smarter than boys. It just means that girls and boys are different. Differences do not imply an order of rank. Oranges and apples are different, but that doesn't mean oranges are better than apples. Ovaries and testicles are different, but that doesn't mean that ovaries are better than testicles.

Girls' brains not only mature differently from boys' brains. They may function differently as well. Based on their studies of magnetic resonance imaging (MRI) scans and brain connectivity in 949 individuals 8 to 22 years of age, researchers at the

University of Pennsylvania School of Medicine concluded that "male brains are structured to facilitate connectivity between perception and coordinated action, whereas female brains are designed to facilitate communication between analytical and intuitive processing modes."[6]

In view of the research demonstrating large and robust differences in the development of girls' brains compared with boys' brains, you might expect to find that teachers and school administrators are trying hard to accommodate girl/boy differences in learning. But if that's what you expect, you will be disappointed. Most teachers and most school administrators are not familiar with this research. Instead, many have been taught that gender is nothing more than a "social construct," no different from race or social class.

Imagine visiting a 21st-century kindergarten—which is to say, a kindergarten where children are expected to do what 1st-graders were expected to do 30 or 40 years ago, a kindergarten where children are expected to sit quietly and learn about digraphs and diphthongs. It's common to find that the teacher has divided the children into two groups. Over here are the kids who are ready to learn for the grind of phonics: mostly girls, with a few of the older boys. Over there, on the other side of the room, are the other kids: the kids whom the teacher has (correctly) recognized are not ready to sit for hours learning about digraphs and diphthongs. That group is mostly boys, with a few of the younger girls.

There's one thing 5-year-old girls and boys are equally good at: figuring out who's in the Dumb Group. By November, the kids in the Dumb Group are aware of their inferior status, and they don't like it.

"I hate school," Brett tells Mom.

"Why, honey?" Mom asks.

"I just hate it. It's stupid."

After further questioning and coaxing, Mom finally extracts what sounds like the real explanation. "That teacher doesn't like me. That teacher hates me," Brett tells Mom.

Mom gets on the job. She's going to figure out whether the teacher really doesn't like Brett, and if so, why. She gets permission to visit the kindergarten. But after two visits, she can't find a shred of evidence to support Brett's accusation. The teacher is friendly and encouraging to all the students. In fact she seems genuinely fond of Brett. "Brett isn't ready to sit still for hours at a stretch, so we don't ask him to," the teacher explains to Mom. "The reading drills can be awfully dull for some of the kids. We understand that. So we let Brett play in the play corner with the other boys."

The teacher's intentions are good. But most 5-year-olds are keenly aware of their status in the eyes of the grown-ups. A boy whom the teacher has relegated to the Play Group (a.k.a. the Dumb Group) may think the teacher doesn't like him. He's figured out that the smart kids are in the Accelerated Reading Group. He wasn't chosen to be in the elite group. He knows that the teacher was responsible for that choice. So he may decide that the teacher doesn't like him. That's unfair and illogical, but he is not a grown-up. He's a 5-year-old child, and 5-year-olds are often illogical. Many 5-year-olds, whether girls or boys, are likely to believe that the teacher likes the kids in the Smart Group better than she likes the kids in the Dumb Group.

Professor Deborah Stipek, dean of the school of education at Stanford University, has found that kids form opinions about school early. Imagine asking a boy who has just finished kindergarten two questions: "Do you like school? Do you think the teacher likes you?" I asked Brett those questions. He answered: "I don't like school. I hate school. And that teacher hates me."

Once that young boy has decided that the teacher doesn't like him, Stipek and others have found, he's likely to generalize that belief to other teachers and other classrooms.[7] He is likely to go to school next year with a negative attitude. When he's put in the Dumb Group again (which is almost inevitable, because the kids in the Smart Group now have a year's head start on him), he may decide that school just isn't for him. "School is dumb," he may say. And he means it. Return four years later and ask him the same questions. Brett is now 9 years old. Ask him: "Do you like school? Do you think the teacher likes you?" The answers you get are likely to be the same: "I hate school. And all the teachers hate me. Except for Mr. Kitzmiller, the gym teacher."

Critics of American education often point out, quite accurately, that the United States spends more money per pupil than most other developed countries and yet accomplishes less. On the international test most widely administered around the world, the United States ranks at #24 in reading, well below countries whose per-pupil spending on education is much lower, such as Estonia (#11), Poland (#10), and Finland (#6).[8] Finland, incidentally, consistently scores very well on these international rankings. What's special about public education in Finland? Here's one interesting feature: Children in Finland don't begin any formal schooling until they are 7 years old.[9] Nevertheless, by the time they're teenagers, Finnish children are beating American children by large margins on the same test. In the latest round of testing, for example, the average 15-year-old in Finland scored 519 in math; 15-year-old American students taking the same examination scored 481. In science, the average Finnish teenager scored 545, while the average American teenager scored 497. I am old enough to remember when American students led the world in science. Today, on the science exam, American students lag behind students in Australia, Austria, Belgium, Canada, the Czech Republic, Denmark, Estonia, Finland, France, Germany, Ireland, Japan, Latvia, Liechtenstein, the Netherlands, New Zealand, Poland, Singapore, Slovenia, South Korea, the United Kingdom, and Vietnam.[10]

But I think the case of Finland has special value for us. How could starting kids in school at age 7—two years later than we do—lead to superior performance when those children become teenagers? Simple. If kids start school two years later and are taught material when they are developmentally ready to learn, kids are less likely to hate school. If kids don't hate school, it's easier to get them to learn. If kids do hate school, as many American boys do, then the teacher is starting out at a major disadvantage before even stepping into the classroom.

Waiting until 7 years of age to begin the formal, "rigorous" reading and writing curriculum of today's kindergarten might reduce or ameliorate a significant fraction of the problems we see with boys and school. For many boys, there's a huge difference in readiness to learn between age 5 and age 7—just as there's a huge difference in readiness for a girl between 3 and 5.

Hold Him Back So He'll Get Ahead

Many parents have figured out that the accelerated pace of today's kindergarten is not a good match for their 5-year-old sons. Particularly in affluent neighborhoods, it's become common for parents to enroll their sons in kindergarten one year later than the district would normally enroll that child. In those neighborhoods, it's not unusual to find that half the boys, or more, are enrolled in kindergarten at age 6 rather than at age 5. In low-income neighborhoods—where many working parents simply can't afford to keep their children home another year—it's less common to find parents holding their kids back.[11] One reason that boys from low-income neighborhoods are doing so much worse in school than boys from more affluent neighborhoods, beginning early in elementary school, may be that the boys from more affluent neighborhoods are starting school at a later age, on average, than the boys from the poor neighborhoods.

Addressing the issue of holding kids back, Dana Haddad, director of admissions for an exclusive private elementary school in Manhattan, says, "It's become a huge epidemic." Most of the parents at Ms. Haddad's school are waiting a year to start their boys in kindergarten; some are even holding their girls back, just to be on the safe side. "The gift of a year, that's what I always say to my parents," says Betsy Newell, director of another prestigious private elementary school in Manhattan. "The gift of a year is the best gift you can give a child."[12]

Way back in 2001, I published a scholarly paper suggesting that simply starting boys in kindergarten one year later than girls might prevent many boys from deciding, very early, that school isn't for them.[13] Doing something earlier doesn't necessarily mean that you will do it any better. In fact, it may mean that you do it less well in the long run.

The pace of education has accelerated, but boys' brains don't grow any faster now than they did 30 years ago. That's one part of the first factor leading boys to disengage from school. But schools have changed in other ways as well. To understand these other changes, and how they might affect boys differently from girls, you need to understand how girls' motivation to succeed in school often differs from that of boys.

What Are Little Girls Made Of?

The first question we will try to answer is why the acceleration of the early elementary curriculum might affect boys differently from the way it affects most girls. As I have already suggested, Reason #1 may be that the brain develops at a faster tempo in girls compared with boys in most of the brain regions related to reading and writing. As a result, the average 5-year-old girl is better able to adapt to the academic character of 21st-century kindergarten than the average 5-year-old boy is. Even for girls, I don't think that the accelerated curriculum of today's kindergarten is best—I believe it leads ultimately to a narrowing of girls' educational horizons, as I explained in my book *Girls on the Edge*—but it is less likely to alienate them from school altogether. Many 5-year-old girls are able to do what the kindergarten teacher wants them to do. They can sit still. They can be quiet for ten whole minutes without interrupting or jumping up and down. They are more likely to possess the fine motor skills required to write the letters of the alphabet legibly and neatly.

Reason #2 has to do with the question of motivation, the huge blind spot of contemporary educational psychology—about which I'll have more to say in just a moment. Girls and boys differ in their desire to please the teacher. Most girls are at least somewhat motivated to please the teacher. Many boys don't share that motivation.

Let me share with you a story that a middle school teacher told me. It was the first day of school. She was greeting her homeroom students for the first time. "Good morning everybody. My name is Ms. Jackson," she said. "I'd like to welcome all of you to 8th grade. I'll be your homeroom teacher." She turned to write some information on the whiteboard at the front of the room.

While her back was turned, one of the boys, Jonathan, took the small stack of textbooks from his desk and dumped them on the linoleum floor, making a loud noise. Some of the boys laughed.

Ms. Jackson turned, startled. She saw the books scattered on the floor next to Jonathan's desk.

"Aw geez, I'm sorry, Ms. Jackson," Jonathan said with a snort. "I had no idea those books would make such a racket."

Three boys at the back of the room sniggered. Ms. Jackson wasn't sure what to say. But Emily, the girl sitting next to Jonathan, was not amused.

"Jonathan, you are such a dweeb," Emily said. "Can't you at least wait a day or two to show us what a total loser you are?"

When I heard this story, it brought to mind a study of chimpanzees living in the jungles of Tanzania. Three anthropologists—Elizabeth Lonsdorf, Lynn Eberly, and Anne Pusey—spent four years watching chimpanzees in their natural habitat in the wild. These particular chimpanzees have their own particular way of doing things. For example, they like to "fish" for termites. Adult chimps break a branch off a tree, cut the branch to the desired length, strip the leaves off the branch, stick the branch down into a termite mound, wait a minute or two, and then carefully pull the stick back out for a yummy snack of fresh termites.

Lonsdorf, Eberly, and Pusey found consistent sex differences in how young female and young male chimps learn from their elders—for example, in learning to "fish" for termites. Girl chimps pay close attention to the adult who is showing them the procedure. The girl chimp then does just what the adult demonstrated: she breaks off a branch, cuts it to the same length as the adult had done, strips the leaves as the adult had done, inserts it into the termite mound just as the adult did, and so forth. But the young males ignore the grown-ups; they prefer to run off and wrestle with other young male chimps, or to swing from trees. As a result, girl chimps master the art of "termite fishing" up to two years earlier than boy chimps.[14] The same researchers have now cataloged a variety of sex differences in the behaviors of boy chimps compared with girl chimps: boy chimps are more likely to wander off than girl chimps are, and more likely to run in front of their mothers while girl chimps remain with their mothers, for example.[15]

Are gender differences primarily hardwired—by which I mean that gender differences derive primarily from genetically programmed differences between girls and boys—or are they learned primarily from social cues? I still encounter people who insist that most of the sex differences we observe between girls and boys are not hardwired. Instead, they believe that girls and boys behave differently because our society expects them to. We expect boys to be noisy and to throw things, while we expect girls to behave like little ladies. Or so the story goes.

One reason I think it's useful to study our close primate relatives such as chimpanzees, gorillas, bonobos, and orangutans is because it gives us a more complete context in which to consider such questions. If sex differences were primarily socially constructed—if girls typically behave better than boys do because girls are taught to play with Barbies while boys are encouraged to play with lightsabers—then we wouldn't expect to see sex differences in the behavior of juvenile female chimpanzees compared with juvenile male chimpanzees. But sex differences in our primate cousins are just as pronounced, or more pronounced than, sex differences in our own species. Juvenile female chimps and juvenile male chimps behave in different ways, despite the fact that girl chimps have never played with Barbies and boy chimps have never played with toy guns.

In human females, the sex chromosomes are XX; in human males, they are XY. The same is true in chimpanzees. As a human male, I share many genes on my Y chromosome with a male chimpanzee that I do not share with any human female, because females—whether human or chimpanzee—do not have a Y chromosome. Recent work comparing the human genome with the chimpanzee genome suggests that I share 99.4 percent of my genes with a male chimpanzee—slightly more than I share with a human female.[16] That does not mean (I hope) that I am in general more like a male chimpanzee than I am like a female human. But in certain specific ways—for example, in the way I see, hear, and smell—I may actually have more in common with a male chimpanzee than I have with a human female.[17] And those areas of commonality are important to understand.

Profound sex differences are characteristics of most primate species. Young male monkeys, like young male humans, are significantly more likely to engage in aggressive rough-and-tumble play than are young females.[18] Likewise, young female primates are far more likely to babysit a younger sibling than a young male primate would be.[19] That's true in our species as well: girls are far more likely to babysit a younger sibling than their brothers are, and that difference is robust across cultures.[20]

Girls are more likely to affiliate with the adults. They are more likely to share common aims and values with the grown-ups. Boys and young men, on the other hand, are less likely to be sympathetic to adult aims and values and are more inclined than girls are to engage in delinquent behaviors such as smashing mailboxes, street racing, mooning police officers, and so forth. A boy who smashes mailboxes "just for the fun of it" will raise his status in the eyes of at least some other boys. A girl who smashes mailboxes just for the fun of it is unlikely to raise her status in the eyes of most of the other girls. Girls are more likely to listen to what the grown-ups are saying, and to do what the grown-ups ask, particularly if there are no boys around. (If boys are around, some girls become more likely to misbehave, perhaps because they perceive that disrespecting the adults will raise their status in the eyes of at least some of the boys.[21])

Girls are more likely to see a situation from the perspective of the grown-ups. In one study, investigators examined 20 cases where students were plotting a school shooting but the plan was detected and stopped before any violence occurred. In 18 of those 20 incidents, girls—not boys—alerted school officials or other adults to the plot. All the potential shooters were boys. "Boys feel like snitches if they tell on a friend, [while] girls [can] more openly seek out adults with their concerns," said James McGee, author of the study. Boys' first allegiance is to other boys. Girls are more likely to see the situation from the grown-ups' perspective.[22]

Some of these differences diminish as children grow up. Some don't. Women are more likely to take their medication the way the doctor prescribed; men are less likely to comply, and men are less likely to go to the doctor in the first place.[23] Most girls and most women are comfortable asking for directions if they get lost;

many boys, and many men, would rather wander for hours than stop and ask for directions.[24]

Why might it be the case that among most primates—including humans—juvenile females are more likely to affiliate with the grown-ups than the juvenile males are? Here's one possible explanation. Among primates generally, females are more likely to live near their parents after they are fully grown up, while the males are more likely to move away. In the great majority of primate species, "females reside in their natal groups for life, whereas males disperse around puberty and transfer to other groups," say primatologists Michael Pereira and Lynn Fairbanks.[25] There are some exceptions. Among the muriqui—also known as the woolly spider monkey—many young females leave the troop at puberty, while most of the young males stay with the troop into which they were born, for life. But the muriqui today are found only in a few isolated forest tracts along the Atlantic coast of southeastern Brazil. The latest estimate of the total number of living muriqui is fewer than 1,000 individuals.[26]

If you expect to live near Mom for the rest of your life, you might make more of an effort to get along with her. Most girls seem to grow up with a desire to get along with the grown-ups— and that's true not just for *human* females, but also for females from most primate species. Primate females appear to have some built-in tendency to try to please the grown-ups, to adapt to the grown-up culture. That's also true among humans, or so the evidence seems to show. Young girls are more likely than young boys are to pay attention to what the grown-ups say, to follow the rules, to care about what the grown-ups think. Likewise, researchers have found that little girls are significantly more likely than little boys to stay close to Mommy and to do what Mommy says.[27]

It's easy to see how these sex differences are relevant to education. Most girls will do the homework because the teacher asked them to. Boys are more likely to do the homework only if it interests them. If it bores them, or if they think it's "stupid," then they are more likely to ignore it. Girls are significantly more likely than boys to do the assigned homework in every subject.[28] Even the highest-achieving boys are significantly less likely to do the homework than comparably achieving girls.[29] Girls at every age get better grades in school than boys do, in every subject—not because girls are smarter, researchers have found, but because girls try harder.[30] Most girls would like to please the teacher, if possible. Many boys don't care as much about pleasing the teacher or about getting straight A's—and boys who do try to please the teacher and who do care about their grades may lower their status in the eyes of the other boys.[31] Girls are more likely to assess their work as their teachers do. Boys are less likely to care what the teacher thinks of their work. That divergence leads to an enduring paradox: at every age, girls do better in school, but are less satisfied with their achievements, compared with the boys.[32] Researchers at the University of Pennsylvania reported that girls' greater self-discipline and self-control—perhaps deriving from their greater motivation to please the teacher—appears to be a key distinguishing factor that has enabled girls to survive and thrive in the accelerated world of 21st-century education.[33]

The acceleration of the early elementary curriculum, with its emphasis on phonics and reading drills, by itself might well have created a minor gender crisis in education. But unfortunately this acceleration is not the only major change in education over the past 30 years. Education has changed in two other substantial ways that have exacerbated gender differences.

The Tree of the Knowledge of Good and Evil

In English, the verb *to know* can have two very different meanings, reflecting two different kinds of knowledge. Consider these two sentences:

I know Sarah.
I know pediatrics.

We English speakers use the same word, *know*, in both sentences. As a result, English speakers may not fully appreciate just how different these two meanings are. My knowledge of my daughter, Sarah, is very different from my knowledge of pediatrics. My knowledge of Sarah is experiential knowledge. I know that Sarah likes to jump in the waves at the beach, but she doesn't like roller coasters. I know that she likes broccoli and red beets, but she doesn't like peach pie.

In biblical Hebrew, the word *know* refers primarily to experiential learning. When we read that "Cain knew his wife," it meant that he had "carnal knowledge" of her: they had sexual intercourse. In English, we read about "the tree of the knowledge of good and evil," but the Hebrew might be better translated as "the tree of the *experience* of good and evil." Adam and Eve are forbidden to eat from that tree. They are forbidden the actual experience of evil.

Most European languages use two different words for these two kinds of knowledge. In French, "to know" in the sense of knowing a person is *connaître*; "to know" in the sense of knowing a subject in school is *savoir*. In Spanish, "to know" as in knowing a person is *conocer*; "to know" in the sense of book learning is *saber*. In

German, knowledge about a person or a place that you've actually experienced is *Kenntnis*, from *kennen*, "to know by experience"; knowledge learned from books is *Wissenschaft*, from *wissen*, "to know about something."

English	German	Spanish
I know Sarah.	*Ich **kenne** Sarah.*	***Conozco** a Sara.*
I know chemistry.	*Ich **weiss** um Chimie.*	*Sé química.*

There is a fundamental belief running through all European pedagogy that both *Wissenschaft* and *Kenntnis* are valuable, and that the two ways of knowing must be balanced.

My wife and I accompanied a class of Swiss 3rd-graders on a field trip through the Dolder forest, high above Zürich. The teacher divided the children into pairs. One child in each pair blindfolded the other. Then the blindfolded child was led to a tree, at least ten paces away, and was instructed to feel the tree with her hands, from the ground up; and also to smell it. (Some children even licked it.) Next the child was spun around and led away from the tree, at least ten paces in a different direction. Then the blindfold was removed and the child was asked: Which tree were you just feeling? The point was "*ohne Augen zu sehen*," the teacher told me: to see without your eyes.

Such an experience would be rare for American schoolchildren today. American students may occasionally go on field trips, but the trips are almost invariably didactic in tone. Pupils learn the difference, say, between an oak leaf and a maple leaf. It's all *Wissenschaft*. American education, today more than ever before, is characterized by a serious lack of understanding of, and respect for, *Kenntnis*. It's hard to overemphasize how much most Europeans value *Kenntnis*. When I smiled, perhaps somewhat patronizingly, at the Swiss children feeling and sniffing their trees, the teacher frowned at me. She insisted on blindfolding me herself and leading me to a tree, and having me touch it and smell it without being able to see it. Then she led me ten paces away from the tree, turned me around, removed the blindfold, and asked me: "Where is your tree?" I looked, and immediately recognized "my" tree from the dozens of others. It was an unfamiliar, exhilarating experience.

There is more than 60 years of research on the importance, for child development, of multisensory interaction with the real world. This work began with the investigations of the psychiatrist René Spitz into "hospitalism," the syndrome of stunted emotional and cognitive development that was seen in abandoned children raised in sterile and impersonal hospitals after World War II. This research demonstrated that children must have a rich, interactive sensory environment—touching, smelling, seeing, hearing the real world—in order for the child's brain and mind to develop properly.[34] Without such real-world experiences, the child's development will be impaired.

Kids need to experience the real world. Only in the past decade have developmental psychologists come to recognize that a curriculum that emphasizes *Wissenschaft* at the expense of *Kenntnis* may produce a syndrome analogous to the neglected children documented by Dr. Spitz. Richard Louv, author of *Last Child in the Woods*, has coined the term "nature-deficit disorder" to refer to the constellation of symptoms seen in a child whose life has been spent indoors.[35] You can easily find high school students in America today who can tell you about the importance of the environment, the carbon cycle and the nitrogen cycle, and so on, but they've never spent a night outdoors. They have plenty of *Wissen-schaft* but not a trace of *Kenntnis*.

For boys, in particular, emphasizing *Wissenschaft* while ignoring *Kenntnis* may seriously impair development—not cognitive development, but the development of a lively and passionate curiosity. "Nature is about smelling, hearing, tasting," Louv reminds us.[36] The end result of a childhood with more time spent in front of computer screens than outdoors is what Louv calls "cultural autism." Defining it, he writes: "The symptoms? Tunneled senses, and feelings of isolation and containment [and] a wired, know-it-all state of mind. That which cannot be Googled does not count."[37]

Boys who have been deprived of time outdoors, who have spent more time interacting with screens rather than with the real world, sometimes have trouble grasping concepts that seem simple to us. Louv quotes Frank Wilson, professor of neurology at Stanford, who says that parents have been deceived about the value of computer-based experience for their children. Dr. Wilson says that medical school instructors are having more difficulty teaching medical students how the heart works as a pump,

> because these students have so little real-world experience. They've never siphoned anything, never fixed a car, never worked on a fuel pump, may not even have hooked up a garden hose. For a whole generation of kids, direct experiences in the backyard, in the tool shed, in the fields and woods, has been replaced by indirect learning, through [computers]. These young people are smart, they grew up with computers, they were supposed to be superior—but now we know that something's missing.[38]

Kenntnis and *Wissenschaft* are fundamentally different kinds of knowledge. Each is important. Let's go back to when my daughter, Sarah, was a baby. Let's suppose she is crying. Let's suppose further that a world-renowned expert on infant and child development, perhaps Dr. T. Berry Brazelton himself, has just walked into the room. If I handed Sarah to Dr. Brazelton, how effective would he be in calming her down? Probably not very effective. He wouldn't know how Sarah likes to be rocked or bounced. All his knowledge about child development counts for nothing if he doesn't have some *Kenntnis* to go with his *Wissenschaft*. That principle generally holds true in the real world, I have found, at least as far as the practice of medicine and of psychology is concerned. Book learning is essential. But without *Kenntnis* you'll go far astray.

Louv provides a compendium of research demonstrating that when there is a profound imbalance in a child's early experiences—when nature has been replaced by computer screens and fancy indoor toys—the result is an increased risk for ADHD. For example, Louv cites a Swedish study in which researchers compared children in two different day-care facilities. One facility was surrounded by tall buildings, with a brick pathway. The other was set in an orchard surrounded by woods and was adjacent to an overgrown garden; at this facility, children were encouraged to play outdoors in all kinds of weather. The researchers found that "children in the 'green' day care had better motor coordination and more ability to concentrate."[39] Similarly, researchers at the University of Illinois have found that putting children in an outdoor environment, where they can actually put their hands in the dirt and feel and smell real stuff, as opposed to interacting with sophisticated computer simulations, is helpful in treating ADHD.[40] Ironically, the outdoor alternative is cheaper than the program with the fancy computers.

Boys are at least twice as likely to be treated for ADHD compared with girls, and the rates of diagnosis of ADHD for both girls and boys have soared over the past three decades.[41] One wonders to what extent the shift from *Kenntnis* to *Wissenschaft* may have contributed to the explosion in the numbers of children being treated for ADHD.

The mental-health benefit of getting your hands dirty is not a new insight. As Louv observes, Dr. Benjamin Rush, one of the men who signed the Declaration of Independence, declared more than 200 years ago that "digging in the soil has a curative effect on the mentally ill."[42]

We have forgotten what our grandparents knew: all children need a balance of *Wissenschaft* and *Kenntnis*, a balance between sitting and standing, a balance between classroom work and field trips. That's true for girls as well as for boys. But if girls are deprived of that balance, if girls are saddled with a curriculum like ours today, all *Wissenschaft* and no *Kenntnis*, they will still do the homework—because for most girls, as we discussed a moment ago, pleasing the teacher is a significant reward for its own sake. Not so for most boys. If boys are deprived of that balance between *Wissenschaft* and *Kenntnis*, they may simply disengage from school. If you ask a boy to read about the life cycle of a tadpole metamorphosing into a frog, but that boy has never touched a frog, never had the experience of jumping around in a pond in his bare feet chasing after a tadpole, he may not see the point. The shift in the curriculum away from *Kenntnis* toward *Wissenschaft* has had the unintended consequence of diminishing the motivation of boys to study what they're asked to learn.

How could such a change happen? How could the intelligent, well-educated people who write school curricula push the school format into such an unhealthy imbalance?

The answer is simple: computers.

How Is a Child Different from a Programmable Computer?

Imagine a really good robot, the best robot money could buy, with the best possible "brain" and "eyes" and "ears." How would a human being differ from that robot?

Or to put the question another way: Will we someday—someday soon, perhaps—have robots that are able to simulate humans—simulate human behavior, maybe even feel emotions?

The entertainment industry offers us a continual diet of movies like *Ex Machina* and *Chappie* and *Bicentennial Man* that portray robots (always played by human actors) that are indistinguishable from humans.

It's just a matter of time before reality catches up with science fiction, right?

Maybe not. Like the search for peace in the Middle East, the goal that we were once assured was nearly within grasp keeps receding further into the distance. Today, the idea of a fully mechanical device that can actually experience human emotions—and not merely simulate such an experience—seems more distant than it did 30 years ago.

I enrolled in the PhD program in psychology at the University of Pennsylvania in 1980. The period from the late 1970s through

the late 1990s was the era when cognitive psychology ruled supreme. Cognitive psychology is that branch of psychology that
focuses on how we process information.[43] And the University of
Pennsylvania was a haven for true believers in cognitive psychology. For two decades, roughly 1977 through 1997, cognitive psychologists were optimistic that their approach was the best way
to understand human learning, development, and behavior.

Throughout that period, cognitive psychologists insisted that
everything we do, everything we *are*, can be represented formally
as a computational process, and therefore could theoretically be
transposed to a computer. Humans are just complex computers—
or so the story went. The mind itself is a sort of computer program
running on a very sophisticated computer made of neurons instead of microchips.

This way of thinking about the human mind, and human
learning, continues to be influential among educators. If humans are sophisticated computers, and learning is in some way
equivalent to programming that computer, then teachers are in
some sense merely computer programmers. If we give teachers
the correct set of instructions, or programs, then all we should
need to do is flip the "on" switch, and children should learn, in-
fallibly and efficiently. The 1990s saw the widespread adoption
of programs such as Direct Instruction, in which teachers were
expected essentially to read from a script for an entire class, with
students answering questions in unison and by rote. If the script
is written correctly, and the teachers do as they are told, then
good results are inevitable.

Foolproof.

Failsafe.

. . . provided only that children are pretty much the same as programmable computers.

Which they aren't.

It turns out that a great deal was missing from the cognitivist perspective. This is not the place for a thorough critique of the arid cognitivism of the 1980s and 1990s. But for our purposes the most obvious and key deficiency of the cognitivist point of view was its failure to grasp the importance of motivation and emotion.

Type an address in your Web browser and hit "Enter." If your computer is functioning properly, it won't talk back. It will do what you tell it to do. Your computer won't say, "I don't feel like it," or "Why go there?" or "How about if we go outside and play instead?"

Computers don't have to be motivated to do what you tell them to do.

But children do.

The colossal error of 1990s' cognition-based educational strategies—many of which are still with us today—is that those strategies ignore the crucial question: What *motivates* kids to learn?

The first thing that happens when you ask kids to do stuff they have no interest in doing is: they stop paying attention. In 1979, researchers estimated that only about 1.2 percent of American kids—12 out of 1,000—had the condition we now call ADHD, and which was then known as "hyperkinetic reaction of childhood."[44] But according to recent data from the Centers for Disease Control and Prevention, 110 kids out of every 1,000 have been diagnosed with ADHD. That's an increase by nearly a factor of ten, from 12 per 1,000 to 110 per 1,000.[45]

As we'll see in chapter 4, many kids who are being diagnosed with ADD/ADHD today are misdiagnosed. They're not paying attention, true, but their deficit of attention isn't due to ADHD: it's due to a lack of motivation in the classroom. That's not ADHD. Those boys don't need drugs. What they need, first, is a curriculum that is developmentally appropriate; and second, teachers who know how to teach boys. We'll return to these points in chapter 4.

The second thing that happens when you ask kids to do stuff they have no interest in doing is they get annoyed. They get irritable. They withdraw. "I hate school. It's stupid." Anything associated with school becomes uncool. Reading a book becomes uncool. Caring about school becomes uncool. Being interested in learning becomes uncool.

Computers don't have to care about frogs or be interested in frogs to learn about frogs. But children do. If children are not motivated to learn, they may stop paying attention. That's especially true for boys, for reasons we discussed earlier in this chapter. Computers are all about *Wissenschaft*. They don't need *Kenntnis*. But real children do—especially boys. The lack of respect for *Kenntnis* over the past three decades is an important part of the answer to the question, "What's behind the massive disengagement of so many boys from school?"

Good News: The Boys' Crisis Is a Myth!

In 2006, a nonprofit group called Education Sector released a study that proved, according to front-page coverage in the *Washington Post*, "that widespread reports of US boys being in crisis are greatly overstated and that young males in school are in many ways doing better than ever. [T]he pessimism about young males seems to derive from inadequate research, sloppy analysis and discomfort with the fact that although the average boy is doing better, the average girl has gotten ahead of him."[46] *New York Times* columnist Judith Warner, in a column entitled "What Boy Crisis?," wrote that the study confirmed that the "boys' crisis" is a myth, after all. The facts, wrote Warner—echoing the *Washington Post*—are that boys are "doing better than ever on most measures of academic performance," with the possible exception of black and Hispanic boys from low-income households.[47] Seven years later, Warner repeated her claim in a column for *Time* magazine, asserting that "the real 'crisis' in America is one of class (income and education level), not gender."[48] *Time* also published a cover story entitled "The Myth About Boys," which asserted that "young men are better off, socially and academically, than ever."[49]

Is it true? Is the boys' crisis really a myth? Does social class matter more than gender?

It depends. It depends especially on which measure of achievement you choose to measure. If you focus solely on high school graduation rates, then social class does appear to be more important than gender. In low-income neighborhoods, graduation rates are not good, and boys are significantly more likely to drop out than girls are.[50] In affluent neighborhoods, almost all the kids graduate from high school, boys as well as girls. So if high school graduation rates are the only outcome you measure, then it's easy to conclude that gender issues are a concern only in low-income neighborhoods.

But if you dig just a little deeper, the gender gap is clearly visible in every community, including affluent white neighborhoods. For example: among 12th-grade white students with college-educated parents, the gender gap has become dramatic: 1 in 4 white boys with college-educated parents today cannot read at a basic level of proficiency, compared with only 1 in 16 white girls.[51]

The National Assessment of Educational Progress (NAEP) is a federal program established back in 1969 to measure academic achievement in all 50 states. The US Department of Education refers to the NAEP as "Our Nation's Report Card," because it is the only assessment administered in every state across different grade levels (grades 4, 8, and 12) to kids from every background. The results can be broken down by race, sex, and eligibility for free school lunches. If you are from a low-income household, then you are eligible for free school lunches. If your family is more affluent, then you are not eligible. The test covers many subject areas; for our purposes, we will look at the Writing exam, and at the most recent scores available.

Let's compare 12th-grade white girls who are eligible for free school lunches with 12th-grade white girls who are not eligible. White girls, not eligible for free school lunches, earn an average score of 168. White girls who are eligible for free school lunches earn an average score of 153. That's a difference of **15 points**, which is equivalent to about 1½ grade levels.[52] It's a big difference.

Why do white girls who are eligible for free school lunches do so much worse, on average, than white girls who are not eligible? White girls who are not eligible come from more affluent households, by definition. They are more likely to have college-educated parents. They are likely to have more books and magazines in the house. They are more likely to have two parents in the household, and therefore to have one parent available to help them with homework, etc. (My mom was a single mom, and she was rarely available to help me or my brothers with homework, because she had to work.) Similar differences in NAEP test scores are seen for other races and ethnicities:

> African American girls, not eligible for free school lunches: 147
> African American girls, eligible for free school lunches: 131
> 147−131 = **16 points**
> Latina girls, not eligible for free school lunches: 149
> Latina girls, eligible for free school lunches: 134
> 149−134 = **15 points**

It's a robust finding. Regardless of race or ethnicity, if you come from a low-income household your score on the Writing exam drops 15 to 17 points, compared to a student of the same race/ethnicity who comes from a more affluent household.

Now let's go back to that white girl, not eligible for free school lunches, and compare her to a white boy not eligible for free school lunches:

> White girl, not eligible for free school lunches: 168
> White boy, not eligible for free school lunches: 153
> 168−153 = **15 points**

The gap separating a white girl not eligible for free school lunches from a white boy not eligible for free school lunches is exactly the same (15 points) as the gap separating a low-income white girl from a more affluent white girl. But when we compare a white girl not eligible for free school lunches with a white boy not eligible for free school lunches, we are literally comparing sisters and brothers from the same household, from the same demographic. And I have encountered precisely this dynamic in venues all across the United States. At one parents' presentation, a husband and wife spoke to me afterward and told me that their daughter works hard, does the homework, earns good grades, and *cares* about earning good grades. But their son is a goofball who's more concerned about getting to the next level in his video game than he is about getting an A rather than a B in Spanish. Same household. Same parents. Same resources. Yet the gap in academic achievement between that brother and sister is large.

We see a similar gap among African Americans and Hispanics:

African American girl, not eligible for free school lunches: 147
African American boy, not eligible for free school lunches: 133
147–133 = **14 points**
Latina girl, not eligible for free school lunches: 149
Latino boy, not eligible for free school lunches: 136
149–136 = **13 points**

Looking nationwide, there are three major demographic disadvantages in American education:

- **Race/ethnicity:** being African American or Hispanic, rather than white or Asian, drops your NAEP score by roughly 20 points
- **Low household income:** being eligible for free school lunches drops your NAEP score by roughly 15 points
- **Gender:** being a boy, rather than a girl, drops your NAEP score by roughly 15 points

In the United States, we devote substantial resources and research to trying to remediate and ameliorate the effects of race/

ethnicity and low household income, as we should. Being African American or Hispanic should not pose a lasting handicap in the classroom. Coming from a low-income household should not pose a lasting handicap in the classroom. It is right and proper that we seek to understand exactly why race/ethnicity and low income do constitute a handicap. It is altogether fitting that we should seek to improve the prospects for students of color and students from low-income households.

But there is no similar effort to understand why being a boy, rather than a girl, constitutes a handicap in the classroom comparable to coming from a low-income household. I don't think that's fair.

Don't hold your breath waiting for the federal government, or any other major institution, to launch a serious program trying to understand why boys—regardless of race, ethnicity, or social class—do less well compared with girls from the same demographic. You and I will have to do this work ourselves.

Here's one thing I have learned: *motivation* is key to understanding the gender gap in academic achievement. There's growing evidence that the intensive reading drills that now characterize early elementary education may actually lead many students to disengage, particularly boys. What's important, as neurologist Judy Willis has observed, is "for students not only to learn the mechanics of reading, but also to develop a love of reading." She cautions against any "approach that puts phonics first at the expense of intrinsic appeal and significance to the young reader."[53]

In order for kids to understand many of the topics we expect them to grasp, they have to be reading a wide range of material. Kids need to be reading in their spare time. Kids need to read for fun.

Boys used to read for fun. Mark Bauerlein, former director of research for the National Endowment for the Arts, and his colleague Sandra Stotsky published an important article on what teenagers do with their spare time. The National Endowment for the Arts surveyed a demographically representative sample of teenagers around the United States for 25 years, from 1980 through 2004: rich and poor kids; urban, suburban, and rural kids; white, black, Asian, and Hispanic kids. Bauerlein and Stotsky found that girls have always been more likely to read for fun than boys. But that gender gap widened dramatically between 1980 and 2004. It has grown so wide that it has now become "a marker of gender identity," these authors found. "Girls read; boys don't."[54]

The gender gap did not widen because girls are reading more; they're not. In fact, girls are slightly less likely to read in their spare time today than they were in 1980. But roughly nine out of ten boys have stopped reading altogether. Why?

At least one part of the answer, I think, is that changes in education over the past three decades have created a negative attitude toward education among many boys. Boys are less likely to read today simply because *they don't want to read*. And that change in motivation is, at least in part, a consequence of the gender-blind changes in education over the past 30 years.

So far, I've identified two ways in which education has changed in the past 30 years to make it likely that boys will disengage from school more so than girls:

1. the acceleration of the early elementary curriculum, and
2. the shift from *Kenntnis* to *Wissenschaft*

We turn now to one other important change.

"How Would You Feel If You Were Piggy?"— and Other Questions Unfriendly to Boys

Your son is now 12 years old. His latest report card was a mess: an A in math, C's in social studies and Spanish, and D's in reading and English. "You can do better than this," you say to your son. "Your English teacher told me you didn't turn in even half the homework. Am I going to have to supervise you to make sure you do your homework every night?"

"I'm not gonna do that homework. It's stupid," your son says.

"What's stupid about it?" you ask.

"It's TOTALLY stupid," he says.

"What do you mean by that? Can you give an example?"

He shrugs. "Do you want to see it?" he asks.

"Sure," you say.

He rummages in his knapsack, then produces a crumpled piece of paper. After smoothing it out, this is what you read:

In *Lord of the Flies*, a group of boys finds themselves stranded on a tropical island. One of the boys, nicknamed Piggy because he is overweight, is the victim of vicious bullying by the other boys. Write a short essay in the first person, in Piggy's voice, describing how you feel about the other boys picking on you. Be sure to

- include lots of detail,
- describe specific scenes from the book, and
- mention specific boys.

"See what I mean?" he says, a note of triumph in his voice. "It's totally stupid!"

"What's stupid about it?" you ask.

"'Write an essay in Piggy's voice,'" he paraphrases. "That is total stupidness!"

"Why is it stupid?" you ask again.

"I'm not Piggy. I'm not some pathetic fat loser who can't even pick his own nose. If I'd been on that island, I'd have smashed his face in myself!"

THIS HOMEWORK ASSIGNMENT BOILS DOWN TO: *HOW WOULD YOU feel if you were Piggy?* When I spoke with the teacher who assigned this homework, she explained that she wanted to teach the children about empathy. With all due respect to the teacher, I submit that this assignment didn't teach this particular boy anything about empathy. Instead, the message the assignment reinforced for him is that doing homework is for girls, not for real boys. No self-respecting boy, in this boy's frame of reference, would do such a homework assignment.

Deborah Yurgelun-Todd and her associates at Harvard Medical School found that the regions of the brain associated with negative emotion in teenage girls are closely associated with the language areas of the brain. In boys of the same age, by contrast, brain activity associated with negative emotion is localized primarily in the amygdala, a nucleus with comparatively scant connections to the language areas of the brain.[55] It's easy for most middle school and high school girls to answer a question like "How would you feel if you were X?" because the area of the brain where the feeling is happening is closely linked to the area of the brain where talking happens. For boys, that's not the case. For boys like the one who refused to write about how Piggy might have felt when the other boys were being mean to him, it's not easy to answer, in a genuine and articulate way, the question "How would you *feel* if . . . ?" If he were motivated to do the homework, he may attempt to produce the answer he thinks the teacher wants to hear, but it would be a chore. A better question for most boys would be "What would you *do* if . . . ?" That question may sound similar, but it's actually a different question, and much more boy-friendly—for most boys.

School Has Become Unfriendly to Boys

I attended public schools in Shaker Heights, Ohio, from kindergarten through 12th grade. During the winter months at my elementary school, Lomond Elementary, we would put on our winter coats, go outside, and—more often than not—throw snowballs. The teachers would often come out and join us. Students versus teachers. I remember one teacher by name: he was a great shot. He'd get you right between the eyes every time.

Those are some of my favorite memories of elementary school. But that doesn't happen anymore. Across North America, most schools now strictly prohibit the throwing of snowballs on school property. "Snow is to stay on the ground at all times."[56] If two boys start throwing snowballs at each other on school property, the odds are good that a teacher or administrator will yell at them: "What are you guys doing? You're not allowed to throw snowballs on school property! If you want to throw snowballs, go somewhere else!" The message these boys will hear is loud and clear: *school is not the place for you. Go somewhere else.*

I understand why today's schools usually don't allow kids to throw snowballs at each other: the school leaders are concerned about liability. But there is a way to accommodate liability concerns without pushing boys who want to throw snowballs off of school property. I first encountered this strategy at St. Andrew's, a boys' school in Aurora, Ontario, just north of Toronto. At St. Andrew's, they have a simple rule: if you want to throw snowballs, go to the football field. The football field is on school property, but it's not on the way to anywhere. So, people who don't want snowballs thrown at them are not inconvenienced by boys who want to have snowball fights. And the football field is clearly demarcated. The staff at the school told me that they have never had problems or complaints related to this policy.

I summarize this policy as *in-bounds versus out-of-bounds.* Create a space on school property where the throwing of snowballs is allowed. Throwing snowballs is in-bounds when you are in that space, but out-of-bounds everywhere else. Boys understand in-bounds versus out-of-bounds. When I have assisted schools in the United States deploying this policy, some school administrators have insisted on having parents sign waivers, indemnifying the school in the event of injury. I don't have a problem with that. The school has to take any and all measures necessary to protect itself with regard to liability. But don't prohibit the throwing of snowballs; just redirect it to a safe place. In-bounds, not out-of-bounds.

This principle can be applied across many domains, not just in regard to throwing snowballs. I visited a school where the 10th-grade English teacher asked all her students to write a story about anything they liked. A boy named Jacob chose to write about the Battle of Stalingrad, winter of 1942, from the perspective of a Russian soldier. Jacob carefully researched the battle to get all the details right. In Jacob's story, the Russian soldier was patrolling a street when he was ambushed by a German soldier. The Russian soldier fired his rifle at point-blank range into the face of the German soldier. Jacob then described what happens when a soldier fires a military rifle into another man's face. What happens is that the head explodes: a piece of chin goes this way, a piece of skull goes that way, a chunk of eyeball goes another way.

Jacob was suspended from school. The school counselor told his parents that Jacob would not be permitted to return until the parents had obtained an evaluation by a licensed professional, and a note from the professional assuring the school and the district that Jacob posed no imminent danger to himself or to others.

When the parents shared this story with me, it struck a chord, because I myself wrote a similar story, a story that ended with a description of violent death. Back in 1977, when I was a senior at Shaker Heights High School in northeastern Ohio, our school's lead teacher for English nominated me and three other students to sit for an exam administered by the National Council of Teachers of English (NCTE). The four of us were shown into an empty classroom. The proctor gave each of us a blue essay book and told us to write a story.

In my story, I imagined a family of East Germans trying to escape to West Germany. (When I describe my story to high schoolers today, I have to begin by reminding them that in 1977,

Germany was divided in two, and East Germans were not allowed to travel freely to West Germany. Many American teenagers need to be enlightened on this point.) The East German family is running across the no-man's-land separating East Germany from West Germany. The father steps on a landmine, which—in my story—blows off his left leg up to the hip, and his right leg below the knee. So now he is crawling rather than walking, since he no longer has any feet. I described blood pouring from the mutilated stumps where his legs used to be. The East German guards have heard the explosion and are focusing their search lights on him and shooting, but the bullets narrowly miss. The West German guards are calling out encouragement, but they are prohibited from going into no-man's-land to help. The man reaches the border. The West German guards pull him to safety, to take him to a hospital. But as they lift him off the ground, the man dies.

My own mom died in 2008. Going through her papers after her death, I found that she had kept the certificate sent to our home by the NCTE back in 1977, awarding me the Council's highest honor in creative writing.

Boys have always written stories of traumatic amputation and violent death. In 1977, writing such a story might earn you an award, as it did for me. Today, it may earn you a suspension. Forty years ago, kids could throw snowballs at each other on school grounds without being yelled at. Today, at most schools, they can't. **Boys doing things that boys have always done now gets boys in trouble.** That's what I mean when I say that schools have become unfriendly to boys.

What's the guideline for violent stories? What's in-bounds and what's out-of-bounds? Here's my answer: *generic violence is in-bounds.* "Generic" violence means violence that is intrinsic to that genre of writing. If you're writing a story about the Battle of Stalingrad, there will be blood. The Battle of Stalingrad was all about door-to-door close combat. If you are writing a story about Roman gladiators in the arena, there will be battle-axes and swords and decapitations, because that's what happened when Roman gladiators fought. There is no evidence that boys who write such stories are more likely than other boys to engage in actual violence.

But **personal and threatening** *violence is out of bounds.* If Ethan writes a story about a boy named Ethan who stabs a boy named Noah, and there is a boy named Noah in Ethan's class and the two boys are not getting along, then that's personal and threatening. That's out-of-bounds.

What about "zero-tolerance" policies? When a teacher or principal tells you that the school has a zero-tolerance policy for students writing violent stories, ask whether the same policy applies to what students *read.* If students are not allowed to read violent fiction, then the librarian will have to remove novels by Hemingway, Steinbeck, Dostoyevsky, Tolstoy, and many others from the library shelves. If the school is really going to ban Hemingway and Dostoyevsky, then that school has some pretty serious problems. But if they're not going to ban Hemingway and Dostoyevsky, then on what grounds can they reasonably prohibit boys from trying to *write* in the same genre that they're allowed to *read*?

There is no evidence that zero-tolerance policies have any beneficial effect in reducing actual violence; instead, such policies merely increase discipline referrals.[57] More suspensions, more expulsions. More boys who conclude, quite reasonably, that school is not the place for them.

The Right Kind of Competition

I've already pointed out how using the computer metaphor to describe how brains work fails to capture the importance of motivation. It also falls short in another important respect: it doesn't accommodate the enormous individual differences between one student and another. The differences between a PC and an Apple computer are trivial in comparison with the differences between Brett, who plays every kind of competitive sport, and his younger sister, Emily, who occasionally watches football games with her older brother but feels bad for the losing team, no matter who they are, because "it must hurt to lose."

Some kids—both boys and girls—thrive in a competitive atmosphere, even if they often lose. Others wilt and collapse, or withdraw, under the stress of competition. Is competition good or bad? It depends on your child. That's why there may be no such thing as "the best school." The best choice for Emily may be a disaster for Brett. The school that is best for Brett may be a poor choice for Emily.

Think for a moment about boys who thrive on competition (not all boys do). Consider how changes in our schools and in our society over the past 30 years may have undermined the motivation of boys to engage with a wide domain of school activities, including gym. Gym class used to offer many opportunities for boys to experience "the thrill of victory and the agony of defeat"—even if the game was just kickball or dodgeball. But over the past 30 years, many school districts have eliminated sports such as dodgeball, in the belief that dodgeball and similar sports reward violence. Likewise, competition has been systematically eliminated from many districts' physical education programs, in the belief that competition alienates some kids from sports. And perhaps it does. But some boys need the zest of competition as a motivator.

A parent recently told me about her son's experience in 2nd grade. The gym teacher had announced that there would be a big race, one week from Friday. All the students would run four times around the school track. This boy took the challenge very seriously. He began training. Every day, at recess and at lunch, he would run around the track. Then finally the big day arrived. It was time for the race. "Ready, set, go!" This boy ran as hard as he could and he came in second out of the 35 kids. He was very happy about that result—until the teacher gave every student a "First Place" ribbon. He came home in tears, tears of anger. "The teacher tricked us!" he complained to his parents. "The teacher said it was going to be a real race. I'm never going to run a race again!"

In older grades, a different problem arises: not enough spaces for all the boys who want to play. Many schools have ballooned in size over the past 30 years. I commonly visit middle schools with 2,000-plus students and high schools with 4,000-plus students. One problem with a high school of 4,000-plus students is that only the most elite athletes get to play on the school team. In a typical school district in the United States, maybe 1 boy in 5 would like to play football. In a coed school with 4,000 students—that is, about 2,000 boys—there might be 400 boys who would like to play on the football team if they could. But even big schools often have only one bus for the varsity and one bus for the JV team. That means only 36 boys can make the varsity team, and another 36 can be on the JV. The other 300-plus boys are out of luck. Most of those boys probably won't even try out: they know that only the best athletes can make the team, and they don't want to be embarrassed. So they stay home.

If your son is one of those boys who thrive on competition, and he can't make the team, what should you do? In the short run, you might transfer your son to a smaller school, or you might help him transition to a different sport. More fundamentally, though, I think we need to change the mindset of American sports. I believe every kid who wants to play on a school team should have the opportunity to play.

I know what you're thinking: "My kid's high school enrolls 3,000 kids. If 200 boys try out for the team, how can the coach play every boy? Most of the boys will just be sitting on the bench." That would be true if there's only one varsity team, one junior varsity, and maybe one practice squad. But my visits to Australian schools have taught me that there's a different way. At large Australian schools, there isn't just one team, or three: it's common to find five teams, or seven, or ten. How do they do it? Simple: they practice during the school day. One team practices during first period, one team practices during fourth period, and another team practices after school. Even more radical—from the American perspective— is the fact that no team practices every day. No team practices more than three days a week. In Australia, the consensus is that school-based sports should provide decent training to a broad range of athletes, rather than focusing on the most talented few. In the United States, we provide intensive daily training and coaching for those elite few, while leaving the great majority of boys no opportunity to play organized sports at all. Instead, those boys go home and play video games.

KNOW A BOY, LET'S CALL HIM TONY, WHO IS COMPETITIVE IN ABSO-
lutely every aspect of his life. He's only 11 years old, but he finds
a way to make everything a race or some sort of competition. At
summer camp, he organized a contest among all the boys to see
who could pee the farthest. Boys like Tony usually will respond
well to any challenge, so long as:

- there are winners and losers, and
- the outcome is in doubt. Anybody might win and anybody
  might lose. Everything depends on how hard you play.

Satisfy both criteria, and Tony will be on board. If either one of
the criteria is missing, Tony won't see the point. He'll disengage.
He'll lose interest. He'll stare out the window.

Mater Dei School is an all-boys elementary school in Montgomery County, Maryland, where this principle is understood
very well. On enrollment, every boy is assigned either to Blue
Team or White Team. The assignment is arbitrary—in other
words, it's random—and it is permanent. (The only exception to
random assignment is that if a boy has an older brother who attended the school, then the boy is assigned to the same team that
his brother was on.) Once you're a member of Blue Team, you are
forever a member of Blue Team. The two teams compete in every
aspect of school life. When the boys play soccer, it's Blue against
White. On school examinations, it's Blue against White. The team
that scores higher on the exams gets points. The team whose
members donate more food to give away at Thanksgiving gets
points. At the end of the year, the winning team is officially recognized and gets its name—"Blue" or "White"—the year of its

victory, and the names of the team captains emblazoned on a plaque in the hallway. This may seem silly to some people. But for many of these boys, it's highly motivating.

Team competition has another benefit for boys who are motivated by the will to win. Team competition socializes boys. It teaches boys to value something above themselves. It subordinates some of the ego and the egocentricity that competitive boys often manifest.

I've seen team competition engage many boys who otherwise don't care much about school. Individual competition is seldom as successful and is almost guaranteed to cause many boys to disengage. Why is that? Remember the second principle we discussed a moment ago: the outcome must be in doubt. If you have individual competition in academics, for example, Daniel may decide that he's unlikely to win. He doesn't think that he's any good at spelling. For him, the outcome is not in doubt: he's not going to win the spelling bee, regardless. Once he's decided that he's not likely to win, he's not interested in playing. "You think I care about your spelling bee? Ha. I couldn't care less. Go ahead and flunk me."

But if Daniel is a member of a large team, anything can happen. Either team might win. Daniel's performance might determine whether his team wins or loses. Here's an example from a class where the assignment was to read *The Lord of the Rings: The Fellowship of the Ring*. Now there's an oral quiz, Blue Team vs. White Team. All the students in the class will have been warned, incidentally, that answers must be taken only from J. R. R. Tolkien's books, not from a movie version of the books.

The teacher, Mrs. Hofstadter, says: "It's Blue Team's turn. Carlos, you're answering for Blue Team this round. Here's your question: After Frodo is wounded by the Nazgûl and needs to be taken to Rivendell, what is the name of the elf who takes him there?"

"Arwen?" Carlos guesses.

"Wrong!" Mrs. Hofstadter says. "Arwen has that role in the movie, but not in the book. Daniel, you're answering for White Team. After Frodo is wounded, what is the name of the elf who takes Frodo to Rivendell?"

Daniel shouts "Glorfindel!"

"Right!" Mrs. Hofstadter says. Daniel's teammates on White Team give him high fives all around, because this is a high-stakes test for 6th-grade boys. Each member of the winning team in this classroom will get a coupon for free pizza and ice cream at the corner pizzeria.

Daniel may not care that much about his grade in the class or about *The Lord of the Rings*. He may not even care that much about pizza and ice cream. But he doesn't want to let his teammates down. He doesn't want to risk being the one who got the wrong answer, whose one wrong answer cost the whole team the prize.

Why doesn't this approach work as well for many girls? Here's why: most girls value friendship above team affiliation. If Emily and Melissa are best friends, and you put Emily and Melissa on opposing teams, both girls may be uncomfortable. Emily doesn't want to make Melissa sad, so she may be reluctant to beat Melissa. She'd rather play alongside Melissa than try to make her lose. But if Justin and Jared are best friends, and you put them on opposing teams, Justin will happily run down the field and knock Jared down. In that situation I've seen Jared get up, dust himself off, and say to Justin, "You think that was a good hit? Ha! I'll get you better next time." That kind of good-natured competition actually builds their friendship. Boys are more likely to understand that friends don't have to be teammates, and teammates don't have to be friends. And boys are more likely to be invested in the success of their team regardless of whether any of their friends are on the team.

It's easy to see how the competitive team format might engage and motivate boys who otherwise wouldn't be inspired to do their homework or read the assigned text. But I've also seen team competition work in other unexpected ways: for example, to motivate scholarly boys to become better athletes. When I visited Calgary, Alberta, I heard a story involving team competition that took place at a boys' school near Edmonton. At this school, all the boys were assigned to one of three teams. It happened that this particular year, the best athletes were on one team, while most of the best students were on another team.

A 20-kilometer snowshoe relay race was announced. Each team would nominate four boys to race. Everybody expected the team with the best athletes to win easily. But the scholars—the "geeks"— really studied up on snowshoeing. They learned that the key to success in snowshoeing is to run lightly over the surface of the snow. So they nominated their four lightest, fastest boys to represent their team. And those boys trained. The athletes didn't train for this event; they figured they didn't have to, they were already in excellent shape.

When the day of the race arrived, the scholarly boys were ready. They blew the other two teams away: the fourth boy on the scholarly team crossed the finish line about nine minutes ahead of either of the other teams. The strong football players representing the athletic team became bogged down in the snow—their muscular build was a liability rather than an advantage. That event, I was told, raised the status of the scholarly team enormously in the eyes of the whole school. They had beaten the jocks at an athletic event. And the jocks saluted them.

The competitive format of this boys' school in Alberta, or of the Mater Dei School in Maryland, might make those schools a poor choice for many girls (if those schools enrolled girls). And those schools might not be the best choice for some boys. But if your son loves competition—if you can imagine him competing to see who can pee the farthest—then you need to find your son a school like this one. If there is no such school nearby, then I hope you will lend your copy of this book to your school's principal and to some of your son's teachers. Ask whether they might make some effort to accommodate different types of boys. In the 21st century, most North American schools allow little place for team competition outside of athletics. Indeed, any school competition with clearly defined winners and losers is disparaged in many schools nowadays, on the grounds that the self-esteem of the children who lose might be in jeopardy in a competitive environment. We need to change that, and we can.

What About Self-Esteem?

"What if my son loses?" you may be wondering. "What if my son gives the wrong answer and the team loses as a result? Wouldn't that damage his self-esteem?"

To understand the answer to this question, you have to understand something about gender differences with regard to self-esteem. Let me tell you first about a study that was done at Harvard University. The researchers recruited Asian and Asian American women from among Harvard undergraduates. The women were then randomly assigned to three groups. Women in each group were given the same short written math examination. In the first group, the women took the exam, and that was it. Those in the second group were given a questionnaire that emphasized their Asian heritage before taking the math exam. The questionnaire asked what language they spoke at home, whether they preferred traditional Asian foods over Western foods, and so on. On average, the women in this second group scored significantly higher on the math exam than the women in the first group.

The women in the third group were given a questionnaire that emphasized the fact that they were women before taking the math exam. The questionnaire asked whether they preferred to live in a single-sex dorm or a coed dorm, whether they felt that there were adequate protections for women on campus, and so on. The women in this third group scored significantly lower on the math exam than the women in the first group.[58]

Just reminding women of their membership in a category that is negatively stereotyped—i.e., women supposedly aren't as good in math as men are—resulted in a significant impairment of their ability to test well. Reminding women of a different stereotype— the supposed superior ability of Asians in math—significantly enhanced their ability to do well. These women weren't stupid. They were Harvard undergraduates. Similar studies of young girls and teenagers, with even larger effects, have been published.[59] For girls and for many women, if you believe you're smart, you'll actually be smarter—you'll learn better and do better on tests—than if you think you're dumb. A girl who thinks she's good in math will test better than a girl of the same ability who thinks she's bad in math.

But that effect simply doesn't hold true for boys, as a rule. A boy who thinks he's smart in math won't necessarily test better than his equally bright peer who thinks he's not so smart. The boy who thinks he's smart may actually test worse than his peer, because boys who think they're smart in a subject tend not to work as hard studying the subject—just as the athletes at the school in Edmonton didn't bother to train for the snowshoe relay. The correlation between a boy's self-esteem in a subject and his performance in that subject is zero, at best—and may possibly be negative, after controlling for ability.[60]

I know many parents who are uneasy with the idea that their sons need a school with a more competitive format to get motivated. That idea clashes with the politically correct notions of the past 30 years, according to which competition is bad because it is harmful to self-esteem. But those notions were not empirically based. We now know that self-esteem has a value for girls that it simply doesn't have for many boys, while competition—particularly team competition—has a value for many boys that it doesn't have for most girls. Some boys need the challenge and the risk of competition to care about the results. If parents and teachers and school administrators don't understand that fact, they may actually cause these boys to disengage from school.

I met with a woman who has coached both girls' and boys' sports for many years. She has found that most girls, even athletically talented girls, need encouragement. Otherwise, girls are likely to decide they're not good enough, they're not fast enough, they're not strong enough. They give up. "You have to build the girls up," this coach told me. But boys are different. Many boys—especially athletically talented boys—have a tendency to overestimate their skills and their ability. "You have to tell that hotshot that he may have some talent, but he's not nearly as good as he thinks he is. He still has a lot to learn. He's going to need to put in a lot of work if he wants to make it to the next level," she told me. "You have to break the boys down."

I'm a little uneasy with this woman's motto—"build the girls up, break the boys down"—but I have to admit that it captures the essence of the research on self-esteem. For many boys, failure is a spur to work harder. The competitive format gives these boys a structured environment in which they can easily determine whether or not they're making real progress. A noncompetitive format in which "everybody's a winner" is a sure way to make this boy disengage from the whole process.

What About Columbine—and Virginia Tech?

The zero-tolerance policies many school districts have put in place regarding anything that looks or sounds violent didn't spring out of nowhere. They are motivated by concerns about school violence. Some parents ask: "If you let boys write violent stories, and you encourage competition with winners and losers, aren't you creating conditions in which violent activity is more likely to occur?"

Those parents—and the district administrators who wrote the zero-tolerance policies—usually believe that prohibiting violent play or imaginary violence (e.g., boys writing violent stories) will decrease actual violence. There is no shred of evidence to support this belief.[61] We actually know a good deal about the kind of boy who is the most likely to bring a gun to school. For example, that boy is less likely than other boys to participate in contact sports such as football.[62]

We now have very detailed information regarding Dylan Klebold and Eric Harris, the two boys who killed 13 of their fellow students at Columbine High School on April 20, 1999, and then killed themselves. We know that Eric Harris wrote on his website, "God I can't wait till I can kill you people. All I want to do is kill and injure as many of you pricks as I can!" He publicly posted a log describing his work making homemade bombs, and he named particular students he wanted to kill.[63]

We know that in February 1998, more than a year before the killings, Dylan Klebold wrote a short story for his creative writing class. In the story, Klebold described a killer shooting high school students in a way startlingly similar to what actually happened on April 20, 1999. "The smallest details match," according to author Dave Cullen, who wrote a book on the tragedy. "[Klebold's] instructor, Judy Kelly, read it and shuddered. Dylan's protagonist was killing civilians, ruthlessly, and enjoying it. [Kelly] had never been confronted with a story this sadistic." Kelly contacted Dylan's guidance counselor, and his mother and father, to express her concerns about Dylan and the story he had written. All three of them dismissed Kelly's concerns.[64]

Dylan brought that short story with him on April 20, 1999. It was found in his car after the massacre.[65]

If a boy writes a story about killing real people in his own school, glamorizing the killing, with no concern for the victims, such a situation warrants urgent, same-day intervention. Dylan's parents didn't know that. The guidance counselor should have known it, but apparently did not. One of the lessons of Columbine is that boys who tell personal and threatening stories of violence may be at increased risk of actually engaging in such violence, no matter how charming the boy's façade. Such boys should be seen promptly by properly trained professionals.

O N DECEMBER 13, 2005, THE GENERAL DISTRICT COURT FOR Montgomery County, Virginia, found that Seung-Hui Cho was "mentally ill and in need of hospitalization" and concluded that he "presents an imminent danger to self or others as a result of mental illness."[66] Cho was subsequently released from the Carilion St. Albans Behavioral Health Center by an order from Virginia Special Justice Paul Barnett. The order included a directive that Cho undergo continued mental health treatment on an outpatient basis. Cho never obtained the outpatient treatment mandated by the court, and there was apparently no follow-up to ensure compliance. Under federal law, the judge's ruling made Cho ineligible to purchase firearms.[67] He nevertheless managed to purchase firearms anyhow.

One of Cho's professors, Nikki Giovanni, contacted campus police, student affairs, the counseling service, and the police to express her concerns about Cho. "I was willing to resign," she said, rather than have Cho continue in her class. In a writing class, Cho submitted two "profoundly violent and profane plays," which a classmate said were "like something out of a nightmare [with] really twisted, macabre violence that used weapons I wouldn't have even thought of." As a result of the plays, "we students were talking to each other with serious worry about whether he could be[come] a school shooter."[68]

On April 16, 2007, Seung-Hui Cho shot and killed 32 people and wounded 17 others on the campus of Virginia Tech. An investigation by the state subsequently concluded that "while the campus police knew of Mr. Cho's repeated instances of inappropriate behavior and his stay at a mental health facility, that information never reached campus workers who deal with troubled students." The investigators also discovered that Cho had a history of "suicidal and homicidal thoughts in his writings" that had been noticed as far back as his middle school years.[69]

There were plenty of clues that Dylan Klebold and Eric Harris were likely to engage in violence. There was abundant evidence that Seung-Hui Cho posed a danger to others. But a boy who writes a story about the Battle of Stalingrad is not more likely than other boys to kill somebody. That's generic, classic violence; it's not personal and threatening violence. It's in-bounds, not out-of-bounds. Prohibitions on writing stories about World War II do not in any way decrease the likelihood of school violence; they won't stop a Dylan Klebold or an Eric Harris or a Seung-Hui Cho. Such prohibitions accomplish only one thing: they send a clear message that boys who like to write about World War II, or ancient Rome, are simply not welcome at school. To do well at school, that boy must deny his true self and pretend to be someone else. He must become more compliant. More willing to do what the teacher asks. More concerned about pleasing the teacher. In short, more like a typical girl.

Consider these examples:

- In Pennsylvania, 10-year-old Johnny Jones pretended that his pencil was a bow and arrow. He pretended to pull back on an imaginary bowstring and release an imaginary arrow aimed at another boy who was pretending to shoot an imaginary gun at him. Both boys were disciplined and Johnny was suspended. The school principal, John Horton, notified Johnny's mother, Beverly Jones, that another such offense might result in Johnny's *expulsion* from the public school. The attorney hired by the Jones family noted that the school's action amounted to "criminalizing the imagination."[70]
- In Maryland, a 2nd-grade boy was suspended from his elementary school for two days after he chewed his Pop-Tart into the

shape of a gun and pointed it at other students. The family hired a lawyer to get the district to remove the suspension from their boy's record. "No one was hurt," the lawyer noted. "No one was scared." But the district refused to clear the son's record.[71]

- In Alabama, 9-year-old Austin Crittenden was suspended for "possession of a weapon—replica" when he brought a tiny plastic G.I. Joe handgun to his elementary school. The 3rd-grader's principal "had to tape the gun to a piece of paper to keep from losing it," Austin's grandmother reported.[72]

These stories are so outrageous that they made the newspapers. But I can tell you many stories from my own experience that don't make the newspapers: for example, a boy whose story about a family escaping from Zimbabwe was given a C because it included the suggestion of a violent act, while a girl's story of comparable quality in response to the same assignment—but with no hint of violence— received an A+. The end result of these kinds of episodes is the widespread belief among boys that school isn't the place for boys who want to write stories in any sort of violent genre.

In my first book, *Why Gender Matters*, I quoted a famous saying attributed to the Roman poet Horace: "You can try to drive out Nature with a pitchfork; yet she will always return."[73] If your son is motivated by competition, then eliminating competition from his school, throwing out his toy guns, and forbidding him to write stories with violent themes won't change him. He may disengage from school because of those policies, however. The end result may be a boy who feels that the only place he is truly understood, as he really is, is in the world of video games.

And, as we'll see in the next chapter, that world has its own problems.

3

The Second Factor

Video Games

*Y*OUR SON IS NOW *13* YEARS OLD. *HE'S A SERIOUS VIDEO-GAME PLAYER.*
He still plays with a few friends, occasionally, but more and more he prefers to play against other gamers online. Last month he was a runner-up in an online Halo *competition that drew competitors from around the world.*[1] *That's OK, you suppose, but you're becoming concerned about how much time he spends playing, as well as the strangers he plays with online. Who are these people? How come they have so much spare time on their hands?*

His grades are fine, more or less, so far. But he'll be starting 9th grade next fall. You and your spouse have decided it's time to lay down some rules. First of all, homework comes before video games. Your son's going to be in high school soon. No playing video games until all the homework is done.

Before you get to rule number two, you notice that your son isn't paying attention. He's not even pretending to pay attention. He's looking out the window. He's tapping his fingers on the table. Now he's actually humming something. And he's not looking at you. He just keeps looking out the window, nodding his head—not at you, but in rhythm to the song he's humming.

"You're not paying attention," you say.

"Sure I am," he says, still not making eye contact. "No video games until the homework's done. Got it."

"OK, then let's talk about rule number two," you say. "Rule number two is: no more than 30 minutes a night on video games, on school nights. That means Sunday through Thursday whenever school's in session."

Now you've got his attention. He stops drumming his fingers on the table. For the first time he makes eye contact with you. Then he snorts contemptuously. "Not gonna happen," he says. "Sorry. Thirty minutes? That's barely enough time to get powered up and log on."

"But all the time you're spending on video games right now—it must be a dozen hours a week, at least," you protest. "You're spending all your free time on video games."

"But those games are basically the best thing I have," your son says. His tone is simultaneously angry and pleading. "Those games are who I am. I'm not some pathetic nerd geek who's going to spend 6 zillion hours a week studying."

"But those games aren't the real world," you say. "They're just games."

"What's real?" your son says. Before you can answer this unexpectedly philosophical question, he continues: "When I'm playing Halo, that world is more real to me than this one. I'm really good, too," he says, dreamily. "Although I do NOT expect you to have even the slightest clue what that means." He pauses, then adds

softly, almost shyly, "I could win the championship. Next year maybe. Definitely a possibility. But not on 30 minutes a day."

W HERE'S THIS COMING FROM? HOW DID THIS BOY COME TO HAVE such an obsession, such a drive to play some silly game? The answer will take you deeper than you might expect.

Boy World is a weird place. Many boys and young men are wrestling with drives and motivations that a lot of parents, especially mothers, don't understand. Fathers may understand these motivations, but fathers are sometimes disdainful of the egocentricity and unreality that characterize the inner life of many teen and preteen boys. Dads may not want to be reminded that they were something like that themselves, once upon a time, a long time ago.

I am not making some grand statement about *all* boys. I'm focusing only on those boys who seem unmotivated to do their best, boys who don't seem to care much about getting the best grades or getting into a good college, boys who are capable of doing the schoolwork but who just aren't motivated to do it. Many of them *could* be good students, but they don't seem to care about that. What do they want?

Two generations ago, in the age of *Gidget* and The Beatles, boys were more likely to be highly driven overachievers than girls were. Today the reverse is true. But DNA can't change that much in two generations, or even in ten. *Society* has changed. Your son, who seems so unmotivated to succeed at school, may actually be highly motivated to succeed—just not at school, at least not at the particular school he is attending. I hear many parents say things like,

"My son doesn't care about school at all, but he can work incredibly hard at something that he does care about. He'll stay up till 3 in the morning to get to the next level in *Call of Duty*. He just doesn't care about *school*."

Why do some tasks engage your boy's motivational engine, while others don't? It's not sufficient to say that video games are fun and school isn't. That answer begs the question. Why do these boys find video games to be so much more fun than school? Many girls, and indeed some boys, don't get much of a kick out of playing *Call of Duty*. For many girls, and for some boys, the main activity in *Call of Duty*—shooting the (virtual) bad guys while they are shooting at you—would be as tedious as conjugating Spanish verbs in the imperfect subjunctive, or writing an essay on the Federalist Papers.

The answer, I think, lies in a concept that most of these boys have never heard of, something that contemporary psychologists refer to with terms like "the reinforcing effects of contingent paradigms," or "learned mastery." The German philosopher Friedrich Nietzsche was the first to write at length about the reinforcing effect I have in mind here: he called this drive simply "the will to power." To get a better handle on how you might get your son's motivation back in gear, I think you'll find it helpful to understand Nietzsche's concept of the will to power.

First a disclaimer: some unmotivated boys don't fit into the will-to-power category. We'll investigate what might be going on with those boys in chapters 4, 5, and 7.

Let's start with Nietzsche's insight, follow that insight to help us understand the modern research, then figure out where and how 21st-century boys—including your son, perhaps—may have gone astray.

The Will to Power

The simplest way to express what Nietzsche meant by the "will to power" is that individuals want to be in charge of their environment. This characteristic is clearly evident as early as two months of age. In one classic study, psychologists rigged up babies' cribs with motion detectors so that a colorful mobile over the baby's head would rotate for a few seconds every time the baby moved its head. These were two-month-old babies, but they figured out the game quickly. Very soon these babies were moving their heads back and forth and cooing at the mobiles. Other babies were given the same crib and the same colorful mobiles, but the mobiles were programmed to rotate every minute or two regardless of the baby's activity. No motion detectors. These other babies had no control over the movement of the mobiles. They lay still, not moving, not cooing. They appeared bored.[2] Another psychologist, commenting on this study, remarked that "infants, no less than we, prefer to exercise some control over their environments. It appears that even a two-month-old infant wants to be master of its own fate."[3]

If you tell a boy who has a generous dose of this kind of motivation to sit down, he'll stand up. If you tell him to stand up, he'll sit down. He doesn't care so much whether he's standing or sitting. But he needs to know, and he needs you to know, that he's in charge of whether he stands or sits. He doesn't want you to tell him what to do.

Now of course many people will respond, "I know girls just like that. I know women like that, too. They don't like to be told what to do. They like to be in charge." And that's certainly true. But according to Nietzsche, what distinguishes people who are motivated by the will to power from other people is that the will to power *takes precedence over* other drives and other perspectives.[4] For most girls and women, being well-liked and being well-thought-of counts for more than being in charge. But some boys and some men would rather be in charge than be well-liked. That's true for a few women, but not many.

Again, I emphasize that I'm not making any sweeping statement about gender here. We all know girls and women who want to be the boss, and we all know boys and men who are content to follow rather than to lead. What I have found in more than two decades of medical practice, however, is that many of the boys who seem un-motivated, from our perspective, are actually motivated by the will to power. The will to power can best be understood perhaps not so much as a drive per se but as a worldview, a way of valuing traits and characteristics. Secretly, these boys often believe that they are special, that they are unique, that they have a hidden destiny that will be revealed in time. As a result, they believe that the rules that apply to ordinary people don't apply to them. Their "destiny" mat-ters more to them than friendship or academic achievement—more than happiness, for that matter. They often do not expect other people, including their parents, to understand them. They may not even *want* other people to understand them, because they sense (correctly) that their worldview, with all its megalomania, will ap-pear puerile and egocentric to most adult eyes.

Watch a teenage boy playing certain video games, particularly games in which the boy has to shoot and kill his way to victory, such as *Call of Duty* and *Grand Theft Auto*. Such video games offer a quick and easy fix for these boys. They give them the feelings of power and control they crave: the power of life and death. "It's just a game"—but watch the seriousness with which these boys play. What happens when you tell your son that he should stop playing those video games? You tell him that if he spends all his time playing video games, he is less likely to be successful in the real world, less likely to find true happiness. He says he doesn't care about being happy. You tell him that he needs to grow up, put the games aside, and get a real life. He may reply, quoting Nietzsche (but not aware that he is quoting Nietzsche): "This is what I am; this is what I want; you can go to hell!"[5]

I know some boys who don't play video games at all. I know other boys who play them more than 20 hours a week—more than three hours a day, every day, including school days—which often means that their homework ends up being an after-midnight afterthought, if it is not neglected altogether. In this chapter we will ask, "How much involvement in video games is OK for your son, and with what kind of video games?" We'll get to some specifics in a moment, but I can tell you right now that one key is *balance*. Moderation in all things is the key to good health. If time spent on video games is crowding out time spent with friends or time spent on homework, then your son is spending too much time on video games.

Video games aren't all bad. I know families where video games bring parents and kids together, instead of separating them. Shawn Hirsch of Gaithersburg, Maryland, always considered himself an "anti-video-game guy." Then he bought the Nintendo Wii system for his daughters. Now he enjoys playing video-game tennis and bowling with his daughters, especially his 7-year-old, with whom he plays almost every night after dinner. Thomas Morgan of Potomac, Maryland, agrees that the right video game "absolutely reaches across the generation gap."[6]

The will to power also has a positive dimension. It's not hard to see how boys motivated by the will to power might have been successful in earlier generations. They might have grown up to be successful entrepreneurs, daring innovators, explorers, politicians, or soldiers. They could readily create a productive niche for themselves. Most young men I have known eventually outgrow this stage when maturity arrives around age 30 and they gain a broader, less egocentric perspective on life. But some men remain motivated by the will to power for their entire lives. General George S. Patton Jr. was certainly such a man, as were Henry Ford, Howard Hughes, and perhaps Richard Nixon. You may not like any of these men: they were all relentlessly self-centered and almost completely incapable of irony or of good-natured self-deprecating humor. But they each played a substantive role, for better or worse, in American culture and history.

If these men were reborn today, it is less likely that they would undertake a meaningful career. I suspect that a boy born today with the DNA of General Patton would more likely become a video-game addict. He might have a job, but there's a real risk that his drive and his energy would be directed into the video games rather than into his career.

If you haven't played video games in the past ten years, you may not understand how addictive some of them can be, owing to advances in technology—particularly for boys motivated by the will to power. Imagine that you are such a boy, the reincarnation of General George S. Patton. That boy can now play a video game in which he gets in a tank, hears the clang as he closes the hatch, feels the rumble from 300-watt subwoofers as his tank treads crush the rubble of a demolished house, and fires off depleted uranium rounds at enemy outposts as he enjoys the thrill of victory— or the agony of defeat when three enemy tanks blast him almost simultaneously. But the agony of defeat is lessened by the knowledge that he can just hit "Restart" and play it all over again—and again.

Today, any boy with a high-speed Internet connection can play in real time against another gamer across town or on the other side of the planet. Sophisticated headsets allow boys to engage in simulated online combat in teams, arranging coordinated ambushes of enemy fighters using high-tech virtual weaponry. After your son has spent two hours leading a squad of fighters in a raid on terrorist headquarters, issuing commands through his headset-mounted microphone to his online comrades, and raced through a hail of virtual bullets to destroy the enemy power generator, well, studying Spanish grammar from a textbook can seem hopelessly dull. The virtual world is fast-moving, interactive, collaborative, and fun.

And it is *heroic*. For years, Sony's lead advertising line for its PS4 video-game console was: "Greatness Awaits." The official Sony commercial offers some insight. The actor, a young man looking directly into the camera as special effects explode around him, says, "Who are you to be ordinary? Who are you to be anonymous? You—whose name should be spoken in reverent tones, or in terrified whispers!"[7] In the real world, maybe you're just an ordinary, anonymous kid who's not doing very well in school. Not to worry: in the world of the video game, you can be great. The real world of homework and textbooks can't compete—not, at least, for the boy who is motivated by the will to power.

For Better, for Worse

Kids who spend many hours a week playing video games are changed by that experience. Some changes are for the better. Most are not.

Let's look at the plus side first. If you ask, "Do video games improve kids' reaction times when they're asked to push a button every time they see a flashing light?"—then the answer is yes. Kids who play video games will get faster at such a task—by about two-hundredths of a second (0.02 seconds)—compared with kids who don't play video games.[8]

But if you ask questions such as "Do video games help kids to concentrate and focus on academic tasks, as opposed to simple push-button reactions? Do the games help kids to judge risk appropriately? Do the most popular video games help kids to be more caring, more empathic, more tuned in to the humanity of others?"—then the answer is no. Let's look at the evidence

Attention deficit. The most popular video games, such as *Grand Theft Auto* and *Call of Duty*, offer constantly changing challenges, scenes, and characters. Often there are multiple characters on the screen. The successful player must continually be scanning up, down, and sideways for new assailants. Sustained concentration on a single item is a recipe for defeat: you didn't respond to that rustle on the right side of the screen, which was your only clue to an impending ambush. Distractibility is rewarded. Not surprisingly, researchers find that the more time you spend playing video games, the more likely you are to develop difficulties maintaining sustained concentration on a single item. Conversely, researchers find that boys who already have difficulty concentrating and focusing tend to gravitate to video games, where their distractibility is an asset rather than a liability.[9]

Risk-taking. The world of video games is unreal. You can jump off a 20-foot ledge onto the concrete pavement below and continue chasing your enemy: no sprained ankle, no broken bones. You can race your car at high speeds, crash into a wall, and walk away unharmed from the wreck of your car. You can hijack a car in *Grand Theft Auto*—in fact you *have* to hijack a car in order to play the game. Not only is risky behavior allowed in games such as *Grand Theft Auto* and *Call of Duty*, but risky behavior is required and rewarded. If you jump off that high ledge to chase after your opponent, you are much more likely to succeed in killing your opponent than if you "waste" valuable time by running down the stairs instead. Not surprisingly, researchers have found that adolescents who play these risk-glorifying games are more likely to engage in dangerous driving behaviors such as speeding, tailgating, and weaving in traffic; they are more likely to be pulled over by the police; more likely to be in automobile accidents; and more willing to drink and drive.[10] In another study, teens who were playing risky racing video games at age 17 or 18 were more than three times as likely, five years later, to have been involved in an actual car crash, compared with teens who did not play such games.[11]

Obesity. Boys who spend lots of time playing video games are more likely to become overweight or obese compared with boys who spend less time playing video games.[12] There seem to be at least two mechanisms operating here. First, playing video games exercises your thumbs but burns fewer calories than many other activities, such as playing actual sports. Second, and less intuitively, playing video games seems to have a direct appetite-stimulant effect, worse than watching TV.[13] That may be why time spent playing video games is significantly more likely to be associated with obesity and other bad health outcomes compared with time spent watching TV.[14]

Dehumanization / changes in personality. When young people play a violent video game, they not only regard their opponents as less human; they come to regard *themselves* as less human, more of an object. The researchers who documented this effect conclude that "violent video game play diminishes our humanity."[15] In a longitudinal study conducted over four years' time, researchers found that the more time a young person spends playing violent video games, the more likely that person is subsequently to abuse alcohol, smoke cigarettes, and engage in risky sexual behaviors.[16] Playing video games in which antisocial and delinquent behavior is rewarded increases the likelihood that the gamer will subsequently actually engage in delinquent behavior.[17] When high school kids were randomly assigned to play either violent video games or nonviolent video games, playing violent video games appeared to undermine self-control and to promote moral disengagement.[18] Other researchers have suggested that young men who play violent video games may develop a "myopia for the future," meaning that the young men prefer to continue playing the game "despite the negative long-term consequences in social or work domains of life."[19] *Playing* a violent video game has effects on how you feel, how you think, and how physiologically aroused you are that are greater than, and different from, the effects of *watching* that game or watching violent TV.[20]

I HAVE CITED CONSIDERABLE RESEARCH ON *VIOLENT* VIDEO GAMES. AND there is now evidence that violent video games such as *Grand Theft Auto* and *Call of Duty* have effects that are qualitatively different from nonviolent games such as *Zuma* and *Tetris*.[21] Young people who play violent video games change their brains, becoming desensitized to violence in ways not seen in young people who play nonviolent video games.[22] The more realistic the violence, the bigger the effects.[23] Playing violent video games over a period of months and years appears to cause more aggressive behavior and more aggressive thoughts and feelings as well as decreased empathy; that's not true for playing nonviolent video games.[24]

The most serious negative effects of video games are the effects on the gamer's personality, motivation, and connectedness with the real world. These boys may be highly motivated, but their motivation has been derailed. I've seen boys who care much more about their success at *Grand Theft Auto* than about their grade in Spanish. They're motivated in the virtual world at the expense of motivation in the real world. The video-game world is more real to them than the world of homework and sports and friends. Violent video games in particular tend to promote this disconnection, precisely because of the unreality of the violence. Your son knows that he doesn't get to fire rocket-propelled grenades at the kids he doesn't like at school.

Boys who spend many hours each week playing violent video games are at increased risk of disengaging from the real world. One of the most highly regarded researchers in this field, psychology professor Craig A. Anderson, has pointed out that the strength of the evidence linking video games to antisocial behaviors is every bit as strong as the evidence linking secondhand smoke to lung cancer, or lead poisoning in infancy to lower IQ scores. Anderson also notes that the controversy now surrounding video games is reminiscent of the controversy surrounding cigarette smoking in the 1960s or lead poisoning in the 1970s. After all, many smokers will never get lung cancer. And some people who get lung cancer are not smokers and have never been exposed to cigarette smoke. Likewise, he notes, not all boys who play video games 20 hours a week will disengage from real life, and not all boys who disengage from real life are video-game players.[25]

Legislators in California heard about this research. They were especially concerned by studies showing that playing the most violent video games can change personality in children and teenagers, causing kids to become less caring and more hostile. They thought: *There ought to be a law.* So they wrote a law, making it a civil offense—punishable by a fine of up to $1,000—for stores to sell the most violent video games directly to children under 18. Parents could still purchase violent games and give them to their children to play, if they chose, but the law would prohibit a kid from walking into a store and buying the most violent games without his parents' knowledge. Governor Arnold Schwarzenegger signed the statute into law in 2010.

But it never took effect. The video-game industry, supported by the American Civil Liberties Union (ACLU), promptly brought suit. The industry and the ACLU claimed that the California law violated the video-game companies' First Amendment right of free speech. The case went to the United States Supreme Court. In a decision written by Justice Antonin Scalia, the Court ruled in favor of the video-game industry, rendering the California statute null and void.

In a concurring opinion, Justice Samuel Alito expressed his concerns about violent video games. He agreed with the California state legislators that "the experience of playing video games (and the effects on minors of playing violent video games) may be very different from anything that we have seen before." He expressed his horror at video games in which "victims by the dozens are killed with every imaginable implement, including machine guns, shotguns, clubs, hammers, axes, swords, and chainsaws. Victims are dismembered, decapitated, disemboweled, set on fire, and chopped into little pieces. They cry out in agony and beg for mercy. Blood gushes, splatters, and pools. Severed body parts and gobs of human remains are graphically shown. In some games, points are awarded based, not only on the number of victims killed, but on the killing technique employed."[26]

Justice Alito understood the concerns of the legislators and of the parents who had campaigned for the bill. But he joined with Justice Scalia in ruling that the job of deciding what games children will play is not the job of the California State Assembly. It's the job of the parent.

There is no law prohibiting any child from buying any video game, no matter how violent or vicious the game may encourage the player to be. There cannot be such a law, not in the United States, as a result of the Supreme Court's ruling.

No one else can do this job for you. *You must know what games your child is playing.* There should be no expectation of privacy when your son is playing a video game. You should be looking over his shoulder to make sure that the game meets your criteria (we will talk about those criteria in just a moment). If your son is going to a friend's house, you must ask whether they will be playing video games, and if so, then you must find out whether the parent(s) share(s) your concerns about violent video games. If the parents have no idea what you are talking about, or if the parents won't even be home, then you must tell your son no, he is not allowed to go to that friend's house.

"You don't need to tell us about all those academic papers to know that video games are having a negative effect on boys' motivation," one parent told me. "Just listen to the teachers." Patrick

Welsh has been teaching English at T. C. Williams High School in
Alexandria, Virginia, for more than 30 years. He's "worrying about
the young guys who spend so much time divorced from reality and
the life of the mind as they zap away the hours before their video
screens." At first he was amused by the stories of how the boys
camp out all night at the local Best Buy to purchase the latest version of *Grand Theft Auto* or *Call of Duty* on the day the game is
released. Mr. Welsh continues:

> But I didn't think it was so funny when some guys skipped school
> that day to stay home and try to beat the game. Senior Steve Penn
> (who wasn't one of the skippers) told me that the following week-
> end, he played for six hours straight (minus bathroom breaks) at a
> friend's house. When he got home at 1 a.m. on Sunday, he went at
> it for two more hours, fell asleep, got up at 7 and fired up the game
> again. "My mother had to remind me to change my clothes and
> take a shower," he said.

Football coach Greg Sullivan, Mr. Welsh's colleague, says that
he sees fewer and fewer boys playing outside when he drives
around northern Virginia. "They are inside playing video games,"
he says. "More kids are finding real sports too demanding."[27]

I've talked with other football coaches who describe, with amazement, teenage boys who think that because they can win at Madden
NFL, they therefore know something about playing the real-life
game of football. "These guys are five-minute wonders," one coach
told me. "They get out on the field, run around for a few minutes,
and then they're done. They have no endurance. They're in pathetic
shape. And they don't want to do the work that they would have to
do, to train the way they would have to train, to get in shape."

I don't think the blame can rest solely on the scrawny shoulders of these boys. They are the logical product of an educational system that conveys so little understanding of the distinction between *Kenntnis* and *Wissenschaft* that the boys truly believe that because they know something *about* football, they know how to *play* football.

And what about preparing for the real world? In the real world—unless you're a fighter pilot or a military sniper—being able to push a button 0.02 seconds faster than the other guy isn't such a valuable skill. Preparing teenagers for the demands of real life requires helping them acquire skills quite different from the ones they gain while mastering video games. Imagine a young father, in his twenties, let's say, trying to comfort his crying baby daughter. There are no buttons to push, no photon torpedoes to fire. The right thing to do may be simply to rock the baby and hum a lullaby. The chief virtue required may not be lightning virtuosity with a game controller, but merely—patience. If you need to get along with a belligerent coworker, the chief virtue you need may not be blazing speed, but—patience. In most video games, the best way to deal with difficult people is to vaporize them with rocket-propelled grenades. In the real world, what you need most is not high-tech lethal weaponry, but—patience.

The stereotypical pastimes of boys and men in previous generations were pretty good at teaching skills like patience. Thirty years ago, and even more so 50 years ago, it was more common for boys and men to go hunting and fishing together. Boys who go fishing with an experienced fisherman soon learn that a good fisherman has to be able to wait patiently. That sort of patience might serve a young father well. But video games do not teach that kind of patience.

So what rules should you lay down for your son? Professor Anderson has provided some practical guidelines based on the published research.[28] He recommends first of all that you either play the game yourself or watch it being played. Then ask yourself these questions:

- Does the game involve some characters trying to harm others?
- Does this happen frequently, more than once or twice in 30 minutes?
- Is the harm rewarded in any way?
- Is the harm portrayed as humorous?
- Are nonviolent solutions absent or less "fun" than the violent ones?
- Are realistic consequences of violence absent from the game?

If you answer yes to two or more of these questions, then Anderson suggests that you reconsider whether your son should be allowed to play the game. The first consideration should not be how many hours per day or per week your son is allowed to play these games. The first question should be what kind of video games he is allowed to play at all. Violent video games that reward antisocial aggression—games such as *Grand Theft Auto*—should not be permitted in the house. Period. "Antisocial aggression" means aggression such as killing police officers or prostitutes, aggression that runs counter to all acceptable social behavior.

Another consideration, which I mentioned earlier, is what activities are displaced by playing video games. If your son is neglecting his friendships with non-gamer friends to spend more time playing video games, then he's spending too much time playing video games. If he refuses to sit down to dinner with the family because he's in the middle of a video game, that's not acceptable. He may need some help from you getting his priorities straight.

And what about teenage boys having relationships with girls? Surprisingly, especially to those of us over 30, many boys today seem to prefer playing video games to being with girls. Mr. Welsh, the teacher at T. C. Williams High School whom I mentioned earlier, has heard any number of stories along these lines. Girls at his school have told him that at parties they "are often totally ignored as the guys gather around TV screens, entranced by one video game or another." He quotes one junior, Sarah Kell, who told him, "Girls sit around watching the guys play until they get fed up and drive off looking for something else to do." For Sarah, "the games range from 'stupid and boring' to 'disgusting.'" She said: "We try to tell them they're wasting their time, but they just keep going. Some guys stay up playing until 3 in the morning on school nights, and then they try to do their homework."[29]

Do boys really prefer video games over girls? A reporter for the *New York Times* spoke with students at a number of college campuses. She met many young men who seemed more interested in playing their video games than in being with their girlfriends. The reporter interviewed one young woman at college who had broken off her relationship with a young man "in part out of frustration over his playing video games four hours a day." The young woman explained: "He said he was thinking of trying to cut back to fifteen hours a week. I said, 'Fifteen hours is what I spend on my internship, and I get paid $1,300 a month.' That's my litmus test now: I won't date anyone who plays video games. It means they're choosing to do something that wastes their time and sucks the life out of them."[30]

A young man at college today has unprecedented sexual opportunities. Unlike his father or grandfather, he is likely to be attending a school where men are outnumbered by women. Even boys who are not the best-looking or particularly popular now have an excellent chance of finding young women who will accept their advances. Nevertheless, as the *New York Times* reported in a front-page story, college administrators are reporting that more and more young men show no interest in meeting young women (or meeting other men, for that matter). They don't want to meet anybody. They just want "to stay in their rooms, talk to no one, [and] play video games into the wee hours. [Some] miss classes until they withdraw or flunk out."[31]

HERE ARE GUIDELINES FOR THE APPROPRIATE USE OF VIDEO GAMES, based especially on the work of Professor Craig Anderson cited above:

- **Content:** You should not allow your son to play video games in which the player is rewarded for killing police officers or noncombatant civilians. The video-game industry itself provides a rating system for games, assigning an "M" for Mature to this kind of antisocial violence. The M-rated games are not supposed to be used by anyone under 18 years of age. But just because a game is rated "T" for Teen doesn't guarantee that it's appropriate for your son. Familiarize yourself with the T-rated games. Even games rated "E" for Everyone cannot be assumed to be safe. In fact, Anderson's team has found that some of the E-rated games were more violent—and engendered more violent behaviors—than some games rated T.[32]

- **Time:** No more than 40 minutes a night on school nights, and no more than an hour a day on other days—and that's only after homework and household chores have been completed. And your minutes do not roll over. If your son goes three weeks without playing any video games at all, that doesn't mean that he's allowed to spend eight hours on a Saturday playing video games. That's binge gaming, analogous to binge drinking, and it's unhealthy.

- **Activities displaced:** Make sure your son knows where his priorities should be. Family comes first; schoolwork comes second; friends come third; video games are somewhere farther down the list. If your family is one in which most family members still sit down to share a common evening meal, then sitting down to dinner with the family should be more important than playing a video game, more important than talking on the phone with a friend, more important even than finishing a homework assignment. Homework is more important than talking with friends or playing a video game. Taking a phone call from a friend should be a higher priority than playing out a video game, though.

"I'm Not Quitting"

If you've followed my argument about the will to power, you'll understand that just restricting your son's access to video games is, at best, only half the challenge. You want to help find a constructive outlet for your son's need to conquer. In some cases, competitive sports and a more competitive school format—such as the schoolwide team competitions discussed in chapter 2—might provide such an outlet. What kind of free-time activities and hobbies would be the best choices for this kind of boy? How can he best satisfy his need to be tested and to triumph?

Let me share with you the experience of one of my own patients. At age 12, Aaron was an avid video-game player. His behavior bordered on addiction. The defining characteristic of addiction, incidentally, is *loss of control*: the boy knows that he shouldn't be spending so much time playing video games, he may not even want to play that much, but he feels that he just can't help it. So Aaron was spending three or four hours a day playing video games, mostly sports games like Madden NFL. When his parents asked him whether he'd like to try playing real football, though, he said no. He wasn't interested.

His mom and dad, Jennifer and David, decided to sign Aaron up for football anyway and registered him for Pop Warner (a nationwide football organization for youth founded in 1929). They didn't ask Aaron. They just told him that he was going to play. I've found that parents can do this kind of compulsory sign-up for a boy only up to about age 12 or maybe age 13, but generally no later. If you drive a 16-year-old boy to an activity he doesn't want to attend, he may simply get out of the car and walk away. But Aaron's parents judged correctly that their son was still young enough to go to the practice on their say-so.

Once Aaron was surrounded by the other boys who were doing their best to run, kick, throw, and catch, he joined in. After all, the format of the first day of Pop Warner football isn't much different from gym class at school. It's familiar.

On the drive back home that first day, Jennifer wisely did not ask whether Aaron had a good time. Asking whether Aaron had a good time would have been very nearly equivalent to asking him to admit he was wrong and his parents were right. Instead, she just said, "Practice tomorrow starts at 11 a.m., right?"

He nodded.

The practices were every day, Monday through Friday, sometimes lasting several hours. It was hot. The second week, the boys put on their equipment: helmets, shoulder pads, the whole deal. Mom gasped the first time she saw another boy knock Aaron to the ground. But Aaron got up immediately and trotted back to where the coach was explaining the next drill.

The next day was the first scrimmage. Aaron was knocked down several times, one time pretty hard. It was a hot, muggy August day. On the ride home, Aaron was visibly flushed and tired. After driving in silence for several minutes, his mom finally said, "Aaron, if you want to quit, it's OK. Your Dad and I appreciate your making an effort."

Aaron shook his head no. "Coach can kick me off the team if he wants to," he said, "but I'm not quitting."

The words were so corny, so reminiscent of Richard Gere's line to Louis Gossett Jr. in *An Officer and a Gentleman*, that Mom almost laughed. But then she realized that her son had probably never seen *An Officer and a Gentleman*. He was serious.

Aaron stopped playing video games altogether during football season. When the season ended in November and his team didn't make the play-offs, he said, "Maybe next year."

He started playing Madden NFL again, on and off, after the season ended, but seldom for more than 30 minutes a day. "It's nothing like the real thing," he told his mom spontaneously one day. That's the closest he ever came to thanking his parents for signing him up for real-world football.

The Video Game Meets the Mobile Phone

Many boys still play video games on dedicated platforms such as the Xbox and PlayStation. But a growing proportion are playing games on mobile devices such as cell phones and iPads.[33] Many parents who limit their sons' use of the PlayStation may not realize that they are spending hours in their bedrooms playing games on mobile phones or tablets. *Every screen that your son (or daughter) has is your responsibility, as the parent.* You must govern your child's use of devices until your child is 18 years of age. If you inculcate good habits in childhood and adolescence, those habits are more likely to be maintained after 18 years of age. Conversely, in my book *The Collapse of Parenting*, I described how easily unsupervised use of Internet-enabled devices—such as mobile phones and iPads—facilitates the culture of disrespect, as well as allowing kids to waste enormous amounts of time playing games and surfing the Web. I won't repeat that argument here, except to emphasize that you must be aware of everything your son (or daughter) is doing with every device he or she uses. All the time.

In accordance with guidelines from the American Academy of Pediatrics, I recommend that you install monitoring software on every device your child uses. This software should limit or prohibit the installation of new apps or games without your knowledge.[34] The same software will also report to you how the device is being used and how much time is being spent where. There are many such programs around, such as Net Nanny Mobile and My Mobile Watchdog. These programs can be configured to send their reports to your phone and/or your laptop on a daily basis. If you're going to give your child an Internet-enabled device, then you have a responsibility to know what your child is doing with that device. Explain to your child that you will know how they are using the device. Explain clearly what you expect: No pornography. No cyberbullying. No spending hours on video games.

Another alternative is simply not to give your child a smartphone or tablet. When I speak to parents' groups, some parents gasp in horror and amazement when I make this suggestion. I remind those parents that the iPhone didn't even exist until 2007. It is possible to have a rich and fulfilling childhood and adolescence without constant access to a mobile device. In fact, as I argued in *The Collapse of Parenting*, the devices make it more difficult for kids to develop an authentic sense of self.

Don't do what the neighbors do. It's possible that most of your son's friends have such devices. That doesn't mean your son needs one as well. As I explain in *The Collapse of Parenting*, being a good parent in the United States today means doing things differently from your neighbors.

Insight, or Not

When psychologists say that a client has good *insight*, they mean that the client understands the situation and has a good grasp of what needs to be done. Some boys have insight into their own video-game predicament. Others do not.

Jacob did not. Jacob was 22 years old when his parents brought him to see me in the office. Although he has above-average intelligence, he had been a mediocre student in high school, barely managing to graduate. He now worked a few hours a week assisting his father, who worked as an independent contractor doing home remodeling. His parents were concerned by Jacob's complete lack of ambition. He had no job except for the occasional work provided by his father; no education beyond high school; no interest in further education, vocational or otherwise; and no plans for the future. His parents were also concerned about his lack of a social life. He had no girlfriend, indeed no friends at all.

The four of us met together: Jacob, his parents, and me. His parents spoke first. "I've been researching it online, and I'm worried," his mom said. "He has no ambition. No friends. And no *concern* about any of it. I looked it up online and more than one site mentioned the possibility of schizophrenia."

I nodded, although schizophrenia seemed highly unlikely. After listening to the parents for a few more minutes, I turned to Jacob. "What's your favorite thing to do in your free time?" I asked him.

He snorted. "What do *you* think?" he said.

"I don't know. That's why I asked you," I said.

"Well, it depends," he said. "Jerking off is #1 if I haven't done it in a day or two. But you can't jerk off all day long. Believe me, I've tried to, more than once. So when I'm not jerking off, I play video games." (For those readers outside of North America: "jerking off" is slang for "masturbating.")

"How many hours a day do you spend playing video games?" I asked.

Another snort. "As many as possible," he said.

"How about in the past seven days?" I asked. The four of us then worked through the past seven days, going over what Jacob had done each day as near as they could recall. We concluded that he had spent at least 40 hours in the past seven days playing video games. It was the equivalent of a full-time job. His favorites were violent games such as *Halo*, *World of Warcraft*, *Grand Theft Auto*, and *Assassin's Creed*.

"Do you see a problem there?" I asked Jacob.

"None whatsoever," he said with a charming smile.

"Who are your best friends?" I asked.

"I have dozens. Where do you want me to start?" he answered.

"Just tell me the first names of three of your best friends."

"Their names, or their gamer handles?"

"Preferably a real name," I said.

"Well, there's Jonathan," he said.

"When did you last see Jonathan?" I asked.

"I've never seen Jonathan," Jacob said. "He lives in Singapore. He's in my *World of Warcraft* guild."

"When's the last time you had a friend over at your house?" I asked.

"Yeah, I see what you're getting at. The virtual world isn't as good as the real world, right? That's what you think, right?" Jacob said.

"Yeah, that's fair," I said. "I do think real-world relationships are more important than relationships which exist only online or in a virtual world. So when's the last time you had a friend over at your house?"

No response from Jacob. "It's been a long time," his mom said after a pause.

"Years," his father said.

After another 30 minutes of evaluation, I was ready to make a recommendation. "I don't see any evidence that Jacob has schizophrenia or any other major psychiatric disorder," I said. "And he doesn't appear to be either anxious or depressed. I think that the time he spends playing video games, and other online activities, has displaced his real-world activities. He's spending too much time in front of a computer screen."

"That's what I think, too," his father said. "But what can we do about it?"

"If Jacob were younger, if he were 10 years old instead of 22 years old, then it might be reasonable to impose some limits. If he were 10 years old, you could allow him to play video games for maybe 30 or 40 minutes a day. But that won't work at this age, in my experience."

"Why not?" Mom asked.

I turned to Jacob. "If your parents were to limit your video games to 40 minutes a day, would you turn off the game after 40 minutes?"

Another snort. "No way," he said. "I'm just getting started after 40 minutes."

"That's what I thought," I said. "And if you try to turn off the game in the middle of a game, a man 22 years of age can get upset."

"That's an understatement," Jacob said, and for the first time all three of them—Jacob and his parents—laughed.

"Right," I said. "The only effective intervention in this context, with a man 22 years of age who is spending more than 40 hours a week playing video games, is complete abstinence. You have to eliminate all access to video games."

Jacob's face froze.

"You mean we have to remove the Xbox?" his mother asked.

"Remove the Xbox from the house. Destroy it or give it away. Eliminate all access to the Internet, including the cell phone."

Jacob's face unfroze, changing into an angry grimace. "That's totally unacceptable," he said. "I'm an adult. I'm over 18. You can't tell me what to do. My parents can't tell me what to do."

"That's right," I said. "You are an adult. You are free to walk out of your parents' house and make your own way in the world.

But if you leave"—and now I glanced at the parents—"if you leave, your parents are not to support you. You are on your own. Right now you are living in your parents' home, but you're not paying your way. You don't pay rent. They pay for your food. They pay for your Internet access. If you are going to stay in their house, then you have to abide by their rules."

With my encouragement, the parents followed my instructions. They donated the Xbox, and all the video games they could find in the house, to Goodwill. They took away their son's cell phone. They removed the computer from his room. They password-protected their own computer and refused to allow their son to access it.

Four weeks later, they were back, as I had requested.

"It's unbelievable, the difference," Dad said.

"What's different?" I asked.

"Everything is different," he replied. "At work, for example. It used to be pulling teeth to get Jacob to help me at all, and I had to check everything he did. But now he's showing initiative. And to be blunt: he's a lot smarter than I thought he was."

"How do you mean?" I asked.

"Well, take this past week, for example," Jacob's father said. "We were doing an upscale remodeling job. The homeowner wanted us to install this high-tech shower unit with massage jets, body jets, everything, all voice-controlled by computer. I didn't want to tell the owner the truth, which is that I had never done anything like it. I was struggling. Jacob stepped right in, showed me how to do it, and did most of the wiring himself. He figured it out just by reading the instructions. The unit worked perfectly. It was impressive."

Jacob was staring down at the floor, but I thought I saw a hint of a smile on his face.

"It wasn't easy," his mom said. "Not at first. Jacob didn't talk to us at all for the first week. He would make his own meals and take them into his room. But then after about a week he started joining us for supper. And he just seemed to *wake up*. It was as though he had been in a fog, all those years he was playing video games. Maybe he just wasn't getting enough sleep. Now he actually talks at suppertime."

"He just seems smarter now. He understands better. He's got a better attention span. He's got more patience," Dad said.

"What do you think?" I asked Jacob. "Do you agree?"

"No I don't," Jacob said. "I don't feel any different. Not any smarter, that's for sure."

"If it were up to you, would you start playing video games again tomorrow?" I asked.

"Absolutely," Jacob said.

His parents sighed.

Jacob showed no *insight*. No awareness of how his video games had displaced real-world activities.

Don't wait for your son to show insight into his situation. I have seen many parents who expect their 11- or 15- or 24-year-old son to act logically on the basis of the evidence. The parents will say: "Look how much time video games are taking out of your life. See how your friendships have withered since you started spending 20 hours a week in front of a screen. See how tired you are all the time, except when you are playing the game."

Parents consider these points compelling. They expect their son to have *insight* and to act based on the evidence.

Don't wait. You may be waiting months, years. If your son is one of the millions of boys or young men who have allowed video games to displace real life, you must intervene. Remove the device, if necessary. Limit screen time.

If you don't, who will?

B ACK IN 2006, I WROTE AN OP-ED FOR THE *WASHINGTON POST* about the growing problem of unmotivated boys. We'll return to that op-ed, and the response it elicited from readers, in chapter 6. For now I just want to share with you an e-mail I received from a parent in North Carolina:

> Dear Dr. Sax,
>
> I read your article in the Washington Post. I'm not an expert, just a Mom. I have my own theory. I think video games are the main culprits in this phenomenon [of unmotivated boys]. I wish I had somehow shielded my son from such games or at least put a strict limit on them. When I see guys in their twenties who are totally unmotivated, mooching on someone else and lack any social skills that will benefit them in the workplace or in life, I've noticed a common thread: an obsession with video games.
>
> Video games teach these boys that if you manipulate things a certain way, you will get an easy win. These boys have little interaction with people during the years when such interaction is crucial in developing the skills they need to handle themselves as an adult. They shut themselves off to the real world and get caught up in their fantasy worlds. After a while, they prefer their fantasies to the real world. In the real world, things are

not so easy to control. They can't rule with a joystick. In the real
world they have to talk to people. They have to work.

That brings up another point. Laziness. A guy addicted
to video games can waste hour after hour after hour without
doing anything productive. Playing games is easy. Studying is
hard. Taking care of daily chores is hard. Working on a real
job is hard.

We parents are to blame for some of this because it started
out as a way to entertain our kids. We justified it by saying they
were developing their hand/eye coordination. They were home,
we knew what they were doing, they were out of our hair and
not causing trouble. Now they are in their twenties and we are
scratching our heads wondering, "What's their problem?"

I think if you were to research the growing popularity of
video games and compare it to the growing number of young
men living at home, you would find a parallel. I know that
sounds simplistic, but sometimes the answers to complex
questions are as plain as the nose on our face.

Cheryl M.

North Carolina

In this chapter, I've argued that video games are one factor derailing many boys. In the previous chapter, I suggested that
changes in the education system—including the shift away from
competitive formats in school—constitute another factor. But
those changes aren't the whole story. I can think of plenty of boys
who aren't motivated to succeed but who don't play video games
and who don't thrive on competition. They're not motivated by
the will to power. They're just not motivated, period.

What's their story?

4

The Third Factor

Medications for ADHD

FROM THE AGE OF 2, TIMMY WAS FASCINATED BY TRUCKS. HE WOULD bang his toy trucks together, then pick them up and race around the house going *vroom-vroom*. When he was 3, Timmy and the family's yellow Labrador, Miss Demeanor, got into the bad habit of chasing the UPS truck down the street, after the UPS driver had been friendly to them one day. Aside from the fact that 3-year-olds shouldn't be running down the middle of a street, even in our suburban cul-de-sac nestled safely off the main road, the real problem with that habit was that once Timmy was outdoors, he was *gone*. He would start running after the truck and just keep going. He'd forget to come home, and he'd wander, fearlessly and aimlessly, through other people's backyards and driveways, with Miss Demeanor trotting faithfully behind him. It was especially frightening for Timmy's mother, Carol. After driving around the development looking for Timmy and the dog one evening, she considered having an invisible fence installed and putting the collar around Miss Demeanor's neck—and maybe a collar around Timmy's neck, too.

Aside from chasing after delivery trucks, Timmy was the darling of our neighborhood. His energy and enthusiasm for life were contagious.

Then came kindergarten. Timmy's teacher, Mrs. Engelhardt, spoke with Carol after the third week. "Timmy seems hyperactive," Mrs. Engelhardt said.

"Isn't that pretty normal for a 5-year-old boy?" Carol asked.

"Not really. I know you may think so," Mrs. Engelhardt said, before Carol could interrupt. "But as a teacher, I see a whole range of children. I've seen hundreds of children in the 11 years since I started teaching, and I just thought you should know that Timmy may be having some difficulties staying focused."

"You mean ADD?" Carol said.

"Well, I'm not a doctor," Mrs. Engelhardt said. "I don't make diagnoses. I just want you to be aware that Timmy is having trouble staying in his seat. He just can't sit still very long before he starts wiggling. I tell him to sit still, and he does, and then five minutes later he's wriggling in his chair again and giggling. It's very distracting to the other children."

"I'll talk to him," Carol promised.

Carol talked to Timmy, told him that he needed to sit still and be quiet, but Timmy seemed not to hear. By late October, both Mrs. Engelhardt and the school counselor were encouraging Carol to have Timmy seen by a doctor. So Carol made an appointment with Timmy's pediatrician.

On the day of the visit, the doctor's office was crowded with crying children who looked sick. There wasn't any space left in the "well-baby" corner of the office. Carol tried to shield her son from the germs she could almost see wafting through the air. After a half-hour wait, Timmy's name was called.

Dr. Feldman looked over the note from the school. "I see that the school is concerned about Timmy. They think he may have ADHD,"* she said. "What do you think, Carol?"

"I don't see anything really wrong with Timmy," Carol said. "I mean, Mrs. Engelhardt is concerned because Timmy won't sit still. But since when does kindergarten mean sitting still in a chair all day long? I thought kindergarten was supposed to be about singing songs, playing games, that sort of thing."

"You're about 30 years out of date," Dr. Feldman said, but not in a mean way. "That's what kindergarten *used* to be about. Today's kindergarten is pretty much what 1st grade was 30 years ago. Kindergarten nowadays is mostly about sitting in a chair with paper and pencil and learning to read and write."

"But if my son isn't ready to do that, does that mean my *son* has a problem? Maybe the *school* has a problem," Carol protested. "Maybe the problem is with the school expecting a 5-year-old boy to sit still in a chair all day long. You know his school has all-day kindergarten."

"That's a fair point," Dr. Feldman said. "There's some evidence that 5-year-old boys, on average, may be less ready and less able to sit for long periods of time than the average 5-year-old girl." Dr. Feldman's beeper went off. She glanced at it. "That's the NICU," she said. "I'm going to have to interrupt our visit, I'm afraid. But here are the options, briefly. Option number one: no medication,

---

* ADHD = Attention Deficit Hyperactivity Disorder. The older term, no longer "correct," is ADD, Attention Deficit Disorder. However, many parents still use the term ADD, and I use the two terms interchangeably here.

no change in the basic plan at school. Instead, you just work harder with Timmy. Try to get him to behave the way the teachers want him to behave."

"What's option number two?" Carol asked.

"Option number two would be to pull Timmy out of kindergarten now, put him back in pre-K, and try kindergarten again next year," Dr. Feldman said.

"You're saying I should hold him back."

"It's not such a bad idea, really," Dr. Feldman said. "As you yourself said a minute ago, there's something crazy about schools expecting 5-year-old boys to sit still at a desk for six hours a day. Some boys can do it. Many girls can do it. But for many boys—for the boys who aren't ready to sit still in a chair all day long—their first experience of school is one long frustrating bore. And once they get off to a bad start, things can snowball in the wrong direction. One year can make a big difference. Often a boy will be more willing and able to sit still in class when he's 6 than when he was 5. That one year can make all the difference in the world."

Carol paused. Then she said, "But how would I explain to my friends, and my parents, that my son flunked out of kindergarten? They'd think he's retarded. And I know Timmy is bright." Carol saw Dr. Feldman look again at the message on her beeper. "No, I can't do that. I won't hold my son back. What's option number three?"

"The third option is medication. Adderall, Vyvanse, Metadate, Concerta. I usually start with a low dose of Concerta with these boys. If that works, great. If not, we adjust the dose."

"But stimulants like Concerta and Adderall and the others— aren't they harmful?"

"All medications have the potential for harm," Dr. Feldman said, standing up, suddenly impatient. "A child can die from swallowing 20 tablets of Tylenol. I've seen it happen." She looked again at her pager. "I'm sorry, Carol, but I have to answer this page. Think about what we discussed. Call my office if you decide you want to start the medication for your son."

Carol agonized over her decision for a week. She talked to friends. She searched the Internet. Finally she called and asked for the prescription Dr. Feldman had suggested.

Timmy's initial response to the medication reassured Carol that she had made the right choice. Timmy's behavior in school improved instantly, the very first day he took the medication. "You did the right thing," Timmy's teacher told her. "Now we can see how smart Timmy really is. He really is a very bright boy."

Dr. Feldman recommended that Timmy take the medication every day including weekends and holidays. But Carol decided not to make him take it over Christmas vacation. The first two days he was off the medication, she was alarmed by his behavior. The old impulsivity and energy were back, but with an unfamiliar edge. He didn't come inside when she called for him. When she went to bring him indoors, he suddenly threw his plastic hockey stick at her—directly at her, as if he wanted to hurt her. He had never done anything like that before.

The next day, and every day thereafter for the next two years, she made sure he took his medication. Dr. Feldman increased the dose the following fall, in October of 1st grade, when the teachers again said that Timmy wasn't paying attention.

The following spring, Carol heard about a study showing that boys who took medications like Concerta were likely to be shorter as adults than boys who didn't take those medications—3 to 4 inches shorter, if they began the medication at age 5 as Timmy had and stayed on it for ten years.[1] Carol is short, just 5'1" tall, and Timmy's father is on the short side, at 5'8". Timmy was already showing a love for basketball, and Carol didn't want to be responsible for Timmy ending up at 5'7" when he might have been 5'11".

So, when school let out that June, she stopped giving Timmy the medication. As she expected, Timmy showed "rebound." He was more impulsive than ever. But she also noticed something she had never seen before: Timmy had become lazy. It wasn't just that he didn't want to do his chores. He didn't want to do much of anything. Before, he had been enthusiastic about any project she or Timmy's grandparents would propose. He'd go fishing with his grandfather, or pick weeds in the garden with his grandmother, and he would enjoy it. Nothing was boring to him. Now everything was boring, except for video games.

Carol came to me for a second opinion that August. "I just don't know what to do," she said. "If I don't start him back on the medication, I'm dreading what school will be like—the phone calls from the teachers and all that. But I'm really bothered by what I'm seeing in Timmy this summer. He's been off the medication for two months, and he's not getting any better. The laziness—that's something totally new for him. The lack of motivation. Do you think Timmy would have been like that now if he hadn't ever taken the medication?"

"It's hard to say for sure what *might* have happened," I said.

"I stopped his medication because I was worried it might stunt his growth," Carol said. "Now I'm finding out all these other problems. But what other options do I have?"

THE SYNDROME WE CALL ADHD HAS PROBABLY ALWAYS BEEN WITH us. Despite some claims to the contrary, ADHD was not invented by drug companies eager to sell more medications.[2] It's not hard to find accounts of boys written 100 or more years ago who met all of the modern criteria for ADHD. Some of those accounts are in medical journals. Others are in short stories and novels.

Take Tom Sawyer, for example. If you've never actually read Mark Twain's novel *The Adventures of Tom Sawyer*, you may want to read it now—if only to get some perspective on how the normative view of American boys has changed in the past 150 years. The official guidebook containing criteria for all psychiatric diagnoses is the American Psychiatric Association's *Diagnostic and Statistical Manual*, now in its fifth edition—usually abbreviated DSM-5. Some of the official DSM-5 criteria for ADHD include:

- "Often fails to give close attention to details or makes careless mistakes in schoolwork."
- "Often has difficulty sustaining attention in tasks."
- "Often avoids, dislikes, or is reluctant to engage in tasks that require sustained mental effort (e.g., schoolwork or homework)."[3]

Tom Sawyer fulfills these criteria in abundance. He has no interest in school or schoolwork. Any indoor task that requires sustained reading is a task that Tom will probably not do well, if he does it at all. And despite attending Sunday school regularly, he appears not to have absorbed any of the information imparted to him there. He does at one point decide that he wants to win a prize Bible so as to impress Becky Thatcher. Children in his congregation are awarded special tickets when they memorize verses from the Bible. Tom trades knickknacks with his buddies to garner the necessary number of tickets needed to win a prize Bible—corresponding to memorizing 2,000 verses. He turns in the tickets and is awarded the Bible. At the award ceremony, Becky Thatcher's father is about to bestow the award Bible on Tom, when he asks Tom to mention the names of just two of the twelve disciples of Jesus. Tom is at a complete loss. He finally blurts out, "David and Goliath!"

Many thoughtful people have pointed out that Tom Sawyer and boys like him would be diagnosed as having ADHD if they were to show up in a 21st-century American school. These people have suggested, with good reason, that perhaps the pathology lies not in the boy but in the school. In my first book, *Why Gender Matters*, I told the story of a boy who needed to be on multiple medications for ADHD when he was in school; but when he was assisting a professional hunter in Zimbabwe, he didn't need the medications at all, even when he had to sit motionless in the bush for long periods of time. (Update: in the years since I wrote *Why Gender Matters*, that boy has gone on to college and has published his poems and short stories in his college's journals—without taking any medication for ADHD.)

The fact remains that if Tom Sawyer is going to graduate from a 21st-century high school and go on to college, he is going to have to be able to sit still and pay attention in class. To help him do that, his parents may ask their doctor for help. And the doctor is likely to prescribe a medication such as Adderall, Vyvanse, Ritalin, Concerta, Metadate, Focalin, or Daytrana.

Stimulant medications such as Ritalin and Dexedrine have been on the market for over 50 years. Newer versions, such as Adderall, Vyvanse, Concerta, Focalin, and Metadate, have been available only since the 1990s or more recently. There has been an explosion in the use of these "academic steroids" for the treatment of ADHD. American boys in 2013 were roughly 10 times more likely to be diagnosed with ADHD compared with American boys in 1979.[4]

"Why Not Give It a Try?"

How come boys today are so much more likely to be taking these medications compared with 30-plus years ago?

Several factors account for the greater willingness of doctors today to medicate young minds and the greater willingness of parents to accept and even to seek out such medication.[5] One factor is our cultural shift away from individual responsibility and toward third-party explanations. Thirty years ago, if a boy swore at his parents and spit at his teacher, the neighbors might say that he was a rude boy who needed a good spanking. Today, the same behavior from a similar boy is more likely to prompt a trip to the pediatrician or to the child psychiatrist, and the doctor is likely to "diagnose" the boy with Oppositional-Defiant Disorder (DSM–5 313.81). The main criterion for Oppositional-Defiant Disorder is disobedient and disrespectful behavior that persists despite the best efforts of the grown-ups.[6]

Is there really much of a difference between a neighbor saying "Your son is rude" and a doctor saying "Your son may have Oppositional-Defiant Disorder"? I think there is. If another parent whom you respect suggests that your son is a rude boy who needs structure and discipline, you just might consider adopting a more authoritative parenting style. But if a doctor says that your son has a psychiatric diagnosis, then the next step might reasonably be to ask whether a medication would be appropriate.

You can see how the assignment of responsibility differs in these two cases. If your son is rude and disrespectful, then your son and you (his parents) have to take responsibility. You have to own up to the problem. You will probably have to make some changes. But if your son has a psychiatric diagnosis, that means he may have a chemical imbalance in his brain. He—and you—are no more to blame for that imbalance than if your son were diagnosed with childhood leukemia, right? Psychiatrist Jennifer Harris has pointed out that today, "many clinicians find it easier to tell parents their child has a brain-based disorder than to suggest parenting changes."[7]

Another factor has to do with the inappropriate acceleration of the early elementary curriculum. We discussed in chapter 2 how the 1st-grade curriculum of 30 years ago has become the kindergarten curriculum of today. If 5-year-old Justin fidgets and taps his pencil and sometimes stands up in class for no reason, he may be referred to the doctor's office. Mom brings along a piece of paper from the teacher explaining the school's concerns. "They think that Justin may have ADHD."

I obtained funding from the American Academy of Family Physicians to survey doctors in Washington, DC, and surrounding suburbs about ADHD. We asked many questions, but the most important one was: "Who first suggests the diagnosis of ADHD?" Is it the doctor? Some other professional? Mom? Dad? A teacher? A neighbor? A relative? The doctors told us that the person most likely to suggest the diagnosis is the teacher.[8]

Don't get me wrong. There's nothing wrong with teachers referring students with a concern about the student's ability to pay attention. On several occasions, I have visited schools at the request of parents to observe their son in the classroom after a teacher has made such a referral. In every case I investigated, the teacher's observation was correct. Justin isn't paying attention. He's looking up at the ceiling or staring out the window or tapping his pencil. If the teacher says Justin isn't paying attention, then you can be sure: he's not paying attention.

But *why* isn't Justin paying attention? Does he truly have ADHD? Or is there some other reason?

It's the doctor's job to determine whether Justin's lack of attention is due to ADHD or to some other cause. Unfortunately, most pediatricians and family physicians simply do not have the training or experience (or enough time in their schedules) to perform a sophisticated assessment of a 5- or 6- or 7-year-old boy to determine whether that boy's difficulties are due to ADHD or to some other problem. To their credit, just about every pediatrician and family physician who responded to our survey recognized that fact.

So what do the doctors do when asked to evaluate such a boy? We found that in a few cases, the doctor refers the child to a developmental psychologist who is qualified to perform such an assessment. That doesn't happen very often, for several reasons. One is that many health plans in the United States don't cover such assessments, or if they do, they provide only reduced or partial coverage. The out-of-pocket costs for such an assessment usually begin around $1,000, but they can run much higher.

Another reason is that many American doctors believe in the philosophy, "Let's try it and see if it helps." If you think Justin might have ADHD, try giving him a medication for ADHD. If that helps, great. If not, then maybe it would be appropriate to go ahead and spend the money on the formal assessment. Or maybe just increase the dose.

These medications often will, indeed, improve the attention span and academic performance of many of the boys for whom they are prescribed. And for many parents today, that's all they need to know. If their boy is struggling in school, and the teacher suggests that these medications might help, and the doctor agrees—and the parents know three or four other boys in the same class who are already taking these same medications, apparently with good results—why not give it a try? And if the medication seems to help, then everybody is happy.

Back in 2006, I had the privilege of speaking at a conference at Harvard University entitled "Learning and the Brain." I wish I could say that my presentation was the most interesting, the buzz of the conference, but it wasn't. The presentation that had everybody talking was a presentation given by Massachusetts Institute of Technology professor John Gabrieli.

Dr. Gabrieli's team somehow obtained permission to give powerful ADHD medications to normal children. These researchers also obtained permission to withhold ADHD medication from boys (and a few girls) who undeniably did have ADHD. Then Dr. Gabrieli's team tested both groups, on and off medication, to see how well both groups could learn with and without the medication. There was an audible gasp in the audience when Dr. Gabrieli showed us the crucial slide: medication for ADHD improved the performance of normal kids by the same degree that it improved the performance of kids with ADHD.[9]

That's a tremendously important finding. Many times I've been asked to provide a second opinion of a boy who's already been diagnosed with ADHD. The parents come to me for a variety of reasons. Sometimes the in-laws have told them that their son doesn't need, or shouldn't take, medication. Sometimes the parents have seen something scary on TV about these drugs. So I evaluate their son, let's call him Jake. After doing the evaluation, I have sometimes said, "I'm just not convinced that Jake really has ADHD."

One of the parents answers, "But the other doctor prescribed Vyvanse, and it's made such a difference. Jake is doing so much better since he's been on the medication. He's much less fidgety in class. The teacher says he's much better behaved and more focused. And his grades are up."

In other words, these parents—and Jake's doctor as well, in this case—are interpreting the positive response to the medication as evidence to confirm the diagnosis. "If medication for ADHD helps Jake to learn better, doesn't that mean that Jake probably has ADHD?"

As many of us have long suspected, and as is confirmed by Dr. Gabrieli's study and others like it, the answer to that question is no. These medications—Adderall, Vyvanse, Ritalin, Concerta, Metadate, Focalin, Daytrana, and other stimulants—are likely to improve the performance of a normal child just as much as a child who truly has ADHD. Just because these medications improve a child's performance in class does not mean that the child has ADHD.

"But where's the harm?" one parent asked me. "If the medication helps my son to do better in class, and it doesn't seem to be hurting him in any way, why not give it to him?"

Where's the harm, indeed? Many boys do look and feel more or less OK while they're taking these medications. What these parents don't know—and what the doctor also may not know—is that even relatively short-term use of these drugs can lead to changes in personality. As a result of taking these medications, the boy who used to be agreeable, outgoing, and adventurous may become lazy and disengaged.

The Nucleus Accumbens[10]

Professor William Carlezon and his colleagues at Harvard Medical School were among the first to report that when they gave stimulant medications—such as those used to treat children who have been diagnosed with ADHD—to juvenile laboratory animals, the result was that those animals displayed a loss of drive when they grow up.[11] These animals look normal, but they're lazy. They don't want to work hard for anything, not even to escape a bad situation.

The Harvard investigators suggested that the stimulant medications might cause a similar phenomenon in children. Children who take these medications may look fine while they're taking them. They may look fine after they stop taking them. But when they're no longer taking the medication, they won't have much drive. They won't have much get-up-and-go.

The stimulant medications appear to exert their harmful effects by damaging an area in the developing brain called the *nucleus accumbens*, both in humans and in laboratory animals.[12] For neuroscientists, that's not much of a surprise. All these medications work by mimicking the action of dopamine, a neurotransmitter vital in transmitting nerve impulses in the brain—and the nucleus accumbens has a high concentration of dopamine receptors.[13] If you give any of these medications to a child, the medication is likely to bind to receptors in the nucleus accumbens, which may disrupt the development of the nucleus accumbens.

The nucleus accumbens is the brain's motivational center.[14] More precisely, the nucleus accumbens is the part of the brain that is responsible for translating motivation into action. If a boy's nucleus accumbens is damaged, he may still feel hungry—he just won't feel motivated to do much about it. If you damage the nucleus accumbens, the result is likely to be less motivation, less engagement, less drive to achieve in the real world. That may be the end result of long-term use of medications such as Adderall, Vyvanse, Ritalin, Concerta, Metadate, Focalin, or Daytrana.

Many of the studies mentioned here are based on research in laboratory animals, not in humans. But researchers have now documented that stimulant medications prescribed for ADHD may actually shrink the nucleus accumbens and related structures in the *human* brain, although some of these changes may be transient in some individuals.[15] Other researchers have found that even occasional use of these medications results in changes in the structure of the brain.[16] The smaller size of the nucleus accumbens in people treated with medication for ADHD can't be attributed to ADHD itself, because ADHD itself is associated with a slightly *larger*-than-average nucleus accumbens.[17] It appears, then, that stimulant medications for ADHD may shrink the nucleus accumbens in humans.

That's especially disturbing in light of research documenting a nearly linear correlation between the nucleus accumbens and individual motivation. These studies suggest that the smaller the nucleus accumbens, the more likely a person is to be apathetic, lacking in drive.[18]

Lack of motivation is different from, and not necessarily associated with, depression. A young man might be completely unmotivated and still be perfectly happy and content. We'll come back to that phenomenon—the happy but unmotivated young man— when we discuss the "failure to launch" phenomenon in chapter 6.

When I rattle off that list of medications—Adderall, Vyvanse, Ritalin, Concerta, Metadate, Focalin, and Daytrana—you may think I'm talking about seven different medications. In fact, I'm talking about just two medications: amphetamine and methylphenidate. Adderall and Vyvanse are proprietary blends of amphetamine. Ritalin, Concerta, Focalin, Metadate, and Daytrana are each a proprietary version of methylphenidate.

Can we say with 100 percent certainty that these medications cause lasting injury to the brain? Of course not. It's very difficult to say anything in medicine with 100 percent certainty. But our job, as parents, often requires us to make decisions when some doubt still exists about the right course of action. If you wait until we know for sure that these medications are dangerous, your child may be middle-aged.

I generally recommend that parents choose a safer alternative. If a parent is convinced that a child needs a medication for ADHD, then I often suggest a nonstimulant such as Wellbutrin, Intuniv, or Strattera. All medications have risks, but the nonstimulant medications do not pose a risk of damage to the nucleus accumbens. They don't mimic the action of dopamine.

The Drug Enforcement Administration has classified Adderall, Vyvanse, Ritalin, Concerta, Metadate, Focalin, and Daytrana as Schedule II drugs. Among all prescription medications, Schedule II drugs are considered the ones with the highest potential for abuse and addiction. (Schedule I drugs, such as heroin, are not legal for clinical use at all.) I advise parents to avoid Schedule II drugs for their children except as a last resort. There are, as I said, many safer alternatives. Wellbutrin, Intuniv, and Strattera are not Schedule II—and indeed are not scheduled at all. And in case you're wondering, I have no affiliation with, and I accept no payment from, the companies that developed or manufacture Wellbutrin, Intuniv, and Strattera.

What about girls? Would girls be affected in the same way? We don't know for sure. Most of the researchers working with laboratory animals have studied only male animals. There's substantial evidence that the neurological substrate of ADHD in girls and women may differ significantly from the substrate of ADHD in boys and men.[19] So we can't assume that what's true for males holds true for females, or vice versa. More research on sex differences in the consequences of treatment for ADHD, and on the long-term consequences of these medications generally, is needed.

Drug companies spend tens of millions of dollars every year promoting medications such as Adderall, Vyvanse, Concerta, and Metadate. But nobody is buying ads to warn parents and doctors about the possible risks. To be sure, those risks are not proven beyond a reasonable doubt. We have a few studies, but not enough to say with certainty that these medications cause lasting damage to the human brain. I think they probably do. But maybe they don't.

Would you like to volunteer your son for the trial?

"An Antiquated Relic of the Victorian Era"

We have considered a variety of evidence that the stimulant medications most often prescribed for ADHD may adversely affect children. And as we have seen, some studies suggest that these adverse effects may be lasting: studies in laboratory animals, in particular, have shown that taking these medications during youth or adolescence may negatively affect learning and motivation in adulthood.

But I've also had firsthand experience with boys who have proven that these adverse effects can be overcome.

I first met Jared when I did his prekindergarten physical. He was 5 years old: bright, outgoing, and friendly. Kindergarten, 1st grade, and 2nd grade all went well. Problems began in 3rd grade, when Jared was 8 years old. He started complaining about school, calling it "stupid." The teachers were beginning to tell the parents that Jared wasn't paying attention in class. He had tested in the gifted range, especially in creative writing and in art, but the problems actually seemed to have started after he was put into the gifted and talented classes, despite the very small class sizes. And his grades were starting to suffer.

Jared's mother, Deborah, had researched the situation thoroughly. When she brought Jared to see me, she had already diagnosed the problem: Jared had ADHD, "predominantly inattentive type" (she was using the professional jargon quite appropriately). "The reason he doesn't like school is because he can't pay attention, because of his ADHD, so he doesn't do well," she explained to me. "Jared is a perfectionist. He hates to do something if he can't do it perfectly." Jared's mother didn't really even want me to do my own evaluation; she just wanted me to prescribe medication. "I'm concerned that if we don't take action now, while he's still young, the situation could snowball," she told me. "He'll decide he hates school, and he'll start to fall behind. We definitely need to do something."

This encounter took place in the fall of 1996, when I had less confidence in my own judgment and diagnostic skills than I have now. And Deborah was quite determined. I suspect that any doctor might have had difficulty persuading her to change course. I insisted on a brief (30-minute) evaluation. At the end of that evaluation, I still wasn't persuaded that Jared really had ADHD, of any variety. But Deborah said, "Why don't we just try a low dose of medication and see whether it helps?" (Remember, this was ten years before Dr. Gabrieli did his study showing that ADHD medications improve performance even in kids who don't have ADHD.)

So I agreed to prescribe Ritalin, 5 milligrams twice daily. It had no effect—no beneficial effect, at least. Jared and Deborah returned three weeks later.

"He needs a stronger dose," Deborah said authoritatively.

"I'm sorry," I said. "I'm just not persuaded that increasing Jared's medication is the right course of action. I tell you what. How about if you take Jared to see Dr. So-and-so"—and I named a renowned expert on ADHD. "He's a consultant to the National Institutes of Health. He's written a book on the subject. Let's see what he has to say."

Deborah took her son to be evaluated by the famous expert. He agreed with her: Jared needed a stronger dose of medication. When that didn't help, the doctor switched Jared from Ritalin to Adderall. When Jared became even more moody and withdrawn, the doctor said that Jared must have depression in addition to ADHD, and he added Prozac. When Jared began having angry outbursts at school, the doctor added a third medication, clonidine. Jared was now 9 years old, and he still hated school, but now he was on three medications. At that point the family switched health insurance plans to one we didn't accept, and I lost touch with them.

Four years passed. Dad got a promotion, and the family switched back to a plan that included us in its network. One day I noticed that Jared's name was on the schedule for a routine school physical. I looked in the nurse's note under the listing of medications and saw "None."

Interesting.

I walked into the room. I barely recognized Jared. He was a totally different kid: not merely older, but transformed. He was now muscular and tan. But the biggest difference was that he was smiling—a big smile like I hadn't seen on his face since he was in kindergarten. "Hello, Jared," I said. "Nice to see you again. So tell me: What's your favorite thing to do in your spare time?" This is a good break-the-ice question for girls and boys in this age group, I have found.

"My favorite thing to do in my spare time?" Jared repeated, thinking the question over. "Well, right now, my favorite thing to do is to read about ancient Minoa," he said.

"How's that?" I asked.

"Well, maybe ancient Crete. Or Mycenae." He launched into a fascinating lecture about the ancient island of Thera, in the Aegean Sea. This island was destroyed by a massive volcanic explosion around 1500 BC, he explained. "But the people living there must have known the volcano was about to erupt," he told me, "because when you excavate the remnants of the island—which is now called Santorini, but it's really just the caldera of the volcano that used to be Thera—when you excavate the caldera, you find sheep bones and cattle bones but no human bones."

I was just glad I remembered what a "caldera" was.

Jared continued with his lecture. He taught me how that cataclysmic event may have served as the source of the myth of Atlantis, recorded by Plato roughly 1,000 years after the event—a myth about an advanced civilization crumbling into the sea as the result of a natural disaster. I was fascinated. Jared gave me the title of a book on the subject to read so that I could learn more.[20]

I went out to talk with Deborah. "I'm amazed," I told her. "I'm so glad to see—what a tremendous change! Tell me what happened," I said, but before she could answer, I tried to answer my own question. "I bet I know what happened. I bet you stopped the medications. I was so uneasy about such a young boy taking all those medications."

Mom shook her head. "We tried stopping the medication, but he got worse. More withdrawn, more grumpy. The doctor you sent us to was worried Jared might be suicidal and talked about hospitalizing him. So we went back on the medications, even though they really didn't seem to be helping much."

"So what's the secret?" I asked. "What turned everything around?"

Deborah said, "We transferred him from Byron to The Heights."*

Now it was my turn to shake my head. "But Byron is an outstanding school," I said. "And so is The Heights. They're both excellent schools. How could transferring Jared from one excellent school to another excellent school make such a huge difference?"

Deborah matter-of-factly responded, "The Heights is all boys. Byron is coed."

"What possible difference could that make?" I asked—and before she could reply, I said, "Look, I don't mean to be disrespectful, but we're in the 21st century now. As near as I can see, single-sex education is an antiquated relic of the Victorian era. We live in a coed world. School should prepare kids for the real world. The real world is coed. So school should be coed. That just seems pretty straightforward to me."

Deborah responded: "You need to visit The Heights, Dr. Sax. Jared was miserable at the old school. The people at Byron had

---

*The name I have given the coed school, "Byron," is fictitious; "The Heights," in Potomac, Maryland, is the true name of the school to which this boy transferred.

determined, quite correctly, that Jared is gifted in art and in creative writing. So they put him in special advanced classes in art and creative writing—where he was the only boy, or sometimes just one of two boys. Most of the other kids in the class were always girls. So the other boys teased him. 'You like art, you must be a fag,' they said. Jared asked to drop out of the art class. He came to feel that school was a waste of time. His talents just led to him being made fun of. But he couldn't pretend to like the things that the other boys like, that boys are 'supposed' to like at a coed school. So he was just miserable. At The Heights, he's just blossomed. Obviously all the kids in the art class at The Heights are boys. Same with the creative writing class. And it's just amazing how rapidly his interests have expanded in the years he's been at The Heights. Not just academically. His favorite teacher, the history teacher, is also the lacrosse coach. So Jared decided to try lacrosse, and you know what? He's pretty good! We were able to stop the medications after a few months at the Heights. It was clear he just didn't need medication. He needed a different school."

This was an epiphany of sorts for me. I attended only coed schools. I had always thought of single-sex education as an out-of-date relic of a bygone era. Maybe I would have to reconsider.

I wanted to share this true story with you for two reasons. Most important, in the context of this chapter, I think it's important to stress that despite all the scary news about Adderall and Vyvanse and Concerta and Metadate, the fact that a boy has taken these medications does not mean that he is doomed. In the many years since Deborah told me about the benefits of a boys' school for her son, I've seen many other similar cases: boys who were put on medications when they attended a typical coed school, who were able to stop those medications after switching to a boys' school or a boy-friendly school, and who blossomed into well-rounded students and athletes after making the transition. Those cases have led me to believe that, in many cases, boys are being put on these medications to fit the boy to the school. I've come to believe that we should not medicate boys so they fit the school; we should change the school to fit the boy.

Which leads me to the second reason I think this story is important. In Jared's case, the school was his salvation. Switching schools made all the difference. The parents were as dedicated and concerned and involved as any parents can be, all along, but until they transferred Jared to a school that was a better match for him, Jared was heading in the wrong direction.

I'm not saying that The Heights is a "better" school than Byron. I know other families who prefer Byron to The Heights. They feel that The Heights is too strict, or that it has too strong a religious affiliation. Recall the point I made in chapter 2: there's no such thing as the "best" school without specifying the particular child who will be attending there. The best school for Jared may be a bad choice for his brother Jason. You have to know your child and then find the school that is the best match for your child.

ONE OF THE CENTRAL QUESTIONS WE ARE TRYING TO ANSWER IN THIS book is why we are seeing so many boys today who just don't seem motivated. What has changed in just the past 20 to 30 years that might account for this emerging phenomenon? So far, we've identified three factors:

1. Changes in educational format and curricula over the past
   30 years—in particular:

   - The acceleration of the early elementary curriculum
     (e.g., phonics in kindergarten)
   - The shift in emphasis away from *Kenntnis* to *Wissen-*
     schaft (e.g., screens replacing field trips)
   - The abolition of competitive formats (everybody getting
     a trophy)
   - School becoming less friendly to boys (no throwing snow-
     balls, no writing stories about the Battle of Stalingrad)
2. The advent of realistic, immersive video games
3. The overprescribing of stimulant medications

Both video games (factor #2) and medications (factor #3) may
undermine the motivation to accomplish and succeed in the real
world. Video games can undermine motivation, as we discussed
in the previous chapter, by shifting motivation out of the real
world into the virtual world. The boy who is spending many hours
a week playing video games may come to care more about getting
to the next level in *Grand Theft Auto* than he cares about earning
an A in English. And the medications can undermine motivation
by having a direct effect on the brain, shrinking the nucleus accumbens. In either case, the result is boys who look normal, who
feel normal, but who just don't see the point of working hard to
achieve some objective in the real world.

But when I first wrote about this topic for publication, I hadn't
identified any of the three factors listed above. My first article on this
topic followed a completely different line of inquiry and evidence,
which has now become my fourth factor: endocrine disruptors.[21]

5

The Fourth Factor

Endocrine Disruptors

Fish on the Wild Side

For 19 years, I lived in the outer suburbs of Washington, DC. For the last 14 of those 19 years, the medical office where I worked was located only a few blocks from my home. I could walk or ride my bike to work. On some mornings, I would indulge my taste for *schadenfreude* by listening to the traffic reports on the radio. The Woodrow Wilson Bridge was often featured on those reports. The Wilson Bridge is the longest bridge on the Capital Beltway, crossing the Potomac River just south of Washington. It's often a bottleneck. "And of course, the approach to the Wilson Bridge is stacked up again this morning. It's stop and go. You can expect about a 20-minute delay between Route 210 and the Wilson Bridge."

Back in 2006, scientists studying fish in the Potomac River reported an unsettling discovery. Collecting fish near the Wilson Bridge, the scientists found that the females were normal, but the males weren't. When the scientists examined the male sex organs, they didn't find sperm, they found eggs.

This weird finding wasn't confined to the congested and polluted areas around the Wilson Bridge. The scientists collected fish from all seven tributaries of the Potomac, extending 200 miles up the Shenandoah River into Virginia and more than 100 miles up both the Monocacy River and Conococheague Creek in Maryland. At every one of these seven sites, the scientists found that at least 80 percent of the male smallmouth bass they examined were feminized: the sex organs in the male fish were making eggs instead of sperm.[1]

This news was reported on the front page of the *Washington Post* for the excellent reason that most of the readers of the *Washington Post* get their drinking water from the Potomac River. What was in the river water that was causing the male fish to become feminized? Could that something, whatever it is, affect boys and men in a similar way? What about girls and women?

Dr. Vicki Blazer, a veterinary pathologist who specializes in fish, acknowledged that the results were "striking." She concluded that the Potomac River and its tributaries clearly have significant levels of "endocrine disruptors": substances that mimic the actions of hormones, specifically female hormones. The hormones themselves were not present in the river. In fact, Dr. Blazer and other scientists haven't been able to figure out exactly which chemical or combination of chemicals has been causing the problem among the fish in the Potomac. "There is this sort of widespread endocrine disruption in the Potomac, but we don't know still what are the causes," Dr. Blazer told the *Post*.

Local agency officials were quick to assure the public that the water was safe to drink. But some consumers were skeptical. "If they can't tell us what the problem is," said Ed Merrifield, executive director of the environmental group Potomac Riverkeeper, "then how can they tell us that they've taken it out of the water?"[2] More recent research by Dr. Blazer's team has shown that the feminization of male fish is not confined to the Potomac River. They have now documented the same phenomenon in rivers across the United States. The more exposure a particular river has to manmade chemicals, the greater the likelihood that the fish will be feminized.[3]

The *Washington Post* also reported—in a seemingly unrelated story—that more and more young men attending colleges and universities are struggling with impotence, and even losing interest in sex.[4] Again, this phenomenon is not confined to the Washington area. It's nationwide. Dr. Keith Brodie, former chair of psychiatry at Duke University, has been counseling young men since the 1980s. Back when he started, none of the young men were mentioning anything about erectile dysfunction. But he told the *Washington Post* that "about a quarter" of college men now say they have difficulty achieving or maintaining an erection. Likewise, Dr. Jon Pryor, a Minnesota urologist, reports that about 30 percent of his patients with erectile dysfunction are now under 30 years of age.[5]

The fact that American river water now often contains a substance or substances that can emasculate males puts the story in a new light. But at least those impotent young men aren't making eggs.

As I said, this problem is not confined to the Potomac River estuary or tributaries. This problem is more widespread. Stories of feminized or emasculated wildlife, including a diverse array of mammals, birds, and reptiles as well as fish, have now been described across the United States and around the world: in Idaho and Washington, in central Florida, in the Great Lakes region, in Alaska, in England, and even in Greenland.[6]

What's going on?

And could it be relevant to your son?

This issue obviously affects girls as well as boys. One of the best-documented stories about endocrine disruptors concerns their effects on girls. Let's take a look at that story, and then see how it's relevant to boys.

She's Only Eight Years Old,
But She Could Pass for Twelve—or Fourteen

Doctors in San Juan, Puerto Rico, began noticing something strange as early as 1980. Girls as young as 7 and 8 years of age were going through puberty. Those girls' breasts were developing in ways that would be more typical of 12- and 13- and 14-year-old girls. As reports of these physically precocious girls spread around the city, and as the number of girls reported grew from the dozens to the hundreds and then the thousands, pediatric endocrinologists in San Juan joined together to try to discover the cause of the girls' early development. They tested many hypotheses.

Hormones in beef? One of the first ideas the specialists considered was the notion that hormones in the meat the girls were eating might be partly responsible. For more than 40 years now,

Americans have been eating meat that comes from cattle that have been fed anabolic steroids—male sex hormones—to make the cattle more meaty. These are, in many cases, the same steroid hormones that human athletes are prohibited from using because of the health risks. The doctors conjectured that perhaps these hormones were causing the girls' breasts to develop early.[7] The US Department of Agriculture joined with the Puerto Rico Department of Health to investigate this notion thoroughly, but they found little evidence to support the hypothesis. Compared to normal girls, the girls with premature breast development didn't have higher levels of any hormones linked to the hormones given to cattle. And it wasn't clear how the synthetic *male* hormones fed to cattle could cause precocious development of the *female* breast.

Genetics? The next hypothesis the specialists tested was genetic. Maybe ethnic Puerto Rican girls are just more prone to precocious puberty than girls from other ethnic and racial groups—or so they hypothesized. The doctors carefully compared the frequency of precocious puberty among Puerto Rican girls living in Puerto Rico with Puerto Rican girls living in Philadelphia. They found that the Puerto Rican girls living in Philadelphia were not at risk. Only the girls in Puerto Rico were at risk. Furthermore, girls in Puerto Rico were showing early breast development regardless of their race or ethnicity. Genetics didn't seem to have anything to do with it.[8] The cause of the problem wasn't in the girls' chromosomes: it had to be something in the environment, something in San Juan.

Plastics. Then the doctors heard about feminized alligators in central Florida. Scientists with the US Fish and Wildlife Service had found emasculated male alligators in the wildlife preserves around Florida's Lake Apopka. The alligators had shriveled testicles and high female hormone levels. The scientists had linked the emasculation of those male alligators to manmade environmental toxins.[9]

Clear plastic bottles—the type used for most of the bottled water in the United States as well as for soda beverages such as Coke, Pepsi, Sprite, and Dr. Pepper—are usually made with a synthetic plastic called polyethylene terephthalate (PET). Have you ever left a plastic bottle in your car on a hot summer day? Did the bottle contain Coke or Pepsi or Sprite? Maybe it was just plain bottled water. Did you take a drink from the bottle, and notice that it tasted just a little funny? Just a little—plasticky? When you let one of these PET bottles get warm, chemicals start leaching out of the plastic and into the beverage. The higher the temperature, the more chemicals will leak into the beverage. Some of those chemicals are called *phthalates*.[10]

The doctors in Puerto Rico wondered whether phthalates might be disrupting the endocrine development of the girls in San Juan and accelerating their puberty. After all, girls in Puerto Rico often drink beverages (including bottled water) in plastic bottles. And those plastic bottles are shipped in trucks that are not refrigerated, so the bottles get warm inside the truck. So the doctors tested the levels of phthalates in the girls' blood and compared their levels to the levels in Puerto Rican girls who didn't have early breast development. Bingo. The girls whose breasts had developed early had high levels of phthalates, far higher than the levels in girls whose breasts had not yet developed early.[11]

This story is an extreme case, but many studies now suggest that something like this may be taking place right now, more subtly, among girls throughout the United States and Canada. Girls are going through puberty earlier than ever before. In the United States, the number of girls beginning puberty at 8 years of age has increased so much that pediatric endocrinologists—doctors who specialize in problems of the endocrine system and hormones—called a special conference to decide what should be done about the problem.

Just think of all the options the specialists might have considered. They could have called for more research to determine whether girls who develop adult breasts at age 8 are at increased risk for developing breast cancer 20 or 30 years later, as some have suggested.[12] They could have called for at least a temporary moratorium on clear plastic bottles for beverages served to pre-pubescent children. They could at least have called for an all-out effort to figure out exactly why so many girls are beginning puberty earlier.

But the American endocrinologists did none of those things. Instead they decided simply to redefine what's normal. The experts decided that a girl who needs to wear a bra at age 8 should no longer be considered an anomaly. It's now officially normal for puberty to begin at 8.[13] In my book *Girls on the Edge*, I devote an entire chapter to the harmful effects of early puberty in girls.

But this is a book about boys. Why are we talking about girls?

Puberty Out of Sync

The overwhelming majority of modern chemicals that mimic the action of human sex hormones, curiously, primarily mimic the action of *female* hormones. (For that reason they are sometimes called "environmental estrogens.") As a result, the average child today is practically awash in synthetic chemicals that have the effect of accelerating a girl's sexual development. The effects on boys are more subtle. The net effect appears to be a slowing and/or warping of boys' sexual development. There is now substantial evidence that the same endocrine-disrupting chemicals that accelerate puberty in girls may delay or disrupt the process of puberty in boys.[14]

As a result, middle school has become a very strange place. There has always been a disparity between the sexual development of girls and boys, but 30 or 40 or 50 years ago the gap was measured in months rather than years. In that bygone era, girls began puberty around age 12 or 13, boys around 13 or 14. If you attended a Bar Mitzvah party 30 years ago, you might recall seeing tall, almost adult-looking 13-year-old girls standing next to boys the same age who were six inches shorter than them. Three decades ago, the disparity was most noticeable in the months right around the 13th birthday. Today, the duration of that disparity has lengthened. Girls now commonly begin puberty around age 9. Half of American girls now begin the process of puberty before reaching their 10th birthday.[15] But boys seldom begin puberty earlier than age 12 and sometimes not until 14 or even 15. Many girls now have completed the process of puberty by age 11 or 12—an age when most of the boys are just getting started.

I recently visited a 6th-grade classroom. A 12-year-old boy was sitting next to a 12-year-old girl. The girl could easily have passed for 15 years of age; the process of puberty was complete. The boy could easily have passed for 9 years old; the process of puberty had not yet begun.

You'll see a similar gap in physical appearance among 7th-graders. By 8th grade, some of the boys have started to catch up, but others haven't. Even when you enter a 9th-grade classroom, you can usually still find a significant cohort of boys who could pass for 5th-graders. I've seen this myself at many of the schools I've visited over the past 10 years. Many of the 9th-grade girls could walk into a classroom with college freshmen and pass for college students themselves. Few 9th-grade boys could do that.

There's growing evidence that exposure to synthetic chemicals may disrupt or slow puberty in boys—and only in boys, not in girls. Consider endosulfan, a pesticide that was used widely in the United States and throughout the world from the 1950s through the first decade of the 2000s. In the United States alone, in 2002, more than 1 million pounds of endosulfan were applied to food crops and cotton fields. In 2003 scientists discovered that this common pesticide slows and disrupts the process of puberty in boys—and only in boys.[16] The Environmental Protection Agency (EPA) proposed a voluntary ban on its use within the United States in 2010, and the product is now off the US market. In 2011, the Stockholm Convention on Persistent Organic Pollutants proposed a worldwide ban on the sale and use of endosulfan, which is now being implemented.

But this product was on the market for roughly *50 years* before scientists discovered its effect on puberty in boys, and another 7 years followed before the EPA took action to remove it from the market. Incidentally, the EPA's action to take endosulfan off the market appears to have been motivated not primarily by a concern about boys' development, but by a lawsuit brought on behalf of farmworkers. The suit alleged that farmworkers were being poisoned as a result of prolonged contact with endosulfan.[17] The EPA's notice that endosulfan was being withdrawn did not mention the risk to boys' development.[18]

The EPA and other agencies do not test chemicals for their effects on boys' development. The requirement that new chemicals be proven "safe" means only that those chemicals don't kill you right away or cause cancer. The EPA and other government agencies do not even screen for effects on child development, sexual development, male hormone levels, and the like. You're on your own if you want to limit your child's exposure. Later in this chapter, I will share strategies that experts in the field believe can decrease the risks.

Bottled Water, Pacifiers, and Baby Bottles

What could be healthier than a pregnant woman drinking bottled water? What's wrong with a baby sucking on a pacifier? What's wrong with Mom putting some of her pumped breast milk into a clear plastic bottle so that Dad can feed the baby?

In the past decade, scientists have found that each of these activities may introduce synthetic chemicals, such as phthalates, into the baby's system. Plastic bottles can introduce another dangerous chemical: bisphenol A, or BPA. BPA is used in making polycarbonate, an endocrine disruptor in wide use in all developed countries. Rigid plastic bottles of the sort commonly used worldwide to feed babies infant formula or pumped breast milk are often made of polycarbonate, and therefore they may leach BPA into baby's milk or formula. Some parents use a soft flexible plastic liner within the bottle. Those liners are sometimes made with phthalates. But the manufacturer is not required to tell you that there are phthalates in the liner, and most manufacturers don't reveal that information.

BPA, like the phthalates, mimics the action of female hormones, but another worrisome finding has been detected as well. A team of researchers at the University of Cincinnati found that the low levels of BPA that leach into milk or formula from such bottles irreversibly disrupt brain development in laboratory animals. And the effects on the brain are not confined only or even primarily to the areas involved in reproduction and sexuality. Instead, brain areas involved in memory and motivation are damaged.[19]

Researchers in Italy found that BPA affects males and females differently. They found that when laboratory animals are exposed to BPA when they are young, the animals seem less curious about their environment when they are grown up. Male animals that have been exposed to these chemicals when very young subsequently behave less like males; their activity profile is "feminized, strongly resembling that of control females."[20] Japanese researchers have found that BPA and other endocrine-disrupting chemicals may damage dopamine pathways in the brain, including the nucleus accumbens—the same area of the brain we discussed in the previous chapter: the vital pivot for motivation, the place where emotion gets translated into sustained and purposeful action.[21] Researchers have also found that early exposure to BPA reduces or eliminates the normal sex differences seen in the behavior of laboratory animals.[22]

There is now widespread agreement that BPA exposure, especially in infancy and childhood, disrupts and distorts development in both boys and girls.[23] "But," you say, "I'm careful to buy only those plastic bottles that have a big label on them announcing that they are 'BPA-FREE.'" In recent years, as concerns about the effects of BPA have become better known, manufacturers have begun using alternative plastics to make baby bottles. That's good, right?

Maybe. We don't know for sure. The underlying assumption has been that plastics that are not made from BPA are safer than plastics that are made from BPA. That assumption has recently been tested and shown to be false—or at least, not always true. Some plastics that are BPA-free actually leach *more* chemicals that have *more* endocrine-disrupting activity than plastics made from BPA.[24] According to one estimate, there are now more than 84,000 different synthetic chemicals in the marketplace, and most have never been tested for their effects on the development of girls and boys.[25] "Untested chemicals should not be presumed to be safe," scientists are starting to say.[26]

Avoid plastic. If you want to give your baby or child milk to drink, then use a glass bottle, not a plastic bottle (and don't use a plastic liner in the bottle, either). If you want your child to drink water while on the go, then pour tap water into a steel canteen. We know that glass and steel are safe. With plastic, even BPA-free plastic, we can't be sure.

Endocrine Disruptors, ADHD, and Motivation

Scientists have just begun to recognize the pernicious effects these chemicals have on the brain in ways not previously imagined. ADHD may be one result. The soaring rates of ADHD among North American kids in the past 30 years have only recently been linked to these chemicals. It wasn't until the 21st century that neuroscientists began to recognize the mechanism by which endocrine disruptors such as phthalates and bisphenol A might actually cause ADHD.

Neuroscientists first identified a crucial link between endocrine disruptors and ADHD in 2004. When young laboratory animals were exposed to tiny doses of endocrine disruptors—including bisphenol A and various phthalates—the scientists found that the endocrine disruptors appeared to damage a brain system built around a substance known as PACAP, pituitary adenylate cyclase–activating polypeptide. These laboratory animals were, quite literally, hyper. They just couldn't slow down.[27] In the years since, researchers have discovered many suggestive links between endocrine disruptors and ADHD. For example, in one study, researchers found a significant correlation between phthalates in the urine of kids and the likelihood that those kids had symptoms of ADHD.[28] Other researchers measured the levels of phthalates in the blood of pregnant women; then those researchers checked up on the children of those women when the kids were 4 to 9 years of age. The kids whose mothers had high levels of phthalates in their blood while pregnant were significantly more likely, at 4 to 9 years of age, to have problems with impulsive behavior and attention.[29]

I NFANTS, TODDLERS, AND YOUNG CHILDREN DON'T MAKE SEX HORMONES. Their bodies and brains are not meant to be exposed to those hormones until puberty begins. When young children are exposed to substances that act like sex hormones, the delicate balance is upset, with unpredictable results. Recent research suggests that young children are far more sensitive to these substances than was previously thought, and that the "safe" levels of exposure established by the US Food and Drug Administration (FDA) in the 1990s may be dangerously high. Until recently, concerns about these chemicals centered on the risk of cancer. But with the exceptions of breast cancer, testicular cancer, and (possibly) prostate cancer, these chemicals rarely cause cancer in the amounts to which most of us are exposed.[30] But we now know they may disrupt sexual development and brain development in children even at very low doses.[31]

Why Have Kids Gotten So Fat?

The effects of endocrine disruptors are not confined to the brain and behavior. They may also be contributing to one of our most serious health problems: childhood obesity. Environmental estrogens appear to make kids fat—both girls and boys.

In 1970, only 4.6 percent of American kids 12 to 19 years of age were obese. That proportion quadrupled over the next 40 years: by 2010, 18.4 percent of teenagers were obese.[32] Of course, many blame the increase in the number of chubby teens on teenagers' fondness for pizza, French fries, and potato chips. But teenagers have always been fond of pizza, French fries, and potato chips. Why are teenagers so much more likely to be fat today than they were 40 years ago?

There is more than one right answer to that question. In my book *The Collapse of Parenting*, I described how American parents today often let kids decide what's for supper. When parents let kids decide what's for supper, some kids will choose salmon and spinach. Many other kids will choose cheeseburgers and ice cream. Forty years ago, American parents were more likely to say, "No dessert until you eat your broccoli."

So that's one part of the answer. Kids being less active today— playing video games indoors instead of playing outside, as they might have done in 1970—is another part of the answer.

But here's what's creepy. It's not just humans who are getting fatter. It's cats and dogs and laboratory animals, too. Even wild rats are getting fatter. Using data from the mid-1940s through the first few years of the 2000s, researchers found that the average weight of domestic cats has increased an average of 10 percent per decade, every decade, for six consecutive decades. OK, so maybe people are just feeding their cats more, right? But how do you explain the fact that *wild rats* are getting fatter? It's hard to claim that wild rats are spending too much time watching reruns of *Sex and the City* instead of running around outside. Wild rats live outdoors.

You could argue that maybe we are just leaving more French fries lying around outside for the rats to eat. And maybe we are. But a similar trend has been observed among laboratory animals, from monkeys to mice. And those animals are fed tightly regulated diets that have been carefully documented since the mid-20th century. That diet has not become any higher in calories or fat. Nor are laboratory animals today more restricted in their activities compared with laboratory animals 50 years ago; on the contrary, because of concerns about animal welfare, laboratory animals today often have more spacious accommodations and more opportunities for exercise compared with their ancestors 50 years ago.

But they're still fatter.[33] How come? Researchers who have studied this issue conclude that the most plausible explanation is that chemicals in the environment are changing the way fat cells work, so that they become fatter more easily and are more resistant to weight loss.[34]

Why are so many kids getting so fat? Increasingly, investigators suspect that environmental estrogens may be a major contributing factor. Scientists have known for decades that estrogens regulate the size of fat cells. Young children—whether girls or boys—don't make estrogens in significant amounts. Exposure to environmental estrogens in childhood "may have long-lasting consequences" that increase the tendency to become overweight or obese, according to Retha Newbold, a biologist with the National Institute of Environmental Health Sciences. These chemicals may directly affect fat cells (adipose cells), or they may disrupt the signals between fat cells and the pituitary and hypothalamus (endocrine feedback loops). "We're still trying to determine if it's a direct effect on the adipose cells and how they differentiate or proliferate, or whether it's a disruption of the endocrine feedback loops," Dr. Newbold says.[35] Either way, exposure to these chemicals in childhood appears to increase substantially the risk that a child will be overweight.

Professor Frederick vom Saal at the University of Missouri has highlighted the risk of obesity associated with exposure to bisphenol A. Even very low-dose exposure can activate fat cells, causing them to get bigger, Professor vom Saal warns. He has found that low-dose exposure to BPA early in life causes both male and female laboratory animals to be fatter as adults; it also causes the females, but not the males, to begin puberty at an earlier age.[36]

Exposure to environmental estrogens can lead to both girls and boys becoming overweight. And while exposure to synthetic endocrine disruptors may accelerate puberty in girls, exposure to the same substances can disrupt or slow the process of puberty in boys. Moreover, there is now evidence that these substances may increase the risk of ADHD. How about a triple whammy: all three together? Scientists are now reporting that these three conditions—delayed puberty, overweight, and ADHD—occur together more often than would be expected by chance—but only in boys. In one of the few studies to examine this combination, researchers found that more than 1 in 6 boys who were late to begin puberty also were diagnosed with ADHD, compared with fewer than 1 in 35 girls in the same study.[37] We're seeing a substantial increase in the number of boys who are overweight, inattentive, and late to begin puberty.

Are Boys Now the More Fragile Sex?

My patient, a 10-year-old boy I'll call Steven, tripped and fell on the grass in his own backyard. No big deal, right? Kids fall all the time. But Steven was screaming in pain when he stood up, cradling his right arm in his left. And the right forearm was bent horribly, in a way no forearm should bend. Steven had broken both bones in his forearm—the mid-shaft of both the radius and the ulna—from a trivial fall. He had to have surgery to set the bones in place.

Doctors call such injuries *pathologic* fractures, because such fractures suggest underlying pathology. A boy should be able to fall on the grass without sustaining a complex fracture that requires surgery. In the past, a fracture like Steven's might signify some rare underlying bone disease, such as osteogenesis imperfecta or hyperparathyroidism. No longer. Steven doesn't have any underlying disease. He's a normal boy—which has come to mean that he's a boy who can break his bones just by tripping and falling. In one study, researchers concluded that the risk of fracture for boys had roughly doubled between the 1960s and the 1990s.[38] And that was just the beginning of the trend. Another large study found that the risk of broken bones in childhood increased 350 percent between

January 2004 and December 2009.[39] Steven sustained a fracture of the mid-shaft of the forearm. In a study looking specifically at fractures like Steven's, researchers found a 440 percent increase in fractures of the mid-shaft of the forearm between 2000 and 2009; they also observed that "the increase in the middle-shaft fractures was still accelerating towards the end of the study period."[40]

Why are the bones of boys more brittle today than they were 30 or 40 years ago? Some of this change has been attributed to changes in diet, which is reasonable. Boys today drink less milk and more cola beverages than they did 30 years ago.[41] But that change alone can't account for the dramatic increase in the rate of fractures among boys.

When I present this research to parents, some say "Well, kids are fatter today. And fat kids probably have more brittle bones, right?" No, not right. Increasing weight by itself is associated with *increased* bone density, and this association is stronger in boys than in girls. As a result, heavier boys tend to have stronger bones than skinny boys, when researchers control for other factors.[42]

Environmental estrogens may be the missing factor. There is now good evidence that endocrine-disrupting chemicals in the environment may diminish bone density and distort bone architecture, causing bones to become more brittle.[43] That may help to explain why boys and young men today have bones that are more brittle than the bones of boys and young men a generation ago. The disruptive effect of these chemicals on bone has now been demonstrated in species as diverse as monkeys in the laboratory, alligators in Florida, and polar bears in Greenland.[44] We can't say for sure that these chemicals are to blame for declining bone density in boys. But it's a possibility that merits a closer look.

Neither Male nor Female

Sex differences are not unique to humans. Almost all higher mammals show sex differences in behavior. These differences are particularly pronounced among primates, the mammalian order to which we humans belong. And the differences are present early in life.[45]

Here's what's scary: scientists are finding that exposure to environmental estrogens early in life, particularly in utero and in early infancy, blunts or eliminates sex differences in behavior. Females become less feminine. Males become less masculine. For example, when young laboratory animals were exposed to these endocrine-disrupting chemicals, the males stopped acting like males. They stopped engaging in the rough-and-tumble play characteristic of males, for example. Instead, they demonstrated "play characteristic of females rather than untreated males."[46] Researchers at Tufts University reported that when young laboratory animals were exposed to very low doses of bisphenol A—doses comparable to what a baby might get if her mother is in the habit of occasionally eating canned soup—then the distinctive sexual differentiation of female and male brains was eliminated. Brains of female and male animals that had been exposed to the chemical were no longer distinguishable from one another, unlike the brains of unexposed animals. Likewise, the characteristic sex differences in the behavior and play of the animals were eliminated as well.[47]

There's growing evidence that the end result of our increasingly toxic environment is girls who are both masculine and feminine, and boys who are neither masculine nor feminine.[48] The deleterious effects on girls is a complex topic that I address in chapter 4 of my book *Girls on the Edge*. But right now, we must consider the possibility that the very hardware that makes a boy a boy may be in jeopardy.

Private Parts

Your son may be less than half the man your father was.

American boys today are more than twice as likely to be born with genital abnormalities such as an undescended testicle or *hypospadias* (opening of the penis on the bottom of the penile shaft instead of on the tip of the penis) compared with American boys 40 or 50 years ago.[49] Young men today have significantly lower testosterone levels than their grandfathers had.[50] Male infertility is on the rise, and the evidence suggests that exposure to endocrine disruptors may be at least partly to blame.[51] In recent decades, according to one comprehensive study, there has been

> a synchronized increase in the incidence of male reproductive problems, such as testicular cancer, genital abnormalities, reduced semen quality and subfertility. Temporal and geographical associations, as well as frequent combination of more than one problem in one individual, strongly suggest the existence of a pathogenetic link. The association of male reproduction problems is probably not coincidental but reflects the existence of a common underlying cause.

The authors of the study conclude that the most likely underlying causes are "adverse environmental factors such as hormone disruptors."[52]

The problem may start very early. I have already mentioned that clear plastic bottles made from PET may leach endocrine disruptors such as phthalates into water or soda. If that's so, then if a woman drinks water or soda from a clear plastic bottle while she's pregnant, the baby boy growing in her womb may be adversely affected.

That's a testable hypothesis. Epidemiologist Shanna Swan and her colleagues across the United States set out to test it. They analyzed the urine of pregnant women to see which women had high levels of phthalates in their system and which did not. Then they studied the sons born to those women a few weeks or months later. The researchers were careful to recruit women from diverse areas of the country—California, Minnesota, and Missouri—to make sure their results were not confounded by regional effects.

Dr. Swan and her colleagues found what they had feared. Mothers who had high levels of phthalates in their system were roughly ten times more likely to give birth to boys whose genitals were not quite right. The most common malformations in American boys were smaller-than-normal penises, undescended testicles, and hypospadias—which as I mentioned earlier is a condition in which the opening at the tip of the penis isn't at the tip, but farther down the shaft of the penis.[53] These results led Dr. Swan to conclude that in these boys, "the process of masculinization was incomplete."[54] Dr. Swan's findings did not come as a big surprise, because previous research had already clearly demonstrated a causal association between phthalate exposure and genital malformations in laboratory animals—but only in males.[55]

Dr. Swan was already well known in this field because she had previously published her research demonstrating that in many industrialized countries, including the United States, sperm counts had significantly declined over the second half of the 20th century.[56] More recent studies have confirmed and extended this finding.[57] Dr. Swan has also shown that men living in communities with low exposure to fertilizer and pesticides have the highest sperm counts, while men living in communities with high exposure to these chemicals have the lowest sperm counts. Curiously, the urban vs. rural distinction doesn't seem to play much of a role. Farmers living in the country—where they may be heavily exposed to pesticides and fertilizer—have lower sperm counts than men living in some big cities.[58] Other scholars have reported a direct association between exposure to phthalates and sperm quality: the more exposure, the lower the quality.[59]

Moving to the country, then, is not the solution. You have to fix this problem where you are.

Jane Fisher, a toxicologist at the University of London, has assembled a disturbing array of evidence indicating that boys today just aren't growing up to be the men their fathers and grandfathers were. Young men today are more likely to have problems with fertility than their fathers and grandfathers; boys today are more likely to have congenital abnormalities, and boys and young men today may be as much as ten times more likely to develop testicular cancer.[60]

Declining male hormone levels affect more than just sperm counts. Testosterone fuels *ambition* in boys and men. That's less true, or not at all true, for girls and women. In recent years, scientists have begun to understand that the fountainhead of motivation is very different in girls and boys. In boys, testosterone fuels more than sexual interest: it also fuels the drive to compete, to achieve, to be the best. Successful, high-achieving boys have higher testosterone levels than boys who are content to come in last. Girls can be just as competitive as boys, but competitive girls don't rely on hormones for their drive. Competitive, high-achieving girls do not have higher testosterone levels than less competitive girls, as a rule.[61] This sex difference may be one reason why the flood of estrogen-like chemicals in which today's children are immersed seems not to have impaired the drive or motivation of girls. But the boys are slowing down.

H ERE ARE SOME SUGGESTIONS TO HELP YOU SAFEGUARD YOUR children, and yourself, from the damaging effects of environmental estrogens:

- Don't give your baby son or toddler soft vinyl toys or pacifiers made with phthalates—look for products labeled "PVC-free" and "Phthalate-free." Some manufacturers have slapped the label "BPA-free" on their pacifiers, but BPA has never been used in the production of pacifiers, so that's misleading.
- Don't microwave food for your children in plastic containers or in any sort of plastic packaging. Many frozen foods now come in "boil in the bag" packaging. Take the food out of the plastic bag and put it in a glass or ceramic bowl instead.
- When heating or reheating a meal in the microwave, don't allow a plastic cover to contact the food. Use a dish instead. If you must use a plastic cover, then put the food in a bowl rather than a plate so that the plastic wrap does not come in contact with the food.

- Avoid plastic bottles for your own beverages and for your children's beverages, including water. Use glass instead.
- Don't use clear plastic baby bottles. Use glass instead.
- Don't allow your dentist to put sealants on your children's teeth unless the dentist can assure you that the sealants are phthalate-free.[62]

In the closing chapter, I will put these recommendations in the context of an overall program for safeguarding your son.

6

End Result

Failure to Launch

L ET'S START WITH A LAWYER JOKE.
So there's this lawyer. He lives in a big mansion in an exclusive suburb. His toilet clogs up. He tries using the plunger. Doesn't do any good. So he calls the plumber. The plumber arrives, fixes the toilet, and writes up the bill. The lawyer takes one look at the bill and protests. "You've put down a charge of $250 for labor," the lawyer says. "But you spent less than half an hour doing that repair. You're billing more than $500 an hour! That's more than I bill my clients, and I'm a lawyer!"

The plumber nods sympathetically. "I used to be a lawyer too," he says.[1]

What Happened to Money?

Neal Brown started a plumbing business more than 20 years ago, in northern Montgomery County, Maryland, near the border with

Frederick County. Mr. Brown was having trouble finding any young men (or women) who wanted to learn the plumbing trade.

"We approached Frederick County Public Schools," Mr. Brown told me. "We asked them whether they would help us set up an apprenticeship program in plumbing. They said fine, provided that we could recruit 12 students in the county for the program. Frederick County has over 40,000 students spread over 60 schools. How hard could it be to find 12 students, just 12?"

"How hard was it?" I asked.

"We found 10. In the whole county, only 10 students wanted to learn plumbing. Ten boys, no girls. We couldn't persuade any girls to give it a try."

"I guess the idea of fixing backed-up toilets didn't appeal to the girls," I said.

"Actually, we hoped that at least some girls would be interested," Mr. Brown said. "We figured they might like the independence of being able to take care of plumbing problems without having to call someone. But we didn't get any girls. Not a one."

"I understand that most girls have a better sense of smell than most boys have," I said.[2] "So what did the school district say when you told them you only had 10 students?"

"They said fine. Ten was enough. And the need for trained plumbers is so great in our area, we told every one of those boys that we would *guarantee* them a job if they just stuck with the program. Even an apprentice plumber can earn $50,000 a year right now if you're willing to put in some hours. And a master plumber—"

"What does it take to be a master plumber?" I asked.

"Four years as an apprentice, two years as a journeyman, then you take the exam. If you pass, you're a master plumber," Mr. Brown explained.

"And a master plumber can earn how much?"

"$80,000 a year, easy, and that's just working 40 hours a week. If you're willing to put in overtime, you can crack $100,000, no sweat."

"Without a college degree?"

"Without a college degree," Mr. Brown said. "And we explained this to every boy in the class. We said: Just stick with this, learn this trade, and you are literally set for life. No college loans to pay back. You're set. Your job is secure. No engineer in Bangalore, no factory worker in Shenzhen is going to be able to fix somebody's toilet in Buckeystown, Maryland. If you learn this trade and you do honest work, you are set for life."

"What happened?" I asked.

"After one month, more than half the boys had quit. They had no interest in working. They just didn't care. Earning lots of money just seems to have no appeal to them. We were down to three boys by the middle of October. That's when the district shut us down."

"I would have thought young men would have been motivated by the prospect of earning lots of money straight out of high school. Not many 18-year-olds can earn $50,000 a year," I said.

"I would have thought so, too," Mr. Brown said.

John Craft's Dilemma

John Craft (not his real name) never went to college. He started working in home construction right out of high school, 35 years ago. Twenty years ago, he started his own company specializing in custom remodeling of luxury homes. It's been a good business for him. "Most of the jobs I do now start at half a million.

Quite a few run more than a million dollars," he told me. "And I've got a waiting list of work that's more than a year long. Now, of course, I don't take all that money home. Most of it goes for expenses, subcontractors, all that stuff." But John isn't complaining. His personal income is more than $300,000 a year. Not bad for a guy who never went to college.

But John has a problem. He can't find good help. "It's been more than 10 years since I've been able to hire any young man born in the USA and keep him for more than a month. Number one, these young guys nowadays have no idea of craftsmanship. Number two, they don't have any interest in learning. None whatsoever."

John has a crew of six men, all in their forties and fifties, most of whom have been with him for ten years or more. "I figure I'll keep everybody together another 5, 7 years, 10 years tops, build up my retirement fund, then I'm done. When my guys are ready to retire, I won't have any way to replace them." He paused. "Boys today are lazy," he said at last. "They don't want to work. They'd rather play video games. They just don't have any motivation."

"But human nature can't change in one generation," I said. "If boys today are lazy, it's because our generation or our society made them that way. So what did we do wrong? What should we be doing differently?"

MILLER & LONG IS ONE OF THE LARGEST CONCRETE CONTRACTORS in the United States. Miller & Long built the huge football stadium for the Carolina Panthers. When the Internal Revenue

Service decided to build new headquarters, Miller & Long poured the concrete for the IRS's 1,275,000-square-foot complex. In recent years, Brunei, Egypt, Ethiopia, Ivory Coast, Singapore, and Turkey have all built new embassies in Washington, DC, and guess who was hired to pour the concrete in each case? Miller & Long.

Miller & Long also built a small health clinic in El Salvador. That seems a bit strange, because Miller & Long does no business in El Salvador. The firm is headquartered in Bethesda, Maryland. So why did this huge company build a clinic in a foreign country, at its own expense?

"More than three-quarters of our workforce is from El Salvador," is the answer I received from Myles Gladstone, vice president for human resources at Miller & Long. "They live here in the USA, but they still have family back home, and they're naturally concerned about their family back home. Building this clinic was one way we can support their community. Miller & Long also built about 100 homes in El Salvador after the big earthquakes there. The company spent a lot of money on that project. But Miller & Long wasn't the only company down there. All the big American construction companies were down there, helping out. All the companies get a big chunk of their workforce from El Salvador."

"So you have trouble recruiting young people from the United States?"

"That's right," he says. "We're doing several ongoing projects to try to recruit young people, men and women, to get them to check us out. We work with the local high schools. We also recruit men and women who have just been released from prison."

"How successful have those programs been?" I asked.

"Terrible," he said. "We have maybe half a dozen success stories. They're the poster boys for these projects. Only half a dozen."

"Half a dozen out of how many recruits?" I asked. "Fifty? One
hundred?"

"Hundreds," he said.

This was starting to sound familiar.

I first heard about Miller & Long's good works in El Salvador
from Jeff Donohoe, who was a neighbor of mine at that time. He
and his relatives operate a large commercial contracting company,
Donohoe Construction Company. For several years, Mr. Donohoe made valiant efforts to recruit young people to enter the
trades: to become electricians, plumbers, welders, and other types
of skilled craftsmen. He would visit local high schools. He began
his talks by asking students: "How many of you plan on going to
college?"

Almost all the students would raise their hands. Then he would
ask, "How many of you can tell me *why* you're going to college?
What do you want to do that requires a college education?"

Usually only about 5 or 6 students, mostly girls, would raise
their hands to answer this question. So he would continue: "For
those 20 of you who plan on going to college, but don't know
why you're going to college, I'd like to make a few suggestions
before you take on $20,000 or $30,000 or $40,000, or more in
student loans. I'd like you to consider a career in the trades. If
you become a licensed electrician or carpenter, you can earn as
much as your friends who go to college. You'll be earning good
money right out of high school, and you won't have any college
loans to pay back."

He seldom found any student who was interested. In fact, he's
given up doing the talks. "I just don't get it," Mr. Donohoe told

me. "Most of these kids have no particular interest in going to college. They can't even tell you *why* they're going to college. But then when you explain that there are good jobs in the trades that don't require a college education, they just give you a blank look. I don't understand it."

"How come nobody wants to go into the trades?" I asked. Mr. Donohoe replied:

I think it starts with the parents, and the teachers. They look down their noses at what they call "blue-collar" work. They think we're just digging holes and throwing bricks around. They don't have a clue that modern construction techniques are more high-tech than most desk jobs. We upload the architect's plans directly into our earthmoving equipment, which uses laser guidance and GPS systems to grade the site to extremely close tolerances. It's more like brain surgery than it is like building sand castles at the beach. But the parents and the teachers think that if a kid doesn't go to college, that kid's a failure. We require smart people, highly motivated people who totally understand what they're doing. We're just not able to find those people in this country anymore. So we have to hire people from El Salvador or from Mexico or Guatemala, and train them.

Mr. Donohoe isn't alone in his observation. The social critic Dr. Charles Murray has observed that many high school students from middle-class families "go to college because their parents are paying for it and college is what children of their social class are supposed to do after they finish high school."[3] Those kids may have very little idea what they want to do at college. Few of them have given any thought at all to the trades.

Dr. Murray's analysis is harsher than Mr. Donohoe's. "A bachelor's degree in a field such as sociology, psychology, economics, history, or literature certifies nothing," he writes. "It is a screening device for employers. The college you got into says a lot about your ability, and that you stuck it out for four years says something about your perseverance. But the degree itself does not qualify the graduate for anything. There are better, faster and more efficient ways for young people to acquire credentials to provide to employers." Murray observes further that we have entered a peculiar age, an age in which physicians and lawyers are more plentiful than good plumbers.

> The spread of wealth at the top of American society has created an explosive increase in the demand for craftsmen. Finding a good lawyer or physician is easy. Finding a good carpenter, painter, electrician, plumber, glazier, mason—the list goes on and on—is difficult, and it is a seller's market. . . . [M]aster craftsmen can make six figures. They have work even in a soft economy. Their jobs cannot be outsourced to India. And the craftsman's job provides wonderful intrinsic rewards that come from mastery of a challenging skill that produces tangible results. How many white-collar jobs provide nearly as much satisfaction?[4]

Fifty years ago, even 40 years ago, there was no shame in a young man choosing a career in the trades. Beginning in the early 1980s—and particularly after the publication of *A Nation at Risk* in 1983—a consensus grew in the United States that every young person should go to college, regardless of their ability or aspirations. "Vocational education" lost whatever prestige it had and came to be viewed in some quarters very nearly as a dumping ground for the mildly retarded. Principals and superintendents began to see classes in auto mechanics or welding as expensive and high-liability diversions from the school's core mission of ensuring that every student would go on to college.

The consequences go beyond plumbers who charge exorbitant rates. The downside is a growing cohort of unproductive young men who see no meaning or purpose in their lives.

The Lesson of the Pribilof Islands

Back in 2005, Professor Judith Kleinfeld of the University of Alaska at Fairbanks invited me to spend time meeting with Native American leaders in her area who are concerned about what's happening to Alaskan Native boys. A growing proportion of those boys are disengaging from school; they're dropping out as early as 6th or 7th grade, drinking beer, and getting in trouble. Larry Merculieff, an Alaskan Native and deputy director of the Alaska Native Science Commission, made a comment during one of these meetings that I found disturbing. I stayed after the meeting to ask him to explain what he'd said.

"When I was growing up," he told me, "I learned to hunt the sea lion with the older men of my tribe. I learned about patience. I learned about using my senses. All my senses. I would go out on the ice with the older men and we would sit for hours, waiting for the sea lion. Hours."

"What'd you do while you were waiting?" I asked. "Play a game? Talk?"

Larry shook his head. "Think of a Buddhist monk meditating," he said. "That's the closest thing to what we were doing. We were silent. We were aware. I could sense the sea lion approaching when it was still five miles distant. I can't tell you how I did that, but there is no doubt that I knew, with absolute certainty, when the sea lion was approaching."

"So how did you actually do it? Kill the sea lion, I mean," I asked.

"Our traditional life depended on the sea lion," he answered. "You must kill the sea lion at precisely the right moment. Its lungs must be filled with air. Otherwise, the animal will sink to the bottom when you shoot it, and you will not be able to retrieve it. You must be patient. You can't shoot it as soon as you see it. You must wait for it to take that deep breath. You may have to wait several minutes after you spot it. Then the leader will give the signal."

"He tells you when to shoot?" I asked.

"He doesn't say anything. You watch him out of the corner of your eye. He fires first—then all of us fire within a tenth of a second of his shot. All the shots hit the animal in the head. That's how it is supposed to be. And that's how it was, every time. The animal dies instantly, floats on the water, and we retrieve it."

"So what's different about the young men you saw?" Larry had said something during the meeting about how the young men in his tribe now insist on going out on their own. They don't want any guidance from the older men, and the lack of guidance shows in the way they hunt the sea lion. I wanted to hear more about that.

"Those young men were talking. Laughing. Joking. Punching each other. Drinking beer," Larry said. "They weren't watching the sea. They weren't paying attention to the wind. They were never quiet. A sea lion appeared and they didn't even notice. Then one of them saw it and yelled. They all grabbed their guns and started shooting wildly. They didn't kill it. They wounded it. It swam away. You could see the blood trail in the water. That's the worst possible outcome. A wounded animal. The sea lion will die, but when it dies it will be of no use to the tribe."

Fifty years ago, Larry explained, young men and old men spent whole days and nights together in traditional underground structures they called "men's houses." In these small, confined spaces—only somewhat larger than the sweat lodges used by Native American tribes in the southwestern United States—the art of hunting was passed from one generation to the next. "Then the missionaries came. They destroyed the men's houses," Larry said. Because Native religious ceremonies were occasionally conducted in the men's houses, the missionaries regarded the houses as pagan temples that had to be demolished. Larry believes that the destruction of the men's houses was a factor in the severing of the bond between the generations.

But, as Larry explained, many other factors contributed to the isolation of the younger generation. The introduction of grocery stores probably did more than the razing of the men's houses to wipe out the original Alaskan Native way of life. Once an Alaskan Native woman could go to the store and buy food, she no longer needed the men of the village to hunt for her. When the men no longer needed to hunt, the central purpose of the men's houses was lost (or so Larry and other Alaskan Natives have told me). The nature of hunting changed. The hunt was no longer an activity essential to sustain life. Hunting became a mere entertainment, a pastime.

More fundamentally: the young men of the island no longer see any mission or purpose in their lives. The young women are doing better in school and are usually better qualified for the jobs that are available: jobs as teachers, clerical workers, home health aides. The men don't want those jobs. Professor Kleinfeld told me that Inuit women in Barrow have the same labor-force participation rates as women in New York, while men lag far behind national labor force participation rates.[5] Larry told me that on his island, 70 percent of the young men are either incarcerated, disabled by alcoholism or drug abuse, or dead from suicide before they reach the age of 21. More than two out of three.

The Pribilof Islands are located in the Bering Sea, about 1,000 miles west of Anchorage. The only way in or out is by plane, which is expensive, so most residents are essentially marooned on the islands. They have their own names for the four seasons: Tourist Season (June and July), Almost Winter (August and September), Winter (October through March), and Still Winter (April and May). The islands are among the most remote and inhospitable locations inhabited by humans.

You and I don't live on the Pribilof Islands. So what does this story have to do with us?

Professor Kleinfeld sent me an e-mail about an analysis of young men who don't want to work. The author of this analysis had suggested that the disengagement of so many young American men from the workforce is due to changes in the North American economy. We've all heard about these changes already: there are fewer good jobs in factories, and the good jobs are now primarily in the service sector.[6] Professor Kleinfeld wrote: "Let me add a complexity based on my unique vantage point in Alaska, where traditional male jobs in construction and natural resources and mining have NOT declined. Many young men are not taking these jobs. . . . Many are floundering. Many don't want jobs requiring physical strength and hard labor. Even apprenticeships which offer high wages and benefits are going begging."

What's Going On?

A team of reporters for the *New York Times* documented a growing trend among young and middle-aged men throughout the United States: more and more able-bodied men are out of work and are not even looking for work. These men aren't included in the unemployment statistics because they've given up looking for a job. They may be from middle-class families, most of them are white, and many have some college education. Their ranks are growing rapidly. In Michigan, 18 percent of able-bodied men between the ages of 30 and 54—almost 1 man in 5—are not working and not looking for work. In West Virginia, that figure is now up to 24 percent, almost 1 man in 4. Forty years ago, in the same age group, only about 1 able-bodied man in 20 was unemployed and not looking for work. Today, nationwide, it's about 1 man in 7. Most of these men could find work if they had to, according to the *New York Times* investigative team. But these men "have decided they prefer the alternative [i.e., not working]. It is a significant cultural shift from three decades ago. . . . [These men are] in the prime of their lives [but] have dropped out of regular work. They are turning down jobs they think beneath them."[7] Instead, they live off the income of their wives or families, or off donations from parents or other family.

The *New York Times* investigation was conducted back in 2006, during economic good times, and well before the economic collapse of 2008–2009. In December 2015, the Bureau of Labor Statistics issued the latest numbers, comparing 2004 with 2014. In 2004, among men 25 to 54 years of age, 5,644,000 were not working and not looking for work. In 2014, that number had increased 25 percent, to 7,058,000.[8] (You can't attribute that increase to an increase in population, because the population increased by only 9 percent over the same period, from 293 million in 2004 to 319 million in 2014.) In my work as a family physician, I have encountered many such men. They often offer reasonable explanations: they were laid off, they can't find another job. But it's hard to escape the impression, in some cases (not all), that they're pretty comfortable at home. The stigma of not working, of living off your wife's income, which would have been severe in a previous era, doesn't seem to bother some of these men.

The traditional male provider roles—hunting among the Alaskans, factory work and the trades for many other American men—have been eliminated or made obsolete, or, as in the case of the trades, have simply lost their appeal. The new jobs in the service industry, as a home health aide for example, don't interest many men. For most, the situation is not as dire as that of the Native Alaskans of the Pribilof Islands. Not yet. But the more I listened to Larry and other Alaskan Natives, the more I saw parallels between their situation and the rest of the country.

I am not suggesting that we should try to turn back the clock to the days when the man was usually the sole or chief provider for the home. But I am suggesting that the emerging 21st-century economy, in which many women earn more than their husbands—if they have husbands at all—requires a rethinking of the role of men. If a 30-year-old man is not the principal wage earner in his home, then what is his role? Certainly he could take over the principal responsibilities for child care. But men who stay at home full-time in order to provide child care, clean the house, do the laundry, and cook the meals are still uncommon in North America.

So what is the man's role, if his wife is the principal wage earner? The answer, in too many cases that I have personally witnessed, is that this man becomes a parasite in his own home. The wife is still saddled with many or most of the child-care responsibilities and housekeeping chores in addition to the burden of being the chief breadwinner. Tension between husband and wife commonly ensues.

Let me stress that I fully endorse the idea of a full-time home-maker father. I applaud a man who makes the choice to stay home and raise the children *and* clean the house *and* do the laundry, and so forth. But I haven't seen many men who make that choice. More often, the stay-at-home dad is not vacuuming the carpets; he's seldom making more than a token attempt to do the laundry; and he's not preparing the meals and cleaning the kitchen. He may not even be taking primary responsibility for child care. I have seen some stay-at-home dads who are great at *playing* with their kids but not so great at taking them to the doctor's office for a checkup or a sore throat. They leave those chores for Mom. Mom's working full-time while Dad's working part-time or not at all, but nevertheless Mom is stuck with more than her share of the chores. That's a situation many moms will put up with for only so long. Sooner or later it occurs to her that she might just be better off single.

The Changing American Household

Within the literary genre of "chick lit," there is a fast-growing sub-genre of books about productive young women saddled with un-derachieving boyfriends or husbands. One of the most successful of such books in this genre is Allison Pearson's *I Don't Know How She Does It.* The heroine is a woman named Kate Reddy. She's a hedge-fund manager working 70 hours a week and earning a salary in the high six figures. She is also the mother of two small children. Her laid-back husband earns a small fraction of her income but does less than half of the child-care chores. There's lots of dark comedy in the story because her husband just doesn't understand what motivates her. If you're so tired and overworked, he asks her at one point, why not just call in sick and sleep late? (In the movie version, Sarah Jessica Parker played the role of Kate Reddy, and Greg Kinnear was the laid-back husband.) At Christmas, her husband wonders why the nanny received a much nicer present than he did. Because the nanny is more important in my life, and helps me more than you do, is Kate's response.

For all the popularity of this genre, it's not what the future holds. Not many young women willingly sign up for Kate Reddy's position—earning most of the money and still having to do most of the child care. What's actually happening is different. The marriage rate among young Americans has been in a decades-long downward spiral, and the spiral is still plummeting. The household of the future—indeed, the household of the emerging present— does not look like Kate Reddy's home. The emerging norm is young and middle-aged men who have never married and are unlikely ever to marry, on one side; on the other side are young women, with or without children, who, when they do have children, use professional help (nannies or day care) to raise them. When one investigative team asked college students whether it was better to get married or to go through life single, two-thirds of the young men said it was better to get married. More than half the young women said it would be better to go through life single.[9]

The American household is changing. In 1930, 84 percent of American households were led by a married couple—and most of the remaining 16 percent were led by a widow or widower.

Households led by single, never-married adults were rare. Not anymore. The US Census Bureau reports that married couples with children now make up just 20 percent of American households. The greatest demographic change over the past 50 years has been in the surge in the number of adults living alone. Adults living alone now make up 27 percent of American households.[10]

It used to be unusual to find a man between the ages of 25 and 34 who had never married. In 1970, only about 1 in 6 American men aged 25 to 34 had never been married. But in 2010, 52 percent of American men aged 25 to 34—more than half—had never been married.[11]

These changes in the American social fabric have profoundly altered the lived experience of kids growing up in the United States. Isabel V. Sawhill, a senior fellow at the Brookings Institution, has concluded that "the culture is shifting. . . . [Before 1970], if you looked at families across the income spectrum, they all looked the same: a mother, father, kids, and a dog named Spot." But not anymore. Marriage with children has become "the exception rather than the norm." And there's no sign of this trend tapering off. Examining the numbers, University of Michigan sociology professor Pamela Smock has no doubt that "the percentage of children born outside of marriage is also going to increase."[12]

The decline in marriage rates cuts across all demographic groups. "It is a mistake to think of this [drop in marriage rates] as just happening to the underclass at the bottom," says Christopher Jencks, professor of sociology at Harvard.[13]

Likewise, the proportion of young men aged 25 to 34 living at home with parents has surged. In 1970, only 9.5 percent of men in that age group were living at home with parents. In 2011, the proportion was 18.6 percent, nearly double. By comparison, in 1970, 6.6

percent of women aged 25 to 34 were living with their parents; in 2011, the proportion had increased, but only to 9.7 percent. In other words, the proportion of young men (aged 25 to 34) living at home with parents is now almost double the proportion of young women in the same age group who are living at home with parents.[14]

Young women and young men are now following different life scripts. Young women are getting jobs, establishing themselves in the workplace, then (in some cases at least) thinking about having children. But a growing number of young men are just not on the same page. As a consequence, having children without being married—which would have been unusual in previous generations—is now common. In 1950, in the United States, only 4 percent of babies were born to unmarried women. In 1969, only 10 percent of babies were born to unmarried women. In 2013, more than 40 percent of American babies were born to unmarried women.[15] Right now, for the first time in American history, there are fewer adult women who are currently married than there are women who are unpartnered (either single and never married, or divorced and not remarried). Fifty years ago, married women outnumbered unpartnered women by roughly 2 to 1.[16] Some women who might have been married in a previous generation are now living with a man, but are not married to him. The number of heterosexual couples who are cohabiting, not married, more than doubled over the past two decades, from 2.9 million in 1996 to 7.9 million in 2014.[17]

Whatever Happened to Money and Sex?

Traditionally, one of the factors driving Western society has been the fact that women prefer successful, affluent men over men who are less successful. Because men believed that women would be reluctant to marry men who couldn't comfortably support a wife and children, men were motivated to be successful. That simple mechanism has suffered a double whammy in the past 40 years. First, sex has been divorced from marriage. You don't have to be married nowadays in order to find a sexual partner. Second—and here's what's really disturbing to those of us in the over-30 crowd—sexual satisfaction has been divorced from women altogether.

If you don't talk with today's teenage boys on a regular basis, you may not understand the extent to which pornographic images of women have replaced the real thing. In the general population, the best estimates are that roughly 70 percent of 17-year-old boys now masturbate regularly.[18] Among those boys, use of pornography can readily escalate from an occasional diversion to a daily pastime, and finally, to becoming the preferred sexual outlet.[19] In one Harvard study, 69 percent of men who sought help for sexual problems were experiencing "compulsive masturbation"—meaning that they were masturbating more than they thought they should be, and/or that they were sometimes masturbating in inappropriate places or at inappropriate times. Fifty percent of the men in the same study were described as being "pornography-dependent," meaning that they could not achieve an erection without pornography.[20] More and more boys are discovering that they prefer a sexy image on a computer screen to a real live woman with expectations, a woman who has her own agenda, a woman who may say things that the boy doesn't want to hear.

I've been seeing more and more young men in the office—men aged 18 to 28—who are dealing with the consequences of their overuse of pornography by asking for Viagra or Cialis or Levitra, because they find it difficult to get aroused by real women. One in three college-aged men now reports erectile dysfunction.[21] There are increasing reports of young men who use Viagra or Cialis to boost their "sexual confidence, erection quality, and better sexual performance."[22]

And I'm seeing other young men who use a different strategy: they disengage from the dating scene altogether, using pornography as their only sexual outlet. Here's an excerpt from an e-mail I received from a man in his late twenties after I wrote an article for the *Washington Post* related to this topic:[23]

> Dr. Sax, I think you're being very narrow-minded. Recently I've really gotten into Japanese anime, especially the videos. I love the girls in those videos. There [*sic*] sweet and submissive and nice. The real girls I know aren't anything like that. I would rather watch the anime girls than be with real girls. Why is that so bad? It's not my fault. It's the fault of the girls I know. They're too demanding. They expect the guy to do everything, pay for everything, make them laugh, do it all. Why is it so bad to prefer something different?

The technology has gotten so good, and the images are so life-like, that when those girls bat their eyelashes at him it's easy for him to forget that they're just pixels on a computer screen, not real girls. But there is a real danger that the boy may come to prefer the fantasy over the reality. That's unhealthy, in my judgment.

Not everyone agrees with me on this point. According to one scholarly monograph, the young man who prefers masturbation over actual intimacy with real women may merely be responding, appropriately, to "today's fast-paced social life characterized by individuality, impersonality, materialism, and social isolation."[24] Another critic dismissed concerns about pornography as the outdated prejudice of "moralists and religious conservatives."[25]

Recently, a number of critics have bemoaned the extent to which the culture of pornography has been mainstreamed in our society.[26] Lingerie has become evening wear. Young women can take classes at the local fitness club in aerobic striptease. These critics understandably see this development as a sign of cultural decadence, or as a worldwide plot by men to oppress women, or as a backlash against feminism. But I think the critics may have misdiagnosed the underlying dynamic. I asked a 16-year-old girl, as gently as I could, why she was wearing a Hooters outfit to a school Halloween party. Her shorts were very short, and her top displayed her natural endowment in a manner that invited comparison with Kim Kardashian. "Why?" she mused. "If you don't dress like this, nobody will even notice you."

"I Am the New Generation of Masturbator"

In case you haven't heard of him, John Mayer is a pop star. His album *Battle Studies* opened #1 on the Billboard charts in the United States in 2009. His previous celebrity girlfriends include Jessica Love Hewitt, Jessica Simpson, Jennifer Aniston, Katy Perry, and Taylor Swift. Nevertheless, when *Rolling Stone* magazine interviewed him for a cover story in 2012, he volunteered, "I am the new generation of masturbator," which the reporter said was blurted "out of the blue, apropros of nothing." Old-school men prefer having actual sex with actual women, but not John Mayer. He seems to *prefer* masturbation with pornography over having actual sex with actual women. "I have masturbated myself out of serious problems in my life," he continued. "If Tiger Woods only knew when to jerk off . . . ," he said, without further elaboration, but implying that the golfer wouldn't have gotten in so much trouble with his wife, Elin Nordegren, if he had merely masturbated instead of having sex with actual women.[27]

In case you missed the *Rolling Stone* interview, Mayer then gave an interview to *Playboy* magazine. The interviewer asked him, "What's your point about porn and relationships?" Mayer responded, "Internet pornography has absolutely changed my generation's expectations. . . . I have unbelievable orgasms alone. They're always the best. They always end the way I want them to end. . . . I'm more comfortable in my imagination than I am in actual human discovery."[28]

There's nothing new about pornography. Pornography was widely available 40 years ago (or so I am told, by reliable sources). But 40 years ago, when I was a teenager, boys did not boast about their collections of pornography. Instead, they boasted about their sexual exploits with actual human females. Pornography was seen as a second-best option for boys who couldn't get the real thing.

Not anymore. I was speaking to an auditorium filled with middle-school boys. I asked them, "How many of you have at least 1,000 porn photos or videos on your device?"

Almost all the hands went up. Then I asked, "How many of you have NO porn of any kind, on any device?"

Three hands went up, in an auditorium with nearly 400 boys. "Would any of you who just raised your hands care to share with your peers WHY you don't have any porn on your device?"

All three boys raised their hands. "I'm an evangelical Christian," the first boy said. "I believe Jesus Christ is my Lord and Savior, and I don't think he'd want me to mess with porn."

I called on the other two boys, who were sitting near each other. "We're Mormons," they explained. "We're not allowed to have porn."

I don't believe those 350+ boys who raised their hands to claim that they all had more than 1,000 porn photos or videos. I don't believe that all of them truly have so much porn. I suspect that many of them don't. But *that has become the new norm*. If you're an American boy in middle school or high school, and you're not Mormon or an evangelical Christian—in other words, if you don't have a good excuse—then you raise your hand. You don't want to be the weirdo who *doesn't* have porn.

Failure to Launch

Paramount Pictures released the movie *Failure to Launch* on March 10, 2006. Matthew McConaughey stars as a funny, friendly, good-looking 35-year-old who is utterly devoid of ambition. He lives at home with his parents. His mother cooks his breakfast, washes his laundry, and vacuums his room. His character has no clue that his parents want him to leave. Their desperation leads them to hire a professional "interventionist" whose assignment is to motivate McConaughey's character to leave his parents' home and get a life.

Failure to Launch was the #1-top-grossing movie in the United States for three weeks after its release, and it grossed more than $90 million at the box office in the three months between its March 2006 opening and the release of the DVD in June. I was struck by how accurately the movie captured a phenomenon I'd been tracking in my office for seven years. Two days after I saw the movie, I wrote an op-ed for the *Washington Post* entitled

"What's Happening to Boys?" I began by pointing out how the movie captured key features of the phenomenon I'd been seeing in my practice: in particular, the fact that the main character was intelligent. He is perfectly capable of success and achievement, but he simply has no motivation to accomplish anything real.

I wasn't prepared for what happened next. For three consecutive days, my article was the most e-mailed article on the *Post* website. The *Post* invited me to host an online chat on this topic. The chat line was open for just 60 minutes. Staffers at the paper shut the line down after 395 posts, which they told me was more than double the previous record for a 60-minute chat, of about 170 posts.

I was fascinated by the variety of comments I received, some of which were from men who were completely unapologetic about their situation. Here's one, from the online transcript of the *Washington Post* chat, from a 26-year-old living at home:[29]

Well, what IS the problem? If my parents are happy to have me, why shouldn't I stay with them? Why should I be in any hurry to have a career, wife, and children? Am I really obligated to have "direction"—direction towards where? You say there's something wrong with young people like me, but I would say it's worse to imagine that following the prescribed path to career and family will magically transform your life into a constant state of bliss.

Today's hero is not the blazing, iconoclastic industrialist of Ayn Rand, but the slacking, chilled-out Dude of The Big Lebowski. Why is he wrong, while Taggart and Rearden* are right? Until you

---

*"Taggart" is Dagny Taggart and "Rearden" is Hank Rearden, both characters in Ayn Rand's novel *Atlas Shrugged*. Both could fairly be described as "blazing iconoclastic industrialist[s]."

can answer that, the idea that I merit some kind of concerned examination is ridiculous.

But the online chat was only the beginning. Over the next two weeks, my article was reprinted in about three dozen major newspapers around the United States. On April 4, I went to the studios of National Public Radio in Washington, DC, as the featured guest in a 40-minute interview on the NPR program *On Point*, broadcast nationwide.[30] By the end of April I had received over 1,000 e-mails from all around the country.

I threw out my original draft of this chapter. The e-mails I received turned out to be more interesting than anything I could say. In the remainder of this chapter, I'm going to share with you a few of the most provocative, most outrageous, and most profound of those e-mails.

Subject: Shortest Date in History

Dear Dr. Sax,

I read your op-ed in the Washington Post with great interest. I'd like to add a different perspective. I'm a 35-year-old single woman, with my own house, car, career etc. I've worked hard to get where I am, and I've had to move a lot to move up. Now I'm finally in one place for a bit and can actually date. But many of the single men I meet still live with their parents, or else they are STILL figuring out what they want to be when they grow up. Mostly, I just want to smack them. Would that be OK?

Case in point. Two weeks ago I had the shortest date in history. It was at a coffee shop with a guy named Michael. Michael is 32. He's always wanted to be a journalist but quit a couple jobs along the way (red flag #1) and now works writing

proposals for an architecture firm. But he hates that job too
(red flag #2) and is thinking of quitting and getting his MFA
and teaching creative writing. Me: "How can you teach creative writing if you haven't done any?"

I asked Michael how he spends his free time. Mostly he
hangs out at bars with his friends. He hasn't been to any of
the local museums or theaters or anything remotely requiring
intelligence (red flag #3).

He asked if I had an apartment nearby. I said I owned a
home. He freaked. "Wow, you're quite the grown-up, aren't
you?" he said. Well, uh, yeah, dude, I'm 35.

Total date time: 2 cups of coffee. 35 minutes.

I can't tell you how many times this has been repeated. I
go out with a guy, turns out he's a total slacker. I don't want
to date these guys. I want to tell them: Get a grip! Get a job!
Have a dream! Do I need to go all JFK/MLK on their sad
sack selves?

Anyway. Last year, after more bad dates than I can count,
I gave up. I got myself a nice 25-year-old boy toy, whom I call
when I want and ignore when I want. He's not that bright, but
who cares? There's no future. He lives at home with his parents.

Sigh.

Datelessly yours,

Rachel

Dear Dr. Sax,

As a 24-year-old college graduate, I knew that after
graduating, I was supposed to get a job and move out of my
parents' home, so I moved to the other end of the country. I
love the independence, the freedom, and my personal space.

My brother is a different story. I see so much of him in the comments people posted [on the *Washington Post* chat]: especially the young men who added their two cents. My brother went to college, dropped out, worked in a restaurant for a while, broke up with his live-in girlfriend, and ended up back in my parents' basement. He still works in a restaurant, but he doesn't do ANY chores, he never makes any attempt to help out, and he doesn't seem to care about moving on with his life, though he's made some half-hearted attempts. He's got a good thing going: no rent, few responsibilities other than entertaining the family dog, free food, sleeping till noon, and the knowledge that my parents will help pay for college again if he decides that's what he wants.

Why look to the future when he can have a wad of bills at the end of a shift in the restaurant? It's easy money, and it's a lot of money, but it won't get him anywhere. He doesn't care. I think a lot of young men have a very short-sighted view of the future: the next party, the next short-term job, the next free meal. He's not living at home for the family aspect; he's there because it's free and it's easy.

Another example: my boyfriend of over six years. He's never lifted a hand at home. His mother does everything for him: laundry, meals, picks up his dishes (which he leaves scattered in various rooms around the house), she makes his bed, etc. I told him that if he was going to spend time with me, he was going to do chores, especially washing the dishes. I made it very clear that I wasn't going to be his mother and pick up after him. Neither was I going to put up with laziness in getting things done. I've had to explain to him that sometimes you just have to do unpleasant things so you can enjoy yourself later. He wants instant gratification—and I know he gets that from video games. . . . Play more video games and pretend it's mental development. Gladly! It's very frustrating. I'm worried, especially as we intend to move in together this summer, and I like to have a very neat and clean apartment.

Thank you for the chance to comment. I fully intend to show this to my boyfriend. Keep up the good work!

Anna M.

Dear Dr. Sax,

I read your article on the Washington Post website today and I was struck by your description of what I am going through right now. I am a 25-year-old woman, married eight months to one of these "boys." My boy will be 29 in August. I am experiencing what it's like to live with one of these boys after they finally leave their parents.

My husband and I met online. He and I graduated from college the same semester in 2002. I graduated with two majors in four years. He graduated with one major that took seven years. When we met in early 2004, we were both living with our parents. At that time, I was looking to leave the nest. He seemed content to be at home. I fully believe that if he hadn't met me, he would still be there.

He told me that he passed his time playing Nintendo, surfing the Net, watching TV, etc. He lived in luxury with a nice car, nice clothes and spending money—all on his parents' dime. He worked a retail job that didn't pay much, but it fit his laid-back, jovial, "not serious" personality. He claims that he didn't pursue a professional career because he didn't know what he wanted to do. He once wanted to do outdoors work

with DNR [Department of Natural Resources] etc. but he
claims that the chemistry and biology required were too steep
of a price to achieve his dream job. I overlooked all of this as
just being who he was. He is intelligent. I thought the way he
lived was not because of him necessarily, but rather might be
due to the foundation of money and security—and lack of
responsibility—which his parents had set up for him.

I thought this would change when we got married, that he
would grow up and do things on his own: balance a checkbook,
get his own insurance, do at least some of the housework etc.
I have learned that he doesn't know how to do any of these
things. He is so financially inept that he has practically crippled
our young marriage. I am the professional. I make twice what
he does at his job at the mall. Couple that with the late hours
he works, and I am pretty much by myself in running our
household.

It frustrates me that what seemed to me to be a lack of motivation due to others enabling him has developed into a lack
of understanding of adult responsibilities. I am perplexed.
How can such an intelligent person be so utterly clueless? I
feel like his mother. If I relied on him to pay the bills, file our
taxes, get loans, clean up etc. it simply would not get done. We
would be out on the street. As much as I tell him that I need
help with the bills and that I need his understanding and support, the ignorance just gets that much worse. The thing is, his
family always bailed him out and they still try to. I forbid it.
He gets upset that I am upset but he never takes any interest
in things even though he says he will. I think he just believes
everything will magically work out every month like it has in
the past. Luckily, I have made it work so far. But I know that

eventually our reserve finances are going to run out. I can't imagine what will happen then. I don't see any motivation in him to improve. If I try to pull him from the Xbox or the TV, I'm the bad guy. He doesn't seem to realize that his $10/hour salary cannot cover everything that he wants: cable, Internet, car, cell phones. But I magically make it happen every month—because I'm working my butt off. Sometimes I even have to coerce him to shower and to shave.

I love my husband. But I am constantly haunted by something he once told me. He said that I might need to lower my expectations in life because he didn't know whether he could provide them for me. What I find funny now is that I'm the real provider. I don't feel like part of a team. It's wearing on me.

He has no idea.

Thank you,

Sarah C.

Subject: What's Happened to Boys?

Dear Dr. Sax,

I believe that what's happened to boys is directly related to what's happened to girls. Girls today feel that they don't need boys so much anymore. And boys have figured that out. Girls used to give motivation to boys to be successful so that the boys could "take care of them." Without that motivation, what is left for the boys? Video games, where they can still be the hero. Sleeping around—because, as you succinctly stated, girls still have sexual needs—but we've learned how to satisfy ourselves in that aspect, also. No, it's not the same, but it will do in a pinch.

If you'd like to take it one step further: what if women decide that they've had enough of men and their huge egos, and their testosterone-fueled wars, and start stock-piling frozen sperm until they really DON'T need men anymore? Do you think men, at least subconsciously, haven't thought about that scenario?

I love men. As a divorced woman, I really miss a male presence in my home. There's just something about men and testosterone and physical strength that really turn me on. The world would definitely be a worse place without men. But women are evolving, not necessarily in a good way, and men are reacting.

Rachel Riggs

Coeur d'Alene, Idaho

Dear Dr. Sax,

As a 29-year-old woman, I'm smack in the middle of the "failure to launch" generation. I grew up in Northern Virginia. I went to my 10-year high school reunion last year. All of the girls I went to school with have moved out, gone to college, gotten real jobs, etc. Almost all the boys live at home, have menial jobs, and don't know what they want out of life.

I think the boys' laziness started in high school. Honestly I think at least some of the blame lies with parents. All the girls had curfews in high school. We all had to tell our parents where we were at all times. We had to keep our grades up. Not a single boy I knew had a curfew. Most were allowed to slack off in school because they had "difficulty focusing" or they were diagnosed with "sensory integration disorder." The girls had jobs at the mall. The boys got allowances from Mom and Dad. Even within the same family, there were different rules for boys and girls.

Now we've reaped what we've sown. The girls have discipline. The boys have PlayStations.

I'm newly divorced. I'm not sure I want to remarry. There just aren't any worthwhile men out there. My generation of men aren't looking for partners—they're looking for a new Mommy. I'd much rather be on my own than be with a man who can't stand on his own two feet.

Sincerely,

Sharon S.

Dear Dr. Sax,

Thank you so much for bringing attention to this phenomenon. I'm a 28-year-old woman and I've noticed that my friends and I, instead of talking about our future weddings, families etc. are now talking about the fact that having a relationship with one of these boy/men works against our eventual goals: successful careers and having children. Instead we talk about how we're going to work on our careers, and if we haven't found someone by the time we're of a good age, we'll adopt or find some other way of having children on our own and we'll just support ourselves. The "Failure to Launch" phenomenon is precisely the reason for this shift. Why take on some boy/man who would then move into our homes and expect to be taken care of by us?

Thanks again, and keep us all posted if you come across a solid conclusion as to why this is happening.

Allie

Dear Dr. Sax,

I read your Washington Post article and it really hit home. My never-married fiancé who still lives with his mother called off our wedding a little over three months ago. He's a teacher with a master's degree. He pays his mother $250 a month for room and board (way below market rates). He doesn't even have a savings account. He has spent every cent he has ever made on electronics, car stereos etc.

I knew all this, but because we are both Christians, both teachers, and have many things in common, and because I fell in love with him, the thought never occurred to me that he would back out. He kept reassuring me that he would leave home. I thought he meant it when he spent $7,300 on a ring.

Oh well. Now I'm glad he backed out because it would not have worked out.

I have never married. I own my own home.

Thank you for listening.

Maxine C.

Georgia

Dr. Sax,

I sent this to NPR during their interview with you:

Perhaps the men-staying-at-home phenomenon is a reaction to the feminist era. Before that era, there was no other option than men going to work and women staying at home. Now perhaps there are men hoping to be "found" by a rich woman and marry her and not have to work. I know MANY men who want to marry me simply because I am a lawyer. It's gotten to the point that I don't want to tell a man what I do for a living until after we've decided to date steadily. My boyfriend was depressed for a week after I told him I want to practice PUBLIC INTEREST law. "What?!" he said. "There's no money in that!" He never recovered.

Thanks,

Penny

Reston, Virginia

Dr. Sax,

I read your article in the Washington Post and found it very interesting. While you raise some valid points, I find some of your points to be highly culturally biased. I come at this as a native-born American of Pakistani heritage.

In every other country in the world, it is completely normal and expected that children live with their parents in adulthood. This is seen as mutually beneficial. The older generation is revered in those countries, unlike this country. I believe this comes from a joint family system where parents and children are actively involved in each other's lives. Children can live with their parents to save money and they will take care of their parents when they are old.

Many in the United States seem to feel that family ties stop at age 18. Kids can't come home. Those kids will be unlikely to help their parents when they may need help in their old age. We have somehow established that a Mother's Day card and a Christmas card suffice for familial obligations. I believe this generates severe social consequences. Children benefit from growing up close to their extended families or in joint families.

I take your point that kids living with parents can create disincentives to work. I also concur that in some cases, maybe

they do need to be evicted. But I believe it is a case by case
matter. I find your advice to charge rent to be offensive. Families are not money-making endeavors.

Best regards,

Aliya Husain

Washington, DC

I received several responses like Ms. Husain's, mostly from
people who were born and raised outside of North America. These
people observed that in countries as diverse as India, Italy, Paki-
stan, Portugal, Spain, and many Latin American countries, it's
common for adult children, both women and men, to live with
their parents. That's true. But in those other countries, the adult
children are more likely to be integrated into the household. In
many cases, those adult children may help to operate a family
business. The distinctive feature of the "failure to launch" phenomenon is that the American young man is coasting, slacking
off, relying on his parents to provide everything for him while he
has a good time.

This is something new. There is no country with a tradition of
parents working while their adult children slack off at home. In Italy, there is a centuries-old tradition of the *mammoni*, men who
choose to live at home with their mothers for their entire life.
However, such men are still expected to be productive. It would be
unusual for such a man to expect his mother to provide all the
household income while he plays video games and surfs the Net.[31]
Likewise, in Japan, demographers have expressed concern about
the growing number of adult men who are living at home with
their parents, refusing to work, while the young man's mother
serves the son meals and cleans up his room. These boy/men are

referred to as *hikikomori*, literally "pulling away, being confined."
One key difference between the Japanese hikikomori and the
American "failure to launch" is that the hikikomori men themselves are, with a few exceptions, miserable. They wish that they
had more motivation.[32] The American slacker dude, by contrast—
epitomized by McConaughey's character in *Failure to Launch* or
by Owen Wilson's character in *You, Me, and Dupree*—is perfectly
content to be dependent on others.

> I just finished listening to your interview on NPR. I'm 23
> and living at home. I've been wondering why I lack either the
> motivation or the willpower to leave.
>
> Maybe having ADHD as a child has something to do with
> it. I did hear you say that Ritalin and Adderall might cause
> a lack of motivation. That to me is not a huge leap of logic.
> I remember taking the medication at the age of 8 or 10 and
> becoming completely despondent.
>
> The term "slacker" runs through my mind constantly.
>
> If you would e-mail me some information about this sub-
> ject I would appreciate it.
>
> Ian
> Glen Carbon, Illinois

> What does society tell us should be our goal? A career spent
> in a cubicle on the phone trying to convince people that
> Bunco spark plugs are the best spark plugs in the world? And
> then, after 30 years, your company moves to Mexico and cuts
> your pension? No thanks.
>
> From a bored 23-year-old.
> Jeff

Good afternoon Dr. Sax,

I'm male, 27 years old, married, and in grad school, working toward a doctorate in medieval literature. I also teach Latin. My wife and I don't have a TV because of how much time it wastes and how much mindless junk there is on it. However, I have played computer games in some form since my parents got me a computer when I was in high school. Before that I sometimes used to go to friends' houses and play computer games there. Once I got to college, I had more time to play computer games if I wanted to.

I don't think you understand the computer game phenomenon when you talk about it sapping the motivation of male 20-somethings. That's only part of the picture. The other part is that computer games allow people to do things that feel as significant or important as the things they wish they could do in real life but don't see any way of doing. I don't mean that people are playing Battlefield 2 because they wish they could be shooting lots of people. But they do wish that they could be doing something that mattered. When they're playing that game, they can, for a few hours, feel like they're doing something significant.

When I started grad school, I had a rough first year or so. Many times I came home feeling like I was never going to be any good as a scholar, like I had no hope of ever actually doing anything significant, or making any serious contribution even just in the academic community. But I could turn on the computer and play X-Wing and feel like I was helping to defeat the Galactic Empire. If you want to feel significant, feeling like you just destroyed the Death Star helps for a little while. Or a few years later, I would play Morrowind. As I wandered around that world, I could help a wounded traveler, or rescue captives from bandits, or discover a secret upon which the survival of a city depended. And there, at least in that world, I could succeed. One thing that's key in most computer games is that there is positive feedback. In flight simulator games, you don't just defeat the other pilots: you also get a badge. There's an implicit pat on the back. And you get a sense of achievement. If you're not getting a sense of achievement anywhere else in life, computer games are pretty tempting as a way of getting that feeling. It's built into them.

Not only is there the sense of achievement, but there is also in many games beauty and adventure. In Morrowind, you can wander through a really beautiful, detailed, vivid world. Now I prefer reality. But I live in South Bend, Indiana. There aren't lots of places to hike or even to walk. I can't afford to travel much. I would love to wander on a misty shore and hear the waves, or hike through mountains and valleys. I can't do that here. I daydream about the one time I went to the Pacific Northwest, or the years when I lived in Switzerland. Or, instead of daydreaming, I can play a game that gives me something similar, though of course nowhere near as real or as good. The desire for beauty is very strong—so strong that one might accept all sorts of false substitutes if one couldn't find the reality.

Of course the sad thing is that spending lots of time on computer games can keep you from achieving the very things the desire for which sent you to computer games in the first place. Who has time to study and get involved in urban development if he spends all day playing SimCity?

Of course I agree that people should stop wasting time in front of the PC/Xbox and go do something real. But in order to treat a problem it may be helpful to know something about how it seems to those who suffer from it. I hope this is helpful.

Sincerely,

Richard R.

Notre Dame

South Bend, Indiana

Another post from the *Washington Post* chat:

WhatisanAdult: Doc, I fall into that mold. I tend bar for a living. I live at home. I have fun. I pick up more pretty girls than I can count, so what is my motivation to have a family, career, etc.? What if my happiness is defined differently from yours?

I've dated more than one attractive, highly-paid professional woman and stolen her away from her boring corporate boyfriend who makes multiples of my income. The women tell me they are sick of their non-exciting life. The burbs, playing the role of the little home maker.

We have FUN together. We talk about music, art, cool stuff. They don't seem to miss their "successful" exs much at all.

I am not hurting anyone. So why do I need the suit, the tie, kids, stroller, the BMW, just because I am 30? Seems sort of shallow to live that way.

My response to Casanova:

I'm glad that you are enjoying life.

You wrote that you are picking up "more pretty girls than I can count, so what is my motivation to have a family, career, etc.?"

What is, or should be, the motivation for having a family
or a career? The motivation to have a family and a meaningful
career is not (and should not be) grounded in the desire to pick
up pretty girls. It should be grounded, rather, in the desire to be
of use, to serve others, to give your life some meaning beyond
the pleasure of the moment. If those objectives have no real
meaning to you, then nothing I or anyone else says will have
much impact. If FUN (capitalized, as you capitalized it) is the
be-all and end-all, then by that standard you're doing extremely
well.

I think at some point that you may find that having FUN is
not satisfying, and that a meaningful life requires more than
picking up pretty girls. At that point, you may see the point of
having a career and a family.

Or you may not.

But I wonder what your parents would have to say about
this?

Subject: I am that kid

Listening to your interview on NPR today, I needed about
15 seconds before I realized you were talking about ME.
I'm a white, suburban, semi-affluent male who has been on
academic steroids* since the third grade. I have no work ethic.
I'm graduating in a month and a half.

Can I be of service to you?

Max Geller

---

*"Academic steroids" is a reference to prescription stimulants as Vyvanse, Ad-
derall, Ritalin, Concerta, Metadate, Focalin, Daytrana, and so on.

My name is Mike. I'm 33 years old. I don't live at home, but rather in a home paid for by my parents. I'm in graduate school, but my efforts there have been lackluster.

Like many of the young men you mentioned, I play too many video games. I agree that they offer a fantasy world with a beginning, middle, end, and accomplishments. All with no risk, and nearly certain achievement.

I wonder about my lack of motivation. All the way back to grade school, I hated academics. It's not that I dislike learning. On the contrary, I love to learn. I just hate school. Always have. I used to be a teacher at a small private school working with autistic kids. Before that, I had a string of dead end jobs, which seldom lasted as long as a year. My days were punctuated with pot, video games, and beer. I lived hundreds of miles from home, but my parents have sent me money every two weeks for—many years. They make enough that it doesn't impede their own comfortable existence. Still I do have occasional guilty moments.

I was married for a time—for 6 years. Ironically, I always considered her lazy. At the end of a day's work, her favorite thing to do was watch TV and drink beer. It bored me to tears. My answer was to get into video games. That's when my fixation started. I was a late bloomer in the video game world, discovering them in my mid-twenties. Before that, I preferred to get high—or read—or see a documentary—or take in a museum.

My parents are enablers. They make it easy for me to do less than I might otherwise have to do.

I did live for one year once without any support from my parents. It started out exhilarating. I worked hard at a bookstore, earning raises and respect. But eventually I burnt out. Beer and pot sapped my energy. Depression took hold. Yes I was independent, but I was still a self-destructive mess.

Now I am back in the fold. I struggle with motivation. I struggle with depression and anxiety, but I do live a cleaner and healthier life. I have a year and a half of grad school done, but I'll be lucky to make any use of this degree by the time I get it, at the pace I'm going.

I don't think the answer is "your parents are enablers, they should cut you off." Of course you might predict that I would say that. But the issues are complex.

I hope that this is useful information for you. Thank you for the opportunity.

Mike

Dear Dr. Sax,

You've perfectly described my 31-year-old son, adopted in Taiwan at 5 weeks of age. It may interest you that it used to describe his twin sister as well. Both had high IQs and difficulties fitting into the small New England town we lived in. In college they both suffered from depression and dropped out. She found housing near her school, did some entry-level jobs, finally got married and now has some sense of direction. She talks of going back to school, getting a real job etc. He does not. He flunked out several times, came home, pretended to get jobs but never did—until we gave him an ultimatum: either get a job or get out. He got a job. Later he also moved into an apartment. The job moved away and he has not found another for several years. He seems content to exist on his leftover college fund. He plays video games and online role games with a few friends. He's a nice person—but with no ambition and no desires. He has never shown motivation.

I often wonder if the overwhelming importance for males of achievement in sports early in life offers some explanation for this total giving up if one is not oriented toward sports.

[no name given]

I often hear from parents who, somewhat like this mother, are convinced that their son's lack of motivation can be traced to the day when he wasn't asked to play in the pickup basketball game, or when he didn't make the junior high football team, or when he discovered that he just wasn't particularly good at sports. However, I also hear from parents of other boys, athletically talented boys, who are convinced that their son's lack of motivation is due to the fact that he grew accustomed to being the star, the best athlete, the golden boy. Once he finished high school and realized that he was never going to be good enough to play professional sports, he lost interest in life.

I agree that much of mainstream American culture puts a tremendous emphasis on boys being good at sports, just as it puts an overwhelming emphasis on the physical attractiveness of girls. Boys who are athletically talented are far more likely to be popular than boys who aren't any good at sports, just as girls who are slender and pretty are more likely to be popular than girls who are obese. But the "failure to launch" phenomenon appears just as likely to occur in athletically talented boys as in klutzy boys. Although parents often attribute their son's lack of motivation to his athletic prowess, or to his lack of athletic prowess, I think both attributions miss the point.

Another comment from the *Washington Post* chat:

> Missoula, Mont.: Hey, Mr. Sax, being out of the nest isn't so
> great for everybody. My advice to young men: take as much
> time as you need. The real world is very rough. The people
> advising you to move out are the ones who've made it. Others
> may not see it the same way.

My response: I agree that the real world is very rough. My question for you, if you are a parent, is this: What's the best way to help young people to face that reality? If your child is 10 years old, then by all means, shelter him or her from that harsh reality. But what if your child is 21, or 26, or 32? How long is a parent expected to shelter a child who is not mentally or physically handicapped?

My own belief, based in part on more than 20 years of medical practice, is that if parents continue to shelter their adult child after the age of 21 years, the parents may make it less likely that the adult child will ever be willing and able to meet the challenges of the real world.

Of course, one has to make reasonable distinctions. If your son has just graduated from college and he's 22 or 23, looking for a job, I see no harm in his living at home while he's conducting his job search—provided that you and he have discussed, openly and up front, how long this situation can last before you will expect him to find some kind of part-time job to help pay his expenses. One month? Fine. One year? Too long.

> Dear Dr. Sax,
> I have 3 sons. My 25-year-old has an honors degree, a
> good job, he's married and a homeowner. Successful launch.

My youngest is in college. He is very likely to launch: when
he is home during summer we barely see him and he is very
uncomfortable about accepting money from us for tuition or
car insurance or anything else.

Our middle son, now 23, is a classic failure to launch.
Despite 6 years of college, some of it part time, he only has
a 2 year degree. Of my 3 boys, he's the only computer game
player. He is addicted to video games.

I believe that in certain susceptible individuals, playing
video games gives them control of a fantasy world without
the discomfort and uncertainty of real world social interactions. This same son was diagnosed as ADD in first grade.
We tried Ritalin, but after getting to a dose that caused
palpitations without any noticeable behavior changes we
decided that was not his problem. He tested in the gifted
category, did well on the SAT, but his grades were all over
the map due to lack of focus and a bout of depression in his
senior year.

Thank you for focusing on this.

Carol in South Carolina

This e-mail highlights two recurring issues. First: variation
within a family. It's not unusual to find a situation like this one
where one son "fails to launch" while his brother does just fine.
I agree with what Carol said about individual susceptibilities.
Second: reports of depression. It's common to see the boys who
"fail to launch" struggling with depression. It's often hard to say
which comes first. Is the boy depressed because he's unmotivated and failing to launch, or is he unmotivated because he's
depressed?

Dear Dr. Sax,

I listened with great interest to you on NPR yesterday. I'm the mother of a 33-year-old male—handsome, charming, personable, tall, college graduate (that took 6 years and 4 schools).

He has "failed to launch" no matter what my husband and I have done to help him, beginning right after he graduated from college. We bought him a car and clothes for job interviews. He wasn't interested. He liked the good life: hanging out with a bunch of kids he met in college who did drugs and stayed out all night and slept the better part of the day.

Finally, after consulting with a psychologist who encouraged us to let him fall to the very bottom, we let it happen. He became homeless. Out on the street. When he called us in desperation, we offered him yet another opportunity to launch. He joined the Army. He completed Basic and even did months of Advanced Individual Training. Then just as the war with Iraq broke out, he figured out a way to get out of the Army. But we did not allow him to live with us again.

We are still helping him financially or he would not be able to live on his own. He's living in our beach place rent-free for 8 months a year. He has been working somewhat more steadily but he is still not capable of saving for a rainy day or even cover the basic costs of living. He has no aspiration to become anything. He says he dislikes "corporate" America. He is resentful of us, yet at the same time he needs us to help him.

My husband and I have been self-starters, self-made successes. Over the years, with hard work, we have managed to become financially comfortable. We are in our mid-60s, but we still work, because we enjoy what we do.

So how can we help our son to get on with his own life??
And stop leaning on us???? We have told him countless times
that when we die then no one is going to be able to help him
anymore.

I would love to hear from you.

D.G., near Boston

Subject: Failure to Launch

Dr. Sax,

I read your article and the chat in Washington Post online.
I was struck by the pervasiveness of this "Failure to Launch."
Professor Kleinfeld's web site indicated that this trend began
in the early 70's. I find that timing interesting because that's
when the military draft ended and we went to an all-volunteer
force. The draft may have had a significant effect on young
men in ways not readily apparent.

The military was a place for many boys to finish growing up:

- The additional supervised time after high school,
  age 18–24, may have provided the "catch up time"
  boys need to be on the same level with their female
  counterparts.
- Mature role models. Older and wiser heads were in
  positions of authority and exercised that authority.
- Responsibility. Boys learned that they would be held
  accountable. Rewards and punishments were easily
  understood.

The draft—or more precisely, the threat of being drafted—
may have encouraged young men who did not want to do

military time to apply themselves in college. Dropping out of college could lead you to be drafted into service.

I do not advocate returning to a draft. But, programs which give boys a structured environment with more time to mature seem to have merit.

> Regards,
> Mike Cleveland
> Elkview, West Virginia

Dear Dr. Sax,

I heard your interview this morning on NPR. I tried to call but could not get through. I too have a son, 26 years old, who is a "failure to launch." My son's situation is a little different from many of the young men you talk about because he doesn't live with me. He lives in a house that his Dad left to him, with conditions, before his death six years ago.

My son was a smart student who did not apply himself to his studies. He seemed to lack discipline to study and really did not put very much effort into his studies. He scored very well on his SATs though. He entered Northwestern University but dropped out after one year. Now, five years later, he seems to be sliding down the slippery slope of "failing to launch" his life.

My son is a wonderful conversationalist. He is interested in history, biology, space exploration, etc. There is a myriad of subjects that he is really knowledgeable about. He is charming, respectful, polite—and tall and handsome! He has so much enthusiasm for other areas of his life—but it doesn't seem to apply for planning for his own life. What will he become? What will he do? What will be his life's work? It troubles me. It doesn't seem to trouble him at all.

My son has had every opportunity. He has chosen not to return to college. Did he make this choice with full understanding of what it would mean for his future? I don't believe he ever really thinks about the future.

I want him to do something with his life. His Dad would have wanted that for him too. I know that my son misses him very much, but it's been 6 years and he must find a path for himself.

I would so appreciate a reply whenever you have the time.

Thank you.

Sincerely,

A Most Concerned Mother,

Mary W.

From: Kent Robertson

Subject: NPR interview

I thought I would share an epiphany I experienced during your interview.

With 4 sons, teen and pre-teen, this "Failure to Launch" trend is one I need to get in front of. You mentioned that these men are quite content despite their lack of motivation. Well, why the hell not. These man/boys have it all. Their material needs are handed to them. The over-indulgent Moms will see to that (didn't the mother who called in make that clear?). Their emasculated fathers usually have little say.

Here's the epiphany—or confession, if you like. I sense that I am only a marital separation away from sinking into such a funk. When I think how little I would need to be content, compared with how much I produce, it's amazing. But somehow it works. I work ridiculous hours and earn ridiculous

money. Yet I personally expend only about $200 per month
of it on food, haircut, sundries. Whatever new clothes I have
are given to me as gifts, because I have little interest in how
I look. I live in a comfortable home in a pleasant neighborhood, and a whole wonderful busy suburban lifestyle, but
only because I want that for my wife and children. *Take my
dear ones away and I need none of it.* [Emphasis in original]

I have seen many grown men, when their marriage fails,
drift toward the man/boy zero-ambition style of life, living
in a shanty or maybe back home with parents, in pursuit of
personal gratification over everything else, exploiting every
sexual opportunity, not unlike the man/boys you described
on NPR.

You mentioned "the engine that runs the world." As for
me, I think that the engine is the love of a good woman and
the ambitions we have together for the family we are raising
and for the world we want them to inherit.

Has our intellectual elite and our popular culture tinkered
with "the engine that runs the world"? Have we violated
something that the ancients knew intuitively but which we
have arrogantly ignored?

Kent Robertson

7

The Fifth Factor

The Revenge of the Forsaken Gods[1]

H OW DOES A CHILD BECOME AN ADULT? HOW DOES A BOY BECOME A
man? The transition from childhood to productive adulthood involves more than mere biological maturation and the
passage of time. Children take their cues from the grown-ups
they see around them. Girls look to women they know, as well as
to the images they see on television, in movies, and online. Likewise, boys look to the men they see in their lives and in the media. In his memoir *The Tender Bar*, author J. R. Moehringer
describes how he found his community of men at a local bar,
beginning long before he was old enough to buy a drink. The
men at the bar were not model citizens or great fathers or manly
men. But collectively they provided Moehringer with what he
needed. "Manhood is mimesis," Moehringer wrote. "To be a
man, a boy must see a man."[2]

A boy does not naturally become a gentleman—by which I mean a man who is courteous, kind, and unselfish. That behavior is not hardwired. It has to be taught.

B ACK IN MAY 2006, I DELIVERED THE COMMENCEMENT ADDRESS AT Avon Old Farms, a boys' school in Connecticut. I noticed that there were many teenage girls in the audience—far outnumbering the boys. "You guys all seem to have about four sisters apiece," I said to some of the boys.

"Those aren't our sisters, Dr. Sax," one of the boys told me. "Those are friends."

"You mean girlfriends?"

"Some of them are girlfriends, most of them are just friends," he said.

This piqued my interest. I spoke with some of the girls. A few were from Miss Porter's School, a girls' school about five miles away, but most were from the Westminster Academy, a coed school right next door to Avon Old Farms.

"A coed school?" I said. "So what are you girls doing here? Why would you want to hang out here at a boys' school, when you have boys at your own school?"

One girl rolled her eyes. "The boys at our school are all such total losers," she said. "Being around them is like being around my younger brother. They're loud, and obnoxious, and annoying. And they think they're so tough. It's totally—*nauseating*." The other girls laughed and nodded their agreement.

"And the boys here are really that different?" I asked.

They all nodded their heads again. "Totally," another girl said. "The boys here are, like—*gentlemen*. I know that sounds really strange and weird and old-fashioned, but that's just the way it is. Like, they stand up when you come in the room. They open doors for you."

"And they don't interrupt you," another girl said, interrupting. "I hate trying to talk to guys at our school 'cause they are always interrupting you."

"You should come here some weekend, Dr. Sax," another girl said. "You would totally not even know that this is a boys' school. There are probably more girls here than boys on the weekend. We just totally mob the place. Not even to hang with the guys necessarily. Last week a bunch of us girls went down to the indoor hockey rink here at the school just to slide around on the ice. Just us girls."

"But why bother to come to this school at all? You could have just gone to a public ice skating rink," I said.

She shook her head no. "It wouldn't be the same. It's fun to hang out here, because"

"Because it's like we're family," another girl said.

"Because it feels safe," said another.

This school is not unique. I have heard similar comments from other girls who like to congregate at boys' schools—for example, at Georgetown Prep in Bethesda, Maryland. I hasten to add that I have heard very different comments at certain other boys' schools: I have heard girls say that they would never ever in a million years hang out at certain boys' schools. Just establishing a boys' school doesn't make that school a place where girls like to gather. On the contrary, when you put teenage boys together in groups, without the right kind of adult leadership, they can easily become a gang of bullies and thugs, "crashing through several moral guardrails," to borrow David Brooks's phrase.[3] William Golding's novel *Lord of the Flies* exemplifies what can happen: teenage boys without strong leadership can easily become barbarians.

Leadership from responsible adults makes the difference between schools where girls feel safe and welcome and schools where girls feel unsafe. Schools like the one in Connecticut where I spoke don't leave this to chance. They make a point of teaching boys to be gentlemen. At this particular school, the boys are taught the school's eight "core values," which are:

- Scholarship
- Integrity
- Civility
- Tolerance
- Altruism
- Sportsmanship
- Responsibility
- Self-discipline

"It's not enough for a boy to become a man. We want him to become a *gentleman*," the headmaster, Kenneth LaRocque, explained to me. At this school, LaRocque and his colleagues explicitly teach the rules that they believe define a gentleman: A gentleman doesn't pretend to make farting noises to amuse his buddies. A gentleman doesn't harass girls or women. A gentleman doesn't interrupt a girl when she is speaking. A gentleman stands when a girl or a woman enters the room. At this school, all these points are explicitly taught to the boys. "You can't assume that boys today know these things. Many of them don't. But they can be taught," LaRocque said. "A boy does not naturally grow up to be a gentleman. You need a community of men showing boys how to behave. And that's what we provide here."

Almost every culture of which we have detailed knowledge takes great care in managing this transition to adulthood. One example: the !Kung people of southwestern Africa, who call themselves "the harmless people." Their culture is nonviolent: war is unknown. They have no warriors and no tradition of combat. "Yet even here," according to anthropologist David Gilmore, "in a culture that treasures gentleness and cooperation above all things, the boys must earn the right to be called men by a test of skill and endurance. They must single-handedly track and kill a sizable adult antelope, an act that requires courage and hardiness. Only after their first kill of such a buck are they considered fully men and permitted to marry."[4]

Professor Gilmore devoted several years to researching the various manifestations of masculinity in cultures around the world, including the !Kung. "There are many societies where aggressive hunting never played an important role," Gilmore writes, "where men do not bond for economic purposes, where violence and war are devalued or unknown, and yet where men are [even] today concerned about demonstrating manhood."[5]

What happens when a culture—like ours—neglects this transition? For a decade or two, or three, perhaps, the culture can coast along. But after 30-plus years of neglecting this transition, problems begin to develop. If we fail to provide boys with pro-social models of the transition to adulthood, they will construct their own, which may not be so positive and constructive.

Of course, not all enduring cultures follow the same template in guiding boys to manhood. Without doubt, significant attributes of masculinity are constructed differently by different societies. One example has to do with attitudes toward homosexuality. In some cultures homosexuality is seen as a deviant, unmasculine orientation. In other cultures, however, it is seen as a normal masculine or even hypermasculine orientation. Among some Native American tribes, for example, the most masculine men have sex with other men; having sex with women is perceived as less masculine.[6] Likewise, among samurai warriors in Japan, particularly in the period from the establishment of the Tokugawa Shogunate in 1603 to the Meiji Restoration in 1867, the homosexual orientation was held in high regard as a sign of the truest masculinity.[7] A similar cultural bias in favor of homosexuality was prevalent in ancient Sparta.[8]

Each culture differs, then, in what is considered masculine behavior. But these variations in cultural attitudes should not confuse us. There are certain constants. There is no enduring culture in which cowardly men are esteemed, or in which brave men are held in contempt. There is no enduring culture in which lazy men are celebrated while hardworking men are despised.[9]

Enduring Cultures Have One Thing in Common

What do cultures that have lasted for hundreds or thousands of years have in common? Orthodox Jews and Navajo Indians seem at first glance to have almost nothing in common, except that both cultures have endured more or less intact for more than 1,000 years. The religious beliefs of the Orthodox Jew differ fundamentally from those of the Navajo Indian; rules about what may or may not be eaten differ enormously between the two; they dress differently—and so on.

But they do have one thing in common: strong bonds across generations. That's how these cultures teach customs and traditions to their children—and the rules for what is expected of men and women. And both of these cultures, Orthodox Jewish and Navajo Indian—along with almost every other enduring culture that anthropologists have studied—pass this information from one generation to the next in gender-separate communities. Women teach girls what it means to be a woman in their community. Men teach boys what it means to be a man.

I'm not talking about teaching reading, writing, social studies, math, or science. Women can teach these subjects to boys, just as men can teach these subjects to girls. I've visited boys' schools where some of the best and most beloved teachers are women, just as I've visited girls' schools where some of the most effective teachers are men. But when it comes to showing boys how a gentleman behaves—how a gentleman interacts with women, how he responds to adversity, how he serves his community—then there is no substitute for a man. That's where boys can benefit most, in my judgment: from seeing a man, perhaps a teacher or a coach, who loves to read in his spare time, who participates in projects for Habitat for Humanity or in community service with his local synagogue or church. A man who's a regular guy—not a saint, not Captain America, not Batman. Just somebody real.

In some cultures, this process—the transmission of adult gender roles from one generation to the next—is explicit and formal. Shortly after a Navajo girl experiences her first menstrual period, she goes to stay at the home of her grandmother for four consecutive days. During those four days, all of her adult female relatives call on her. She engages in a series of rituals illustrating her new status as a woman in the community. She is welcomed into the community of adult women.[10] Likewise, in this book we have already glimpsed a few examples of the ways in which various traditional cultures guide boys to manhood.

Not all enduring cultures have such formal ceremonies. In many cultures, the transition to adulthood is more gradual and incremental. But in every *enduring* culture, girls are led into womanhood by a community of adult women; boys are led into manhood by a community of adult men. The mother and father play an important role in some cultures, a less important role in others. Among the Navajo, the process is more communal than familial. But there is no enduring culture in which parents attempt this task alone. As the saying goes, it takes a village to raise a child, and that means raising a boy to manhood or a girl to womanhood.

When I speak to parents' groups, I'm often interrupted at this point. "I don't have a community of men to raise my son," one mother told me. "His father is not in the picture, and I wouldn't want his father back in any case. So what am I supposed to do, as a single mom, as far as this 'transition to manhood' business is concerned?"

I suggested to that mother that she must do the same thing that every other parent of a boy has to do: find a community of men that can give her son healthy and prosocial examples of what it means to be a man. This question has been addressed thoroughly by psychologist Peggy Drexler, who has studied how unmarried heterosexual women and lesbians raise sons. Based on her research, she has this advice for women who don't have men in their personal lives: "Actively recruit male figures from [your] family and from the community—including babysitters, tutors, coaches, and Big Brother–type pals—to be in [your] sons' lives. As a result, [your] sons wind up with more, rather than fewer, men upon which to model themselves."[11] It's hard for parents, even happily married parents, to do this alone. The community you choose might be a Boy Scout troop, an all-male Bible study or Torah study, or a sports team coached by men you know and trust.

If a boy does not have a community of men, then he is likely to look elsewhere for his role models. He may look to the media, where he will encounter a blizzard of images of men like Eminem and Akon and 50 Cent—all of whom have made their money in part by writing songs that are degrading to women. He may look to boys his own age. Teenage boys who look to other teenage boys for guidance often become confused and self-destructive. There is no enduring culture in which teenage boys guide one another to manhood. That's what men are for.

Enduring cultures often imbue the transition to adulthood with sacred meaning, as we have seen already from some of the examples I have discussed. We 21st-century moderns smile condescendingly at such traditions. We think we have no need for such rituals. We are amused by the customs of other peoples and other places, customs that are designed to placate gods we don't believe in.

Think twice before you look down at the traditions of other cultures that have lasted far longer than our own. Our culture's neglect of the transition to manhood is not producing an abundance of young men who are sensitive, caring, and hardworking. Instead, there is growing evidence that our society's neglect of this transition results in the "slacker dude" portrayed in movies such as *Failure to Launch* and *The Big Lebowski*, or in the bully, or in would-be gang members or rappers who boast of being, or who pretend to be, convicted felons.[12]

The forsaken gods will have their revenge.

W HEN I SAY THAT "THE FORSAKEN GODS WILL HAVE THEIR REVENGE," I am not suggesting that I believe in the literal reality of the gods and goddesses who oversee the sacred festivals of the native communities that Professor Gilmore describes. Allow me to go back to the final e-mail message at the close of chapter 6, from Kent Robertson. Mr. Robertson asked, "Have we violated something that the ancients knew intuitively but which we have arrogantly ignored?" I think Mr. Robertson is on to something. We ignore the importance of these traditions at our peril. Manhood isn't something that simply happens to boys as they get older. It's an achievement—something a boy accomplishes, something that can easily go awry. If we ignore the importance of this transition, and fail in our duty as parents to guide boys through it, then we may learn the hard way why traditional cultures invest this transition with so much importance.

In all the cultures he studied, Gilmore found

> a constantly recurring notion that real manhood is different from simple anatomical maleness, that it is not a natural condition that comes about spontaneously through biological maturation but rather is a precarious or artificial state that boys must win against powerful odds. [This belief] is found among the simplest hunters and fishermen, among peasants and sophisticated urbanized peoples; it is found in all continents and environments. It is found among both warrior peoples and those who have never killed in anger.[13]

The recurring theme is that "culturally defined competence . . . leads directly to reproductive success."[14] In some cases, such as among traditional Orthodox Jews, "culturally defined competence" is almost completely cognitive and intellectual. An Orthodox

Jewish boy must prove his knowledge of Torah and Talmud. In other cultures the travail is more physical. But the underlying theme is the same.

According to Gilmore, all enduring cultures agree "that regression to a state of primary narcissism is unacceptable in and of itself as a threat to adult functioning."[15] Similar ideas permeated American culture more than a century ago. The explicit motivation behind the founding of the Boy Scouts in 1910 was to "make men of little boys" and foster "an independent manhood."[16] There was no assumption that an independent manhood would just happen naturally. As in other cultures, there was an awareness that boys must be *led* to manhood.

The idea that manhood is conditional was a major theme in twentieth-century American literature, Gilmore observes, at least until the mid-1970s. William Faulkner, Ernest Hemingway, John Dos Passos, Studs Terkel, Norman Mailer, James Dickey, and others all communicated the idea that manhood is something you must *earn*.

American literary critic Alfred Habegger, commenting on the American tradition, notes that masculinity in American literature "has an uncertain and ambiguous status. It is something to be acquired through a struggle, a painful initiation, or a long and sometimes humiliating apprenticeship. To be male is to be fundamentally unsure about one's status."[17] Gilmore found this idea—that manhood is *conditional*—in almost every culture he studied. He adds that the idea that manhood must be achieved is "true of almost all U.S. ethnic subvariants of manhood, not just some hypothetical Anglo-Saxon archetype."[18]

Gilmore points out that "this heroic image of an achieved manhood has been widely legitimized in U.S. cultural settings ranging from Italian-American gangster culture to Hollywood Westerns, private-eye tales and children's He-Man dolls and games." But these gendered images have changed in the past 50 years. Fifty years ago, 60 years ago, these tales of boys becoming men were mainstream cultural stories of real boys becoming real men—by which I mean men you might plausibly encounter in your daily life. Think of movies such as *The Hustler*, or *Rebel Without a Cause*, or *On the Waterfront*. The characters played by Paul Newman, James Dean, and Marlon Brando in those movies were ordinary young men, not superheroes. In each of these stories, an immature, lazy, cocky boy experiences personal hardship and the death of a friend, and matures into manhood as a result of overcoming various trials. Each of these movies was set in its own time. Each story took place in the era in which the movie was filmed, depicting events that might actually have occurred (*On the Waterfront* was actually based on a Pulitzer Prize–winning series of articles for the *New York Sun*).

Such movies are rare today. We still have masculine heroes in some of our movies—think of *Gladiator* and *Avatar*—but scriptwriters seem unable to write a believable story about a boy becoming a heroic man, without supernatural powers, set in our era. The scriptwriters go back 500 years or more, or set their heroic epics in a science fiction past (*Star Wars*) or future (*Avatar*), or in a fantasy world (*Harry Potter*, *Lord of the Rings*).

THE SAMBURU, WHO LIVE IN THE REGION JUST SOUTH OF LAKE Turkana in Kenya, are dairy farmers. When a Samburu boy is on the threshold of manhood, he must solemnly renounce drinking milk. This action "conveys a public confirmation that he has renounced the breast voluntarily in favor of delayed gratifications of work culture. All women will henceforth be treated as receivers rather than givers of food; the boy will no longer need mothering."[19]

Farther south, the Masai tribes, living in the hills along the border between Kenya and Tanzania, likewise view "manhood [as] a status that does not come naturally, but rather is an elaborate idea symbolically constructed as a series of tests and confirmations," according to Gilmore.[20] A high point of Masai male adolescence is "the sacrifice of his first ox. The major portion of the meat is then given to the boy's mother, an act that is described as a thank-you to her for having reared and fed him as a boy. For the Masai, as for the Samburu, the idea of manhood contains also the idea of the tribe, an idea grounded in a moral courage based on commitment to collective goals. Their construction of manhood encompasses not only physical strength or bravery but also a moral beauty construed as selfless devotion to national identity."[21] Many cultures have such beliefs, in which the young man must reject the "puerile cocoon of pleasure and safety"[22] to achieve real manhood.

Our culture used to tell such stories as well.

We no longer do.

American Culture—Toxic to Boys—and to Girls?

Who's better off: the children of new immigrants to the United States, or children born into families that have been in this country for generations?

Imagine two families. Each family consists of a mother, father, daughter, and son. In each family, the mom and dad are in their

40s or 50s; the daughter is 15 years old and the son is 17. The household income is the same in both families. The occupations of the mother and father in household A are the same as the occupations of the mother and father in household B. The two families live in identical homes in the same neighborhood. The only difference between the two households is that in household A, the mother, father, daughter, and son were all born and raised in the United States. In household B, the mother, father, daughter, and son have just arrived in the United States from Bangalore, India.

Now. What is the likelihood that the girl has recently been diagnosed with anxiety, or depression; or is using alcohol, or illegal drugs; or has been diagnosed with an eating disorder; or has engaged in sexual intercourse prior to age 15? On each of those parameters, the girl born in the United States is at much higher risk than the girl who just arrived here from Bangalore.[23]

What is the likelihood that the boy has been diagnosed with a psychiatric disorder; or has been arrested for street racing; or says, "School is a stupid waste of time"? On each of those parameters, the boy born in the United States is at much higher risk than the boy who just arrived here from Bangalore.[24]

There is nothing special about the ages I chose. I just want you to have a very definite picture in your mind, not of girls in general or boys in general, but a girl of a particular age and a boy of a particular age. This new reality—that American kids are now at greater risk of anxiety and depression, more likely to engage in delinquent behavior, and more likely to be disengaged from school, compared with kids who have just arrived here from overseas—is true across all age groups. And the older the child— the more time the American kid has been exposed to American culture—the more true it is.

It was not always so. For most of American history, children who were born and raised in the United States were healthier—both physically and psychologically—than children who had recently immigrated to the United States from overseas. This reality was so robust that it became embedded in American culture. Two generations ago, most experts agreed that when a family arrived in the United States from a country with a different language and culture, the top priority should be for the family to assimilate into the mainstream English-speaking American culture as soon as possible. It was in the best interests of their children.[25]

Some Americans assume that what was true two generations ago is still true today. They assume that when a new family arrives here from Asia or Latin America or Eastern Europe, the children will be best served by learning English quickly and by speedily assimilating into contemporary American culture.

But that assumption—which might have been valid two generations ago—is mistaken today. The evidence is now overwhelming that the new immigrant family should try to hold on to their native language and their native culture, and shield their children from contemporary American culture as best they can. Scholars have coined the term "the immigrant paradox" because it seems paradoxical to them that the children of immigrants today have an advantage over children born and raised in the United States. The American Psychological Association published a 328-page monograph on this topic with contributions from 24 different researchers. The title of the 2011 work is *The Immigrant Paradox in Children and Adolescents: Is Becoming American a Developmental Risk?*[26] The answer to that question is: Yes. Becoming an American now puts immigrant children at risk. The greater the degree to which immigrant children can hang on to their native culture and language, and be shielded from contemporary American culture, the better those children will do in school, the lower their risk of teenage pregnancy, the lower their risk of drug and alcohol abuse, the lower their risk of juvenile delinquency, and so on.[27]

So being foreign, rather than American, provides protection against American culture. But that protection doesn't last. Although children in the families of new immigrants are healthier in many respects and more motivated compared to their American-born peers, "this relative advantage tends to decline with length of time in the United States and from one generation to the next."[28] A panel of experts that convened at Dartmouth concluded that the longer an immigrant child lives in the United States, the more likely that child is "to be less healthy and to report increases in risk behaviors." And "the implication of these findings is unmistakable," they said. "For the children of immigrants, and for U.S. children overall, some of the basic foundations of childhood appear currently to be at best anemic, in the sense of [being] weak and inadequate to foster full human flourishing, and at worst toxic, inadvertently depressing health and engendering emotional distress and mental illness."[29] Incidentally, that Dartmouth panel included Dr. T. Berry Brazelton, the renowned pediatrician; Robert Coles, arguably the world's leading expert on how children learn morality; Dr. Stephen Suomi, who has spent more than three decades studying parent-child bonding; and about two dozen others. The group included leading scholars in developmental pediatrics, sociology, primatology, and adolescent psychology—an extraordinary, interdisciplinary array of talent brought together to take a careful look at what's going on with American children and teenagers.

A LISON COOPER LIVES IN A SUBURB OF WASHINGTON, DC. ONE
Saturday morning, she was sitting in her car in the parking
lot of a local supermarket, talking on her cell phone, when a troubling incident took place:

> A dad and his two sons, roughly 8 and 10, piled into the car next
> to mine, and in so doing one of the boys carelessly flung his door
> open so far that it scraped the side of my car.
>
> I was appalled to see the dad backing out of his parking spot,
> apparently with no intention of stopping. I aborted my call and
> leaped out of my car, screaming at the driver.
>
> At this point he stopped, got out of his car and began [yelling]:
> *It's a ding! This is a parking lot; what do you expect?! What's the big
> deal?! Get some touch-up paint!*
>
> I let him go, feeling slightly sick about the lessons he had just
> taught his boys: (1) When you damage someone else's car, try to
> get away without having to face the owner of the car, and (2) If
> this fails, come out swinging aggressively, minimize the damage,
> and assert that parking-lot dings are a fact of life and therefore are
> nothing to apologize or take responsibility for.
>
> The next day, my 7-year-old daughter pointed out to me fresh
> and severe damage to the bumper. It was badly crunched. We
> were home in our driveway, but the damage could have occurred
> anytime during the previous 24 hours while we were out and about
> on errands.
>
> There was no note on the windshield. I sadly accepted that I'd
> never know who did this to my car.

The following day, a husband and wife come to her home to
explain what happened.

The wife, in halting English, explained that their son had panicked after hitting the car and rushed to his parents. [They] notified their insurance company and then went looking for the damaged car. They provided their insurance information and apologized profusely.

These parents have taught their teenage boy: (1) Take responsibility for your actions, even if you can get away with not doing so, even if it's not convenient or easy, and even though your insurance rates are certain to increase with this acknowledgment, and (2) Don't make excuses, don't lie, be forthcoming and apologize.

I am struck by the contrasting lessons taught by the Bethesda dad [the dad in the parking lot] and the Kensington housepainters [the family that came to the house].[30]

The Kensington family were immigrants. The wife could barely speak English. Some prominent Americans, such as Donald Trump and commentator Lou Dobbs, have argued that we should tighten restrictions on immigration to the United States, because—Trump and Dobbs believe—immigrants are less likely to make a positive contribution to American culture. Stories like these make one wonder whether we should instead encourage immigration so as to improve the moral fiber of young Americans.

The Significance of Gender

Gender was not mentioned in the initial charge to the Dartmouth panel referenced above. But as the experts met and consulted with one another about what they were seeing in their research and what they were hearing from adolescents, they kept coming up against one truth: gender matters. "Assigning meaning to gender in childhood and adolescence is a human universal that deeply influences well-being," the panel wrote. They concluded:

> In much of today's social science writing, and also more generally within elite culture, gender tends to be viewed primarily as a set of traits and as a tendency to engage in certain roles. Yet the current weight of evidence suggests that this understanding is seriously incomplete. Gender runs deeper, near to the core of human identity and social meaning—in part because it is biologically primed and connected to differences in brain structure and function, and in part because it is so deeply implicated in the transition to adulthood.
>
> In recent decades, many adults have tended to withdraw from the task of assigning pro-social meaning to gender, especially in the case of boys. For some people, actual and desired changes in sex roles, including a desire for greater androgyny, make some of our culture's traditional gender formulations appear anachronistic and even potentially harmful. We recognize the important issues at stake here.
>
> But neglecting the gendered needs of adolescents can be dangerous. Boys and girls differ with respect to risk factors for social pathology. We recognize the perils of oversimplifying or exaggerating gender differences. But as the medical world has discovered, the risk of not attending to real differences that exist between males and females can have dangerous consequences.
>
> Ignoring or denying this challenge will not make it go away. Indeed, when adults choose largely to neglect the critical task of sexually enculturing the young, they are left essentially on their own—perhaps with some help from Hollywood and Madison

Avenue—to discover the social meaning of their sexuality. The resulting, largely adolescent-created rituals of transition are far less likely to be pro-social in their meaning or consequences.

Young people have an inherent need to experience sexual maturing within an affirming system of meaning.[31]

The Changing American Father

The cultural stature of the father figure in the American family has taken a tumble in the past 40 or 50 years. American popular culture illustrates this point dramatically. Fifty years ago, television shows such as *My Three Sons* with Fred MacMurray and *Father Knows Best* with Robert Young were popular fare. The father figures played by MacMurray and Young were wise, caring, and competent. Fast-forward to the 1980s and watch an episode of *Family Ties*. Michael Gross's character, Steven Keaton, was a wise, caring, and competent father to four children and a loving husband to an intelligent wife. Unlike the characters portrayed by MacMurray and Young, Mr. Keaton was often the butt of jokes, but it was all in good fun. At the end of each show, Dad's stature as the father was never in doubt. *Family Ties* enjoyed steady success from its debut in 1982 through its final year, 1989.

The same year that *Family Ties* signed off, *The Simpsons* went on the air. *The Simpsons* is now the longest-running sitcom in American history, having aired nearly 600 episodes in 27 seasons, and shows no signs of slowing down despite (or because of?) the static nature of the lead characters. In particular, the father—Homer Simpson—is always an idiot, reliably a klutz, consistently the least intelligent character in any episode, with the possible exception of his son, Bart, or the family dog. By contrast, Homer's wife, Marge, is generally practical, although sometimes silly. The most intelligent character is usually the daughter Lisa, who routinely ignores her father's advice, because his advice is often hysterically awful.

I don't want to overstate the importance of a TV show, not even a show as iconic as *The Simpsons*. My own assessment is that TV shows reflect our society more than they shape it. Either way, the success of *The Simpsons* is one illustration of how the image of the American father in the American mind today is quite different from where it was two generations ago.

Our purpose here is not to debate whether it is "good" or "bad" that the popular image of the American father has been transformed from wise patriarch to bumbling buffoon. What's important for the purpose of our investigation here is that this transformation has muddled the idea of mature manhood in the minds of American boys. Fifty years ago, if a boy were told to "grow up!" he knew what that meant. It meant acting like the characters portrayed by MacMurray and Young in *My Three Sons* and *Father Knows Best*, or by Gary Cooper in *High Noon*, or by Jimmy Stewart in *It's a Wonderful Life*, or by Sidney Poitier in *In the Heat of the Night*.

But if you ask a boy today to "grow up!" what does that mean? Who is he supposed to act like? Homer Simpson? Akon? Eminem? Lil Wayne? Justin Timberlake? Justin Bieber?

What does it mean to be a man today, a mature adult man?

B ACK IN 2007, A TENURED PROFESSOR AT HARVARD PUBLISHED A book entitled simply *Manliness*. The author, Harvey Mansfield, was distressed by the devaluation of masculinity he saw in contemporary American culture. As any good scholar ought to do, Mansfield began his book with an attempt to define his terms. Right off the bat, he asserted, without any disclaimer, that "John Wayne is still every American's idea of manliness."[32] He then proceeded with a detailed analysis of what makes John Wayne the epitome of manliness.

When I read that sentence—"John Wayne is still every American's idea of manliness"—I was startled. *Speak for yourself*, was the first thought that came to my mind. Like most film aficionados, I know that the man we call "John Wayne" was born Marion Robert Morrison, and that the real person, Mr. Morrison, bore little resemblance to the "John Wayne" character he played in the movies. Speaking personally, my idea of manliness is epitomized by men such as:

- Joshua Chamberlain, the Bowdoin professor of religion and rhetoric who commanded the 20th Maine Volunteer Infantry Regiment at the Battle of Gettysburg (we'll talk more about Chamberlain at the close of the next chapter);
- Dietrich Bonhoeffer, the German pastor who in 1939 left a comfortable post in the United States to return to Germany to organize resistance to the Nazis, and who was arrested and subsequently hanged at the Flossenbürg concentration camp; and
- Yitzhak Rabin, the Israeli prime minister who had the courage to try to make peace with the Palestinians and was gunned down by a fellow Israeli Jew.

These men differ from John Wayne in many respects, most importantly in that they became famous for things they actually did.

John Wayne was not a real man—he just played one in the movies. Moreover, Professor Mansfield might be startled to learn that most young people today have no idea who "John Wayne" was.

Mansfield defines manliness as "confidence in the face of risk"[33]—an irrational bias "in favor of action over reflection."[34] In his estimation, boldly plunging forward into uncertainty is the very essence of manliness. He claims that "thinking is a challenge" for real men—a claim that comes close to equating masculinity with stupidity.[35]

Plunging forward boldly in the face of uncertainty, without thinking first, when other less risky options might be available, doesn't sound manly to me. It sounds dumb. But it also reflects the confusion surrounding our concepts of masculinity today. Indeed, if this Harvard professor is clueless about what real masculinity is about, how are our sons supposed to know better?

What Does It Mean to Be a Man?

I have made several visits to Georgetown Preparatory School, a.k.a. "Prep," a boys' school in Bethesda, Maryland. In a typical year, the school will send one or more crews of 16 boys with 4 adult men to the highlands of the Dominican Republic for a five-week program called *Somos Amigos*, "We Are Friends." It's hot and humid. There's no air conditioning. The boys live with the peasants, eating what they eat, mostly rice and beans. They sleep on the floor, which is often nothing but mud and straw. There are rats. There's no electricity. There's no Internet.

Every one of the boys I've spoken with about this experience regards it as among the most meaningful of their lives. And I think I know why. Those boys are learning through their sweat the answer to the question, "What does it mean to be a man?" The answer taught by the *Somos Amigos* experience is: being a man means using your strength in the service of others. This school explicitly teaches that message. Every boy at Prep knows the school's motto: "Men for Others." But didactic knowledge, *Wissenschaft*, is not sufficient. The leaders of the school understand that a boy must learn this truth by experience, *Kenntnis*. "You can preach all you like, but there's nothing like putting a shovel in a boy's hands to teach him some lessons," headmaster Ed Kowalchick told me.

After one of the boys from Prep has spent five weeks working from dawn to dusk to build an infirmary or a road or an aqueduct, and the job is done, and he returns home, he can watch NFL football on a Sunday afternoon and see a beer commercial that claims that real men drink Miller beer—and that boy can laugh. He knows that being a real man has nothing to do with drinking any particular brand of beer. Being a real man means using your strength in the service of others.

That definition—giving all you have in the service of others—is an integral part of the Judeo-Christian tradition that has animated Western history for the past two millennia. It is not an original idea. "Greater love hath no man than this, that a man lay down his life for his friends" (John 15:13, KJV).

I am not suggesting that the Judeo-Christian tradition of manliness is the only one. I am aware that the ancient Romans and Greeks had different definitions; the Masai and the Samburu might also see the matter differently. But a culture is defined in part by how it answers the question "What does it mean to be a real man?" Every culture must make choices and value judgments. Indeed, one can almost define a culture by the choices its people make. We must choose, individually and collectively, how we are going to define masculinity. If we abstain from this choice, that failure to make a choice is itself a choice—and the marketplace will make the choice for us and for our children, as the Dartmouth panelists observed.

The end result of ignoring this question is not a generation of androgynous flower children. The result is, on the one hand, young men who have no motivation to work or to serve, young men who feel no shame in living indefinitely in their parents' homes, no shame in taking much and giving little in return. These young men—many of them white men living in the suburbs—don't have any concern about being seen as "real men." It's not important to them. Why should it be? The Internet and the movies are filled with cool slacker dudes who lounge around their parents' homes, not working and not looking for work.

That's one outcome. On the other hand, we are beginning to reap a small but fearful harvest of young men who *do* care about being real men and who—receiving no guidance from the adult community about what that means—are turning instead to gang violence, or street racing, or drug abuse for affirmation of their masculine identity and for their rites of passage. The devaluation and disintegration of the masculine ideal is the fifth factor driving the growing epidemic we've been investigating.

Affluence may have played some role in the decline of the masculine ideal in North America. Gilmore found that the more difficult it was to eke out survival in a particular time and place, the more strongly that culture celebrated traditional notions of manhood and masculinity. Remember the older Canadian man whom I quoted in the opening chapter? He said, "When I was their age, we had to walk to school, three miles each way, no matter the weather." Today, very few North American children have to walk three miles to school. Few middle-class American children have to worry about whether there will be food on the table or a roof over their head. That may be part of the reason why "being a real man" matters less to some American boys than might have been the case a generation or two earlier.

Now what can we do to get boys back on track? That's the subject of the final chapter.

8

Detox

W E HAVE ALREADY CONSIDERED MANY STRATEGIES TO COUNTERACT the five factors that are derailing so many boys and undermining the motivation of many young men. Now we're going to pull those strategies together.

The First Factor: Changes in Education

If you and I had the resources and the authority to remake education, we could set a course that might lessen the harm being done to boys and girls by 21st-century educational practices. The first thing we'd do would be to restore kindergarten as kindergarten, as Friedrich Froebel, the German inventor of kindergarten in the 19th century, intended it to be, so that every child's first experience of schooling could be a positive one. We'd push the emphasis on literacy and numeracy back to where it belongs, out of kindergarten and into 1st and 2nd grade. We'd put *Kenntnis* and *Wissenschaft* back in balance, so that kids wouldn't be asked to learn about frogs and tadpoles until they've had some opportunity to chase after real live frogs and tadpoles—not merely images on a computer screen. We'd give teachers more freedom to reintroduce competitive formats, preferably using team strategies, to engage children who flourish in those settings without disadvantaging those who don't need that approach.

But you and I are not likely to have that authority or those resources anytime soon. What can we do in the meantime? How can you do what's best, right now?

First, know what's going on in your school. If the kindergarten at the school your son will be attending is like most kindergartens today, with an accelerated curriculum focusing on reading and math skills, you should seriously consider not enrolling him until he is 6. That one-year delay can make a world of difference. Visit the school before your son reaches kindergarten age. Talk with the principal. If possible, spend some time observing a classroom. Those activities should give you a good idea of the school's academic expectations and the strategies they employ to achieve them. An emphasis on literacy first, before experiential learning, suggests that the school leadership may have priorities that are not developmentally appropriate for many 5-year-old boys.

Look at the kids. Are they having fun? Is there a playful mood in the room? Do they have a chance to run around? Do they have some contact with nature, preferably outdoors, every day? Looking at goldfish in an aquarium does not count as "contact with nature" for this purpose. Remember that *Kenntnis* requires that a child touch, smell, and really experience the natural object. Just looking at nature through glass, or through the wire of a hamster's cage, isn't sufficient.

Second, find out how the school assesses and tests the students. If the only evaluations that count are pencil-and-paper tests assessing *Wissenschaft*, then the leadership of that school may not understand the importance of balance between *Kenntnis* and *Wissenschaft*. Does the school offer outlets for team competition within the school—not just athletically, but also academically? (Please reread chapter 2 if you're fuzzy on the rationale behind these recommendations.)

A few simple changes can accomplish a great deal. Some years ago in Nebraska, school leaders statewide introduced testing formats that emphasized experiential learning, *Kenntnis*, rather than book learning, *Wissenschaft*. Nebraska began testing its elementary school students on their knowledge of electricity not primarily with a pencil-and-paper test, but by giving them electric circuits to assemble: if they assembled the circuit correctly, a small motor on the circuit board began to whir, and a bell sounded. Nebraska educators were pleased with the results. Unfortunately, the US Department of Education prefers pencil-and-paper tests and considered the Nebraska program subpar.[1] But for a few years, Nebraska school administrators had the courage to give priority to experiential tests instead of pencil-and-paper tests. There's already plenty of emphasis on pencil-and-paper tests throughout the curriculum. The Nebraska school administrators were trying to restore some balance between experiential methods and didactic methods, even—or rather, especially—in testing and assessment.[2]

The Nebraska program was abandoned years ago. It's very hard to sustain such a program statewide in the United States today, where testing is all about *Wissenschaft* and so little value is placed on *Kenntnis*. But you can find individual schools where the teachers and administrators understand these issues. Some of them are Montessori schools. Some of them are Waldorf schools. Some of them are enlightened private schools that happen not to have the words "Montessori" or "Waldorf" in their names, but where school leaders nevertheless understand the importance of experiential learning. Some of those schools are boys' schools. And a few schools, a precious few, are regular public schools.

Third, once your son is enrolled in school, if you see that the school is not providing a good learning experience for him, try teaming up with your fellow parents. Talk to your parent-teacher association (PTA), parent-teacher organization (PTO), parent-teacher-student association (PTSA), or whatever your school calls this group. Don't approach the principal or other school administrators by yourself. One parent is just an annoyance. There's power in numbers. Recruit half a dozen like-minded parents and approach the principal as a group. Six parents can't be ignored. Six parents acting together can change things. Not often, but occasionally.

Try to avoid the adversarial approach. Remember that the teachers and administrators fundamentally want what you want: they want girls and boys to be excited about learning. Lend your principal this book. Buy your son's teacher Richard Louv's book *Last Child in the Woods*, which, as I mentioned in chapter 2, is an excellent testament to the power of nature to enrich children's lives.

But don't hold your breath. I have found that if the principal and the other administrators dig in their heels and refuse to consider

any changes, further efforts by parents are unlikely to produce results. Instead, you may have to move your child to another school.
You might even have to move your family to another state, to find a
school that's a good match for your child. That's what my family
and I did. It's what we felt we had to do.

There's a lot at stake. I personally have been involved with
schools that have seen tremendous improvements for boys with
relatively minor changes in their approach. For example, at some
elementary schools, teachers have reported huge gains in boys'
achievement just by making sitting optional rather than required.
In these classrooms, some boys sit at their chairs, other boys
stand, and a few boys crouch on the floor. At a conference I
hosted near Chicago, teachers Betsy Stahler and Jill Renn shared
how the boys' performance at their Chicago school soared after
they introduced this new policy—*sitting is optional*—along with
adjustable-height desks, which can be lowered to a comfortable
height for the boy who prefers to work on the floor, and raised
above standard desk height for the boy who prefers to stand.[3] At
another school, in Waterloo, Iowa, boys from low-income families became fired with enthusiasm for schoolwork—and their
teacher, Jeff Ferguson, told me that a big reason for that enthusiasm is simply that the boys don't have to sit down if they don't
want to. They can stand, or they can lie on the floor—whatever
they like, as long as they are not whacking their neighbor.

Educators in other countries have come up with imaginative
strategies that are beginning to bear fruit—and which are not
well-known to us in the United States. One particularly exciting
innovation is the *Waldkindergarten* movement in German-
speaking Europe, which includes Germany, Austria, and northeastern Switzerland.

Waldkindergarten means literally "forest kindergarten." These
are kindergartens that have no building, no walls. (Most *Waldkindergärten* do have a run-in shed, or a similar structure, with lightning rods to provide a safe place for shelter in case of lightning
storms. And despite the name *Waldkindergarten*, many of these
outdoor schools enroll children from pre-K through 2nd grade.)
The children meet the teacher in a local park or wooded area every
school day, all year round. They may spend a day, or several days,
just studying a dozen trees: sniffing each tree, playing in the leaves
if it's autumn, learning about the seasonal cycles and life cycles of
these trees, making a seesaw out of fallen tree limbs.

The first questions American parents often ask when they hear
about the *Waldkindergarten* are: "What do they do when the weather's bad? What if it snows? What if there's a blizzard?" The answer
the Germans give is always some variation of *Es gibt kein schlechtes
Wetter, nur ungeeignete Kleidung*: "There's no such thing as bad
weather, just unsuitable clothes." If you watch these children playing in the snow, you realize how true that is. We parents don't like
blizzards because bad weather slows us down. But 5-year-olds love
blizzards. (Google "Waldkindergarten" and "Iglu"—that's German
for "Igloo"—to see some of the things the kids do with the snow.)
With proper supervision, a 5-year-old playing in snow is in no
more jeopardy than a 5-year-old on a playground in summertime.

Roland Gorges, a professor of education at Darmstadt College,
south of Frankfurt, assessed children in 4th grade, several years
after they had left the *Waldkindergarten*. He found that the boys
who had started school in a *Waldkindergarten* were less likely to
be diagnosed with ADHD, and typically were more attentive in
4th grade, compared with boys from the same neighborhood who
had attended a conventional kindergarten.[4]

The *Waldkindergarten* movement is growing fast. In 1997, there were fewer than two dozen *Waldkindergärten* in Germany. Today there are more than 1,500 in Germany alone. Some parents express concerns about kids' safety, spending so much time outdoors. But Ute Schulte-Ostermann, president of the German Federation of Nature and Forest Kindergartens (Bundesverband der Natur-und Waldkindergärten in Deutschland, *http://bvnw.de*), notes that "there are far fewer accidents than at regular indoor kindergartens because we have fewer walls and softer floors. Leaves and mud."[5]

American educators and parents would do well to learn more about *Waldkindergarten*. And some already have.[6]

The Second Factor: Video Games

In chapter 3, we considered strategies to help your son reengage with the real world, so that he will have less need for the artificial world of video games. Any intervention is more likely to be effective if you provide an alternative outlet for whatever impulse you are trying to redirect. So if you are going to restrict your son's access to video games, you need to give him an alternative that is more exciting, more real, than anything video games can offer.

Let me tell you about RaceLegal.

RaceLegal

I vividly remember unfolding my copy of the *Washington Post* to see a horrifying photograph of a white Ford Crown Victoria surrounded by debris, while emergency personnel carried away a hastily wrapped corpse. Young men had been drag racing on a seldom-used public road in Maryland. The street-racing community had gotten the word that there would be a race. A crowd of more than 50 adults, mostly men, had gathered in the darkness at 3 a.m. to watch. The driver of the Crown Victoria wasn't part of the race and had no idea that people were standing in the street to watch the drag racers speed away. There were no barriers on the street, and nothing to stop the oncoming car from plowing into the crowd of spectators at full speed in the dark. Eight people were killed, and six more were injured. All the dead were men.[7]

Street racing has become a major problem across North America. Despite the best efforts of police to crack down on the problem, each year there's a new toll of dead and injured. Is there a better way?

There is. The solution has a name, actually several names: "Race-Legal," or "Beat the Heat," or "Top Cop Racing," or "Street Legal Drags." Here's one story.

San Diego police were seeing a surge of deaths and injuries due to teenage boys racing their cars on city streets. In one year, 14 teenagers were killed and 31 were seriously injured in street-racing accidents. Stephen Bender, then a professor of epidemiology at San Diego State University, said that street racing had become an "epidemic"—and as an epidemiologist, he knew exactly what he was talking about when he used the word "epidemic."

Professor Bender secured funding to launch a legal alternative to street racing, which he named RaceLegal. He obtained permission to use the access road for Qualcomm Stadium, the huge stadium owned by the San Diego Chargers football team, as a venue for the races. Any teenager could race: all a boy needed was a valid driver's license and proof that he had the owner's permission to race the car. Initially, few drivers showed up. Boys didn't see the point of paying to race at the stadium when they could race for free on city streets. So San Diego made the punishment for street racing more severe. Undercover cops began videotaping the races; then they would show up at racers' homes with a tow truck. "We handcuff them, put them in jail, impound the car for thirty days for $1,000, suspend their licenses for one year, fine them $1,500 and put two points on their license," said Sergeant Greg Sloan, who headed the unit. "If you get caught street racing for a second time, your car is forfeited forever—even if it's your parents' or a rental—and you get [more] jail time." The county prosecuted 290 cases under the law in 2001, 155 in 2002, 60 in 2003, and fewer in each subsequent year until 2007, when the program was shut down altogether for lack of business. The key was to create that "closed-loop system, including enforcement and a legal outlet," said Lydia DeNecochea, program director for RaceLegal. "We've had a real turnaround."[8]

San Diego County officials now credit the RaceLegal program with a 98 percent drop in injuries and deaths due to street racing. "There is no doubt in my mind, nor among my colleagues, that the viable legal option of the RaceLegal program has contributed to the dramatic decline of illegal street racing," said Captain Glen Revell of the San Diego County Sheriff's Department. "And we see it as a decline in racing as well as deaths and injuries. We don't see the organized events we once did." Officer Scott Thompson of the San Diego Police Department agrees: "RaceLegal has been truly overwhelmingly effective in addressing the problem."[9]

It's catching on. In Noble, Oklahoma, teenage drivers pay $15 to race on Friday evenings at the Thunder Valley Raceway Park. "Beat the Heat" events on the second Friday of every month match high school kids racing their own cars against Noble's police officers driving police cruisers.[10] "Beat the Heat" now has similar programs operating in 30 states around the United States, as well as in Ontario and British Columbia.[11] A similar program in Tampa, Florida, is called "Top Cop Racing."[12] In Redding, California, "Street Legal Drags" regularly attract about 200 drivers for each event, with more than 2,000 spectators.[13] You will find street-legal racing, open to teens with no special experience or training, at No Problem Raceway Park in Belle Rose, Louisiana; the No Bull Street Car Series in Albuquerque, New Mexico; the Junkyard #1 Dragway in Canton, Mississippi; the Monticello Motor Club in Monticello, New York; and the Firebird Raceway on Highway 16 in Eagle, Idaho, about 30 minutes outside of Boise.[14]

I have seen parents squirm uneasily in their chairs when I praise these programs. Some parents are understandably less than enthusiastic about allowing teenage boys with no special training to race at speeds exceeding 100 miles per hour. I remind these parents that most of these strips are straight tracks just one-eighth of a mile long, with no turns. More to the point: telling boys not to race on the street just isn't effective unless you provide a legal alternative.

What Does This Have to Do with Video Games?

Here's the connection: RaceLegal and programs like it are the best answer to the question, "What do I do after I've thrown my son's PlayStation and Xbox in the garbage?" If your son has been playing a motocross video game for hours, take him out to a motocross track, rent him a motorbike, and let him take some lessons doing the real thing. He may complain. He may say that he prefers the sanitized video-game version over getting on an actual bike and going around an actual track. Challenge him. "Video games are just an imitation. Video games are just pretend," you might say. "This is the real thing. You're a big boy now. You can do this."

Boys who prefer the video-game version over the real thing are making a choice very similar to that of boys who prefer online pornography to interacting with real girls. In fact, it's often the same boy: the boy who spends hours every day on his video-game addiction is commonly, in my experience, the boy who prefers online pornography to real interactions with real girls.

If your son is addicted to first-person-shooter role-playing games such as *Grand Theft Auto*, you might think that this strategy can't be applied. After all, you can't very well let him loose on the streets and tell him to go carjack some late-model sports car and then murder police officers. But these boys usually have at least a smidgen of Nietzsche's will to power (see chapter 3), and often more than a smidgen. They don't shy away from physical confrontation—or at least they like to think they don't. Sign this boy up for a contact sport, such as football or rugby. Colliding at full speed with another boy, hitting him so hard "that the snot flew out of my nose and I couldn't breathe" (as one boy enthusiastically described it to me), goes a long way toward satisfying the same urge that otherwise might drive that boy to play *Grand Theft Auto*.

This point is counterintuitive to many parents, especially mothers. "Why would any boy, especially my son, want to collide with another boy so hard that snot flies out of his nose and he can't breathe?" The answer is: because some boys are like that, and he's that kind of boy. Celebrate the fact. Co-opt that desire to hit hard. Use it to help your son become an athlete, instead of a video-game addict.

In my first book, *Why Gender Matters*, I quoted an experienced school counselor who said, "You can't change a bully into a flower child. But you can change him into a knight." I would adapt that insight in the context of video games. "You can't change a video-game addict into a kid who loves gossiping on the phone for hours. But you can change him into a competitive athlete." I have seen precisely this transition in the case of several boys I have counseled over the years.

The Third Factor: Medications for ADHD

In chapter 4, we saw how easy it is nowadays for a boy to acquire the label of "attention deficit." Putting chapter 2 together with chapter 4, you can see how changes in education have contributed to a marked increase in the prescribing of medications for ADHD. Thirty years ago, most elementary schools didn't expect a 5- or 6-year-old boy to sit still and be quiet for hours at a stretch. Today many do. The result, as child psychiatrist Dr. Elizabeth Roberts has observed, is that "parents and teachers today seem to believe that any boy who wriggles in his seat and willfully defies his teacher's rules has ADHD."[15] Rather than question the wisdom of a curriculum that requires 5-year-old boys to sit still and be quiet, it's easier just to prescribe the medication. After all, what's the harm?

Where's the harm? If you read chapter 4 of this book, you know the answer to that question. The harm is in potential damage to the motivational center of your child's brain. The harm is in labeling a normal boy as having a psychiatric disorder. The harm is in relying on psychiatric medications to fix problems that are not psychiatric in origin. The "try it, you'll like it" school of medicine is not a good choice when it comes to prescribing these medications for your son.

So what should you do when the school suggests that your son has ADHD? First of all, insist on a formal assessment by a qualified professional who is not biased in favor of diagnosing ADHD. In most cases, that person should not be your child's primary care physician, because primary care physicians—pediatricians and family physicians—are usually not well-versed in the diagnostic subtleties involved in distinguishing ADHD from other explanations for why a boy might be inattentive or "hyper" in the classroom. Too often, primary care physicians may suggest a trial of medication "just to see if it works." Bad idea.

Many large school districts today employ psychologists specifically to do this type of assessment. Unfortunately, I have found that these psychologists are generally not a good choice either, although there are exceptions. They often have too many kids to evaluate and not enough time to evaluate them. More importantly, if the psychologist agrees that the boy has ADHD, then his or her job is done, that child's name can be crossed off the list of kids who need to be assessed. Everybody's happy, at least as far as the psychologist's colleagues in the school district are concerned. The dice are loaded: the assessments are biased in favor of making the diagnosis.

If your son attends a private school, a similar process can take place. In my experience, when a boy is referred for evaluation because he isn't paying attention, sometimes the real problem lies with the *school*, not with the boy. But I have found that the psychologists recommended by private schools almost never find fault with the school; instead, they usually conclude that the boy has ADHD.

If the psychologist disagrees with the teacher's assessment and questions the diagnosis of ADHD, that psychologist may quickly get into trouble. As I said: when a boy isn't paying attention, the problem sometimes is not with the boy but with the way he is being taught. You need a psychologist who has the courage and the independence to say to the school: "This boy doesn't have a problem. The school has a problem. The school is making developmentally inappropriate demands on this boy, and the school must change its ways." If a boy can't sit still and be quiet without fidgeting, he doesn't necessarily have ADHD. He shouldn't be put on medication just to keep him still. Instead, the school should recognize that expecting all boys, especially young boys, to sit still and be quiet simply isn't compatible with what we know about child development. If you move that child into a boy-friendly classroom (see chapter 2 for more detail about what that means), then that boy may do very well.

This statement is not conjecture. I have been involved with schools in Chicago and Dallas as well as Deland, Florida, Waterloo, Iowa, and elsewhere, encompassing boys from many different socioeconomic and racial backgrounds, where boys previously labeled as "ADHD" have become high-achieving, academically proficient students—without medication—simply by changing a gender-blind classroom into a boy-friendly classroom. This transformation does not require any change in class size or per-pupil funding, just an improved awareness on the part of the faculty regarding what constitutes a boy-friendly classroom.

I used to stop right there. I used to say to parents, "Find a courageous psychologist to evaluate your child." But it's getting harder to find a psychologist willing to challenge the steamroller that's pushing so many kids onto medications. So if you're not convinced that your son needs to be on medication, and you can't find a brave psychologist in your neighborhood, what can you do?

You may have to do some part of the assessment yourself. So let's call this next section:

A Parent's Guide to Neurodevelopment Assessment, with Special Attention to ADHD, for Boys in Elementary School (we'll take up the question of ADHD first being diagnosed in middle school and high school in just a moment).

In assessing whether or not your child—or any child—has ADHD, you need to understand the five official criteria for diagnosing ADHD, adapted here from the official source, the American Psychiatric Association's *Diagnostic and Statistical Manual*, fifth edition (DSM-5). Here are the five criteria:

1. **Hyperactivity/impulsivity or inattention.** This criterion is generally the easiest to meet. The key point I stress is that it is a necessary but not sufficient criterion for the diagnosis of ADHD. Many boys are hyperactive and/or impulsive and/ or inattentive, but that finding alone does not justify the diagnosis of ADHD.

2. **Onset before 12 years of age.** Problems severe enough to cause significant impairment must have been present before age 12.

3. **Multiple settings.** Impairment due to hyperactivity and/ or impulsivity and/or inattention must be present in multiple settings, not just one or two. This criterion is key to determining which children truly have ADHD. All of us are inattentive from time to time. If you ask me to sit for an hour listening to a lecture about the history of needlepoint, I'll be inattentive, because I'm not interested in needlepoint. A boy who is only occasionally inattentive probably doesn't have ADHD. If your son's reading and language arts teacher says that he fidgets and doesn't pay attention, but his science teacher and gym teacher and math teacher all say he's doing

fine, then it's unlikely that your son has ADHD. Even if
most of the teachers report problems, but your son's Boy
Scout troop leader and your son's soccer coach report no
problems, I would still be hesitant about making a diagnosis
of ADHD. Children who have problems only at school but
not in other settings generally do not have ADHD. Moving
that child to a different school, a boy-friendly school, may
fix the problem.

4. **Significant impairment in social or academic functioning.**
What constitutes significant impairment? The joke I hear in
many affluent suburbs is that every child in town is either
gifted, or learning-disabled, or both. Some parents just don't
want to hear that the reason their child is getting B's and a
few C's is because he's just not that smart. They would rather
hear that their child has ADHD and needs medication than
that their child is merely average, or, God forbid, below
average. But in any group of 100 kids, 49 will be below
average. That's not an insult. It's just a reflection of what the
word "average" means.

5. **Not attributable to another disorder.** Sometimes a child is
inattentive, impulsive, and/or hyperactive for reasons that
have nothing to do with ADHD. Family problems may be the
hidden culprit. At one school I visited—Foley Intermediate
School in Foley, Alabama—a teacher, William Bender, told
me about a student, let's call him Damian, who had been an
OK student the previous year, in 3rd grade, but this year—
4th grade—he had become impossible. Damian was acting
out, running around the classroom, defying reasonable
requests by teachers and staff, or just sitting in his chair like
a lump, ignoring everything that was said to him. After a

few weeks, he opened up to Mr. Bender. "I figure if I'm bad enough, they'll call my father to come whup me," he said with a smile. Damian's father had abandoned the family the previous summer. The father called once a month or less.

Mr. Bender took Damian for a walk around the school building.* "Let me tell you something, Damian," he said. "I need you to hear this. Your daddy doesn't call very often. When he calls, he wants to hear good news about you. He wants to hear that you've been a good boy, that school's going good, that everything's great. If all he hears is your momma complaining about how bad you are, then I guarantee you that he's not going to want to come back. I'm giving it to you straight, son." Mr. Bender knew that boys this age don't want anything sugarcoated.

Damian shaped up. His "attention deficit disorder" vanished as quickly as it had appeared. But please don't take this story as providing any sort of guidance in counseling the children of divorced or separated parents. That's not why I included it. Indeed, some professional counselors would take issue with Mr. Bender's comments to Damian. Some might be concerned that Mr. Bender was encouraging a false hope that Damian's father might return, or saddling Damian with the notion that he was somehow responsible for his father not returning. I include Damian's story simply

---

* Notice that Mr. Bender did not sit Damian down for a talk, face to face. Instead he took Damian for a walk around the building, so they could talk shoulder to shoulder. For more about the advisability of talking with boys shoulder to shoulder rather than face to face, see my book *Why Gender Matters*, especially pp. 83–86. A good place to talk with your teenage son is in your car, with you driving and your son in the passenger seat: shoulder to shoulder, not face to face.

to emphasize that a hyperactive, impulsive boy may be hyperactive and impulsive for reasons that have nothing to do with ADHD.

I've seen similar cases in which the correct diagnosis was childhood depression, or pediatric bipolar disorder, or sleep deprivation, all of which can mimic ADHD almost perfectly. That's why the fifth criterion is all about excluding other diagnoses. Before you start giving ADHD medication to your son, remember that not all children who have a deficit of attention have attention deficit disorder!

Of course I'm not really suggesting that you can learn everything a professional needs to know about neurodevelopmental assessment by reading this book. But I think you should at least know some of the criteria provided here so that you can be a more informed and more capable advocate for your son.

Dr. Kathleen Salyer is a psychologist in the Virginia suburbs of Washington, DC, with many years of experience evaluating boys who have been referred for evaluation for ADHD. She is frustrated by the number of consultants who use fancy computer programs to make their diagnoses seem more persuasive than they really are. The sophisticated software is also used to justify high fees—$3,000 and above for a "comprehensive evaluation." She recently wrote me:

> Computerized programs can be purchased that write a very impressive report and, at minimum, only require the evaluator to put the scores from the various tests administered into the program and then edit the report that emerges so that it reflects the specific child's unique characteristics and behavior. Whether or not a

computerized program is used, psychological reports are often written to explain the scores as if they confirm the diagnosis of ADHD. I can take the same data and very convincingly show that the scores do NOT support the diagnosis of ADHD.[16]

But let's suppose that your son has been assessed and you're convinced that he does in fact meet all five criteria for ADHD. Once the diagnosis is confirmed, it is appropriate to consider medication as one facet in the program of treatment your consultant has prepared. If a parent and consultant are convinced that medication is necessary, I generally recommend starting with one of the safer medications that have been proven effective in the treatment of ADHD in children, a medication such as Strattera or Wellbutrin or Intuniv. All medications have risks, but these medications do not pose the risk to the brain that the stimulant medications pose. I advise them to avoid the stimulant medications: Vyvanse, Adderall, Ritalin, Concerta, Metadate, Focalin, Daytrana, and their generic equivalents, amphetamine and methylphenidate. If Strattera alone isn't effective, they may consider adding a low dose of Wellbutrin, or vice versa. The stimulant medications can be held in reserve. In my experience, the boy with true ADHD who needs 30 milligrams of Adderall every day to function well at school will often do just as well with 40 milligrams of Strattera and 5 milligrams of Adderall. The lower the dose of Adderall or other stimulant medication, the lower the risk of toxicity.

Some parents flinch with horror when I suggest using a low dose of Adderall or Vyvanse. "But Dr. Sax, in *Boys Adrift* you talk about how these medications can cause brain damage! How can you prescribe that medication for my son?!" I explain that the risk is proportional to dose and duration. If a boy is taking a low dose, and taking it only on school days—not on weekends or over vacations—then the risk is small. The parents can start giving their son a safer medication, such as Strattera or Wellbutrin, but if necessary add just a pinch of the stimulant medication. If absolutely necessary.

Many doctors are impatient with this approach. Most American doctors treating children who have been diagnosed with ADHD start with the stimulant medications and stay with the stimulants. Vyvanse and Adderall remain the most frequently prescribed medications for ADHD in the United States, followed by Concerta, Metadate, and generic Ritalin. But all these medications pose a risk to the brain that Strattera and Wellbutrin do not pose.

One Question Makes the Diagnosis

In chapter 2 and again in chapter 4, I stressed that many boys today are disengaged from school. They are not *motivated*. Not caring about school is a major problem, but it's not the same thing as ADHD. ADHD is a *cognitive* deficit. A boy who truly has severe ADHD may want to pay attention in school, but he just *can't*. A boy who hates school may not be paying attention in school, but it's not because he *can't* pay attention, it's because he doesn't *want* to. How can you distinguish the kid who truly has ADHD—a *cognitive* deficit—from the boy who just hates school?

Here's a tip from my clinical practice. Ask this question: "What's your favorite *subject* at school?" Be sure to emphasize the word "subject." A few years back, a teenage boy was referred to my practice. He had been diagnosed by a child psychiatrist as having ADHD, and he was being treated for ADHD, but the parents wanted a second opinion. I asked him: "What's your favorite *subject* at school?" He answered: "Well, I really like math, and art, and music, but I really hate English, language arts, creative writing, all that stuff." That answer was informative. He'd just told me that he didn't like anything that involved the written word. In one visit, less than 40 minutes, I established that this boy had dyslexia. He had escaped detection because he was very bright and had made accommodation on his own. But now, having made the correct diagnosis, we could stop the medication prescribed for ADHD, and engage appropriate resources directed at his actual problem. And he subsequently did very well, without medication.

But I also saw a different boy who was 14 years old. He also was not doing well in several subjects at school. I asked him: "What's your favorite *subject* at school?"

He answered cheerfully, "Lunch!"

If the answer to that question is lunch or recess, then you need to take a step back. This boy knows that lunch is not a subject. If he answers "Lunch," he is telling you that he has no respect for the academic mission of school. And he is telling you that he has disengaged from the whole program. His problem may not be cognitive at all. The teacher is right: he's not paying attention in class. But maybe the reason he's not paying attention is not because he *can't* pay attention (ADHD); maybe it's because he *doesn't want to*, because he thinks school is a total waste of time.

How Often Does a Teenage Boy "Develop" ADHD?

I was asked to evaluate one boy who had been a star pupil in elementary school. This boy, let's call him Brad, had earned nearly straight A's and seemed genuinely to enjoy almost every subject.

Then middle school began, and Brad started to disengage. He stopped raising his hand in class. His mother had to nag him to do homework, which she had never had to do before. Several teachers mentioned that Brad seemed to zone out in class. He just wasn't paying attention, wasn't concentrating, and didn't seem to care.

"We read up about ADHD online, and he seems to fit all the criteria," his mother said to me.

"Was he having problems like this earlier, a year or two ago?" I asked.

"Absolutely not. He was always an honors student in elementary school. In every subject."

Then he doesn't fit the criteria, I wanted to say. Specifically, he doesn't meet criterion #2, "Onset of impairment prior to 12 years of age." But I didn't say that. Instead, I asked his mother, "What's going on with his social life?"

She gave me a strange look, as if to say: *funny you should ask.* "His social life has dried up since he started middle school. He used to have two or three good friends. Megan and Ashley were over all the time, Caitlyn would be over once or twice a month. Now—nobody. And nobody calls, either. He doesn't go anywhere. He doesn't get invited."

"Are Megan and Ashley and Caitlyn at his middle school, in his grade?"

"Yes, that's what's strange about it. His best friends from elementary school are all in middle school with him, but they just don't seem to be friends anymore."

To make a long story short: Brad doesn't have ADHD. He's a gender-atypical boy, a boy who would prefer to knit a sampler rather than play football. Such boys often do very well in elementary school, where they often have at least several good friends—usually girls. In middle school, the girls realize that your popularity is largely determined by who you hang with, and the gender-atypical boys are rarely the cool kids. So the girls leave. And these boys are left alone. Occasionally the isolation motivates them to succeed academically, to show everybody how smart they are. Sometimes the isolation causes them to disengage from school altogether, as happened with Brad.

After evaluating Brad myself, I concluded that he doesn't have ADHD. He's on the border between dysthymia (a mild form of depression) and full-blown clinical depression. He misses his friends. He feels devalued—because his peer group has devalued him. These are serious issues that need serious attention. Ironically, Brad improved somewhat after another doctor prescribed Adderall, not because Brad had ADHD, but (in my assessment) because of the antidepressant effects of Adderall. A better and safer choice, in terms of medication, would be Desyrel, in my opinion. Desyrel is just as effective as Adderall as an antidepressant, but Desyrel is many times safer than Adderall.

More important, however, Brad needs counseling and help in developing a new life strategy. I addressed some of the challenges facing gender-atypical boys in my book *Why Gender Matters*. The main point I want to make here is that when a previously successful boy is first "diagnosed" with ADHD after age 11, the correct diagnosis is seldom ADHD.

The Fourth Factor: Endocrine Disruptors

Cargill is a large multinational corporation, with roughly 140,000 employees in 66 countries around the world. Back in 2005, I spoke to employees at their international headquarters just outside Minneapolis. I learned that Cargill has developed an alternative to plastic. The Cargill alternative is made from corn. It's called PLA (polylactic acid). I drank spring water from a bottle made of Cargill's PLA. That bottle is indistinguishable from regular "plastic," except that you don't taste that subtle plastic taste you get from bottles made from PET, polyethylene terephthalate. Most plastic bottles in the United States and Canada are made from PET.

I met at length with Ann Tucker, who was then director of marketing for NatureWorks, the division of Cargill in charge of developing and promoting the new material. Ms. Tucker used to work for the plastics industry, but she came to Cargill because, as she said, "I want to be on the side of the good guys." Although she and her colleagues are well aware of the health risks of plastic bottles, they are reluctant to stress that point in their marketing because they don't want to offend potential megaclients such as Coke and Pepsi. Instead, they emphasize the fact that their material's cost is stable, whereas the price of PET is unpredictable, because PET is made from petroleum—that is, oil. The price of oil varies wildly from year to year. Corn is usually cheaper. The main factory producing PLA is in Blair, Nebraska, right in the middle of corn country. As of 2014, more than 1 billion pounds of PLA have been sold.[17] That's 1 billion fewer pounds of plastic made from oil.

In the United States, the debate about endocrine disruptors has been politicized. People on the left end of the political spectrum tend to regard big business as the enemy, while people on the right often try to downplay the risks of manmade chemicals. But the risks are real, and Cargill isn't the enemy here. Cargill is, as Ms. Tucker observed, on the good guys' side. Coke and Pepsi aren't the enemy, either. They will introduce safer, more environmentally friendly PLA "plastic" bottles promptly—if enough people insist that they do so. You and I have to drive the conversion of the bottled water and soda industry from PET bottles to bottles made from PLA and similar non-petroleum products.

Avoid plastic made from PET, BPA, and other petroleum derivatives.

The Fifth Factor: The Loss of Positive Role Models

Recall J. R. Moehringer's insight, which we discussed in the chapter 7: "Manhood is mimesis. To be a man, a boy must see a man." A boy is likely to become the kind of man he sees around him. A boy needs real-life models of healthy masculinity, just as girls need real-life models of healthy femininity. If you don't provide a boy with healthy role models, he may choose the unhealthy role models offered by the marketplace, from hip-hop or television or movies or the Internet or social media or video games. The challenge is analogous to nutrition. Left to their own devices, not many boys will choose broccoli and Brussels sprouts over French fries and ice cream. That's why they need parents. It's the job of parents to guide their sons to make the right choice.

What does a good role model look like? What happens when teachers try to teach something about being a good man in a public school?

Some years back, the state of California created a few boys' public schools. The Ford Foundation awarded a grant to three scholars—Amanda Datnow, Lea Hubbard, and Elisabeth Woody—to assess the schools. As a general rule, when researchers evaluate the effectiveness of an educational program, they look at parameters such as grades, test scores, attendance, and discipline referrals. Did the program improve grades and test scores? Did more kids show up for class? Did they behave better in class? Datnow, Hubbard, and Woody asked none of those questions, although they did describe their 86-page report as "comprehensive." Instead, they focused on whether the program strengthened or weakened gender stereotypes.

These three authors condemned the boys' schools on the grounds that the schools reinforced gender stereotypes. One teacher who received particularly severe criticism was a man who had dared to speak to his students—all boys—about what it means to be a good man. The teacher said: "We talked about strength, and we talked about self-control and being able to control your emotions and making sacrifices for others. You know we talked about if you have a family and you only have enough money for two cheeseburgers, you're not going to eat. You know you're going to feed your wife and your kids and you wait."[18]

Datnow, Hubbard, and Woody came down hard on this teacher. They were disappointed that boys "were told that they should learn to be strong men and take care of their wives. In most cases, traditional gender role stereotypes were reinforced, and gender was portrayed in an essentialist manner."[19]

This teacher was trying to provide the boys with a healthy image of what a man should be. He told them that the husband, the father, should wait to eat until he's taken care of his wife and kids. He was trying his best to give those boys some guidance, some idea of what it means to be a man.

Not all traditional gender roles deserve to be condemned. There are life-affirming gender roles, and there are gender stereotypes that are harmful and destructive. The "dumb blonde" is a negative and destructive gender stereotype, as is the "dumb jock." But no one should condemn the ideal of the husband and father who sacrifices himself for the sake of his wife and children. Instead, that ideal should be affirmed as a role model, as one among several.

"Deconstructing" all images of the ideal husband and father is not likely to give rise to a utopia. The more likely result is a selfish young man who doesn't feel any strong obligation to the children he has fathered. In the United States, more than 40 percent of babies are now born to unmarried women.[20] The growing trend away from married couples with children cuts across all demographic boundaries. As we discussed in chapter 6, married couples with one or more children now constitute only 20 percent of American households.[21]

What's troubling about the report on the boys' schools in California is the willingness of the scholars to reject the traditional role of father as provider, while putting *nothing* in its place. That attitude has become very common among American researchers and college professors. Datnow and colleagues have no suggestions for what boys *should* be taught about becoming a man. Their suggestions are entirely negative: boys should *not* be taught to be traditional husbands and fathers.

But nature abhors a vacuum. If the grown-ups do not provide positive instruction for boys, then boys will turn to the Internet and social media. And what they will usually find is a culture of disrespect, a culture in which it's cool for boys to play video games and surf the Web for pornography.

To become a man, a boy must see a man. But that man doesn't have to be his father. In fact, ideally, it shouldn't be only his father. Even if your son has a strong father or father figure in his life, he still needs a community of men who together can provide him with varied models of what productive adult men do.

Restore the Bonds Across Generations

We have already seen that cultures that last are careful to pass the norms of that culture from one generation to the next, often in gender-separate communities. Women teach girls. Men teach boys. That doesn't exclude the possibility of men teaching girls and women teaching boys, of course. But there is no enduring culture where boys have been taught *what it means to be a man* primarily by women.

And there's something even more basic that should be stressed: enduring cultures have strong bonds across the generations. In contemporary American culture, we're seeing those bonds dissolving rapidly, in the span of a single lifetime. The *Washington Post* featured a series of interviews with African American men age 60 and over, which the writer notes is "the last generation of black men who share the memory of being deliberately taught how to walk in the world." For these men, "working hard is the basis for everything": it's "dignity and manhood." These men remember what the community was like 40 years ago, when the young men would congregate at older men's houses. Prince George's County—a middle-class, predominantly African American suburb of Washington, DC—had many boys' clubs that were popular and well patronized back then. "The neighborhood was like another mama and daddy," says one of the older men. Nobody locked their doors.

Then the boys' clubs shut down. Things changed. Teenage boys didn't want to talk to older men anymore. Illegal drugs began making inroads into the community, followed closely by crime. Now these older men are disgusted by the lack of motivation they see in the teenage boys and young men. Some of these young men "wouldn't take a job as a pie taster in a pastry factory," complained one of the older men.[22]

Certainly there were more factors at play here than the closing of the boys' clubs. But when the boys' clubs shut their doors, there was no other convenient venue remaining where grandfathers, fathers, and teenage boys from different families could come together, shoot the breeze, and share their experiences. The typical American teenager doesn't hang out with middle-aged adults on the weekend anymore. The typical American teenager hangs out with other teenagers.

In the story I told in chapter 6—about the young Native Alaskan men who went off to hunt the sea lion, and wounded but didn't kill it—the key point was the severing of the bonds between the generations. Cutting those bonds has an effect similar to cutting a boat loose from its moorings. The young men lose direction and purpose. Many of them will seek the pleasure of the moment. Many will avoid responsibility. Many will be set adrift.

That's already starting to happen in our own culture. As parents, we have to find ways to reconnect the generations. If you belong to a church, a synagogue, or a mosque, talk to your pastor, priest, rabbi, or imam about arranging a retreat for boys with men (and for girls with women). Traditional Judaism, the various Christian denominations, and Islam all have long traditions of gender-separate activities. All these traditions embrace the truth that children and teenagers must be taught by adults, not by one another.

If you're not comfortable with any faith community, contact your local chapter of the Boy Scouts, or get your son involved in year-round competitive sports, or martial arts, or skeet-shooting. Something that can build healthy bonds across generations. Perhaps there's an outdoor nature conservancy organization nearby, such as the Izaak Walton League (iwla.org), with programs to get young people involved with the outdoors. You have to do your homework: Meet the people who are leading these programs. Ensure that the adults who will be working with your son are good people. Most of these programs should have procedures in place to screen out sex offenders, etc. But such procedures are a supplement to, not a substitute for, your own assessment.

If your son likes to shoot things, help him to join a local skeet-shooting club where he can learn to shoot—and, more important, make connections with a community of men of all ages with similar interests. For those parents who don't know, skeet shooting means that a clay target is thrown in the air—today, the throwing is usually done by a machine designed for that purpose—and the shooter hits the target in the air. It's an Olympic event for both men and women. Just enter the word "skeet" and the name of your state or province in Google, and you'll find a club, whether you live in New York, Hawaii, Idaho, Manitoba, or Alaska. A good program should have procedures in place to teach gun safety, as well as ensuring that the teachers are qualified and well-vetted.

Don't wait for your son to ask. If he's like most of the boys I see, he may need a push. That's OK. Just choose an activity in which he can interact with grown men, where he can have opportunities to see how they live, how they relax, and how they serve their families and their communities. In most cases, even a not-quite-perfect choice, even a barely OK choice, will be better—will be more likely to engage your son in the real world—than no choice at all.

A Word of Warning

In the previous chapter, I said lots of positive things about traditional cultures such as the Navajo and the Masai and Orthodox Jews. Now we must say something unkind, but true, about these cultures: they are sexist. A Navajo woman can never become a medicine man. An Orthodox Jewish woman cannot become a rabbi.[23]

Many enduring cultures—cultures that have remained intact for hundreds of years—are sexist. That's unfortunate. Those traditional cultures often push girls and boys into pink and blue cubbyholes. We don't want that. But I don't think the solution is to ignore gender. Three decades of pretending that girls and boys are exactly the same except for their genitalia have not created a paradise of gender equity where boys respect and honor girls. They have given us, instead, Eminem and 50 Cent and Akon: musicians whose best-selling songs degrade and disparage women in ways that would have been unthinkable 30 years ago. Our cultural neglect of the significance of gender—as the Dartmouth panelists correctly pointed out—has resulted in a young-adult culture that has veered off, in many respects, into chaos and confusion.

There has to be a third way. There has to be some alternative besides ignoring gender, on the one hand, and pushing children into narrow and limiting gender roles, on the other.

This third way must begin by recognizing the importance of gender, by affirming and celebrating the gendered nature of the human experience. We must use this new understanding of gender not to reinforce old-fashioned *Leave It to Beaver* notions of gender roles, but instead to broaden horizons for both girls and boys.

The writer and lecturer Joseph Campbell popularized the notion that cultures are defined in large part by the myths they tell.[24] I think there is considerable truth to that idea. If we're going to combat this fifth factor—if we're going to re-create an idea of "real men" that advantages boys without disadvantaging girls—then we must give careful thought to the stories we are going to tell boys and young men.

We must tell true stories that affirm real men and the value of real masculinity, without disrespecting women or devaluing women's accomplishments and importance.

Allow me to share one such story with you.

One Story

Joshua Lawrence Chamberlain was born in 1828 in the small town of Brewer, Maine. He entered Bowdoin College, about 100 miles away, in 1848. Toward the end of his time at Bowdoin, he heard Harriet Beecher Stowe read aloud from the manuscript for the book that became *Uncle Tom's Cabin*. Although Chamberlain had never witnessed slavery firsthand, Stowe's book made a profound impression on him. He became convinced that it was the duty of Christians to abolish slavery.

After graduating from Bowdoin in 1852, he returned home to study at Bangor Theological Seminary, just across the Penobscot River from his hometown of Brewer. In 1855, he finished his studies at the seminary and married Fannie Adams, the daughter of a local minister. Together they would have five children. That same year, Chamberlain accepted an offer to return to Bowdoin as an instructor in rhetoric, religion, and languages. He was fluent in German, French, Latin, and Greek.

With the outbreak of the Civil War in 1861, Chamberlain wanted to join the war on the side of the Union and against slavery. Unlike most of his fellow northerners, Chamberlain actually believed that white men should fight and die for the cause of freeing black slaves. He asked Bowdoin College for a year's leave to sign up. His request was denied. Instead, the college offered to provide him a year's travel with pay in Europe to study European languages, classical and modern. Chamberlain accepted the offer, but with the war escalating, he changed his mind, promptly volunteering his services in the Union Army. He convinced the college to allow him to change the terms of his leave: instead of traveling to Europe, he would serve the country and fight against the Confederacy.[25]

Fast-forward to July 2, 1863, the second day of the Battle of Gettysburg. We find Professor Chamberlain, now a full colonel, leading the 20th Maine Volunteer Infantry Regiment on the top of a small hill just south of Gettysburg: Little Round Top. The men of the 20th Maine were stationed at the extreme left flank of the Union lines. Colonel Chamberlain's knowledge of military tactics was drawn more from reading about the Peloponnesian Wars in the original Greek than from any manual of 19th-century military tactics, but he understood the significance of his regiment's position, securing the left flank and occupying the high ground. He realized that if the Confederates could displace his men and take up positions on Little Round Top, the Confederates would be perfectly positioned to cannonade the main body of the Union forces from the flank and the rear. In that event, the Union forces would most likely have to surrender. The Confederates would be able to take tens of thousands of Union prisoners, and there would be no federal forces remaining between Robert E. Lee's Confederate Army and the District of

Columbia. Many historians believe that the fate of the United States hinged critically on the outcome of the battle for Little Round Top.[26] If the Confederates could overwhelm the 20th Maine and take that hill, they would win the battle and perhaps the war.

Five times on that July day, the men of the 15th Regiment of Alabama Infantry stormed up Little Round Top, and five times they were repulsed by the 20th Maine under Colonel Chamberlain's command. After the fifth charge, Chamberlain learned that most of his men had run out of ammunition. "Every round was gone," Chamberlain was told. Each man had only been issued 60 rounds at the beginning of the fighting that morning, and the five Confederate charges had exhausted their supply.[27]

What to do? Withdraw, and cede the high ground—and probably the battle, and perhaps the whole war—to the South? Or continue to fight?

Fight with what?

"Bayonets!" Chamberlain shouted. A single word, but every man understood what it meant: fix bayonets and charge.

It is a fearsome thing to order 200 men with bayonets to charge more than 500 men with rifles, but that was Chamberlain's order, and his men obeyed him. Not only did they obey, but they charged forward like madmen. The men "took up the shout and moved forward," wrote an eyewitness, "and [with] every man eager not to be left behind, the whole line flung itself down the slope through the fire and smoke and upon the enemy."[28] The Confederates, seeing wild men with bayonets yelling and charging down the hill, concluded that they were facing superior numbers (although they weren't)—so the men from Alabama retreated. "We ran like a herd of wild cattle," one Confederate later admitted.[29] And then night fell.

There is more to the Battle of Gettysburg than the story of Little Round Top, of course, but Chamberlain's courage and audacity in that moment is still a meaningful story to tell boys today. Perhaps more important for our purposes than the story of Little Round Top, though, is another of Chamberlain's orders, which he issued almost two years later at Appomattox.

General Ulysses S. Grant had selected Chamberlain to accept the formal surrender of Confederate colors on April 12, 1865. As Confederate general John B. Gordon led the Confederates to surrender—disheartened, sick, many of them wounded, and all of them wondering what awaited them at the hands of the victorious Union forces—Chamberlain, on his own initiative, gave this command to his men: "Attention! Carry arms!"

Chamberlain's men snapped to attention and presented their arms as a show of respect to the defeated Confederates. General Gordon, in reply, wheeled his horse around and commanded his men to dip the Confederate colors in answer to Chamberlain's courtesy. There was "not a sound of trumpet or drum, not a cheer, nor a word nor motion but awful stillness as if it were the passing of the dead."[30]

Chamberlain's salute was reported in northern newspapers, inciting some controversy. Many on the northern side felt that it was inappropriate for Chamberlain to command his men to salute the defeated Confederates. Some apparently might have liked it better if Chamberlain's men had heckled or abused the rebels. But Chamberlain's education—rooted in the classics—led him to value the magnanimous gesture above the pettiness of revenge or spite. In chapter 7, we discussed the definition of a gentleman. Chamberlain's story adds one more line to that definition: A gentleman is magnanimous in victory.

There are many true stories of heroic men throughout American history. I like to tell the story of Joshua Chamberlain for several reasons. First, his story is not particularly well known. For most of the 20th century, the story of Joshua Chamberlain was an obscure footnote familiar only to historians. There is no statue of Chamberlain at Gettysburg (although there is a small monument to the 20th Maine). He had to wait 30 years before he was finally awarded a medal, in 1893, for his actions at Gettysburg.

The second reason I like to tell this story is that Chamberlain was not a superhero. His deeds were modest in comparison to those of George Washington or Robert E. Lee or Abraham Lincoln or Theodore Roosevelt. And that makes it easier for boys and young men to relate to him. It's hard for a young man to imagine being George Washington or Abraham Lincoln. The demands on those men were so exceptional, the burdens so acute, that it strains the imagination to think, "How would I have acted in that situation?" Chamberlain's predicaments were simpler and easier to comprehend.

I remind boys that Chamberlain didn't have to fight at all. Bowdoin College wanted him to take a year off to go on an all-expenses-paid tour of Europe. He could have done so with no loss of honor. He chose to put himself in harm's way because he thought that it was the right thing to do, because he believed it to be the duty of Christian men to fight against slavery—even though many, perhaps most, of his fellow Christians at that time would not have agreed with him, and he knew it.

Another aspect of Chamberlain's story that I stress to boys and young men today is that Chamberlain was a great leader of men precisely because he was a scholar and a seminarian. He was not a professional warrior or tough guy. He wanted to join the fight not because he was big and strong—he wasn't—but because of his beliefs, which were grounded in his education. He knew what really mattered. And he didn't give orders for other men to fight while he remained safely at home. He himself went and fought.

L ET ME TELL YOU ANOTHER TRUE STORY, ONE THAT IS HAPPENING right now.

Craig McClain was raised in Overland Park, Kansas. His early childhood was OK, but beginning in 4th grade, things began to change. "I went downhill," he told me. School and life became a constant struggle. "My father didn't know how to deal with me," as Craig put it. By the time he was in his mid-teens, Craig was doing "marijuana, heroin, and everything in between." At age 18, he was convicted of misdemeanor theft and was sentenced to 90 days in the county jail. After his release, he found work at a paint factory, then taught himself photography. Over time, he made a business as a professional photographer. He was fairly successful and was able to support himself, his wife, and two children. But he was drifting.

Then, at age 40, he attended a weekend "initiation" for men. "They take away all your stuff. It's a boot camp kind of thing. But we talk. I started crying. Bawling. That weekend was magical. I remembered driving away and thinking, '*Man I needed this when I was 16 not 40.*'"

In 1996 Craig met two other men, Herb Sigurdson and Herb's son Joe. Together they decided to create a similar forum but targeting teen boys rather than adult men. In 1997 they launched their program, which they called Boys to Men. It's always been simple: teenage boys meeting in a room with a few men. Just men. Just a safe place for boys to ask, "What does it mean to be a man?"—and to get answers from real men, nobody famous, just men in their community. (Each mentor is trained and vetted to ensure that they are giving good advice.) They also have a Boys Adventure Weekend that takes place on Palomar Mountain in northern San Diego County. The program now has nearly two decades of data documenting remarkable outcomes for boys who were adrift but began to find their moorings. Managing the program is now Craig McClain's full-time job. He has overseen the program's growth, which has gone from hosting just a few boys in San Diego County to a network with branches across the United States and into Canada, the United Kingdom, and South Africa (www.boystomen.org).

I spoke with Louis Castrejon, a graduate of the Boys to Men program. Louis explained that at the age of 14, he was angry. His parents were fighting with each other, drinking too much, and not paying sufficient attention to Louis and his siblings. Louis had been physically abused, and on one occasion, his older sister's boyfriend almost killed him. But his parents didn't seem to notice or care. During his freshman year at Mount Miguel High School near San Diego, he would come to school on edge. "I'd just wait for somebody to do something—look at me the wrong way—and I'd explode on them." In addition to fighting, he was also using LSD, marijuana, and alcohol. He was suspended from school. Then suspended again. And then he was expelled.

Louis was sent to what we would have called a "reform school" in a previous era: a school for kids who have been expelled from their regular school. In his case, the reform school was the Gateway Community Day School in La Mesa (now closed). One of his friends from Mount Miguel, who had also been expelled, encouraged him—begged him—to come to a meeting of Boys to Men held at Gateway. "It blew my mind," Louis said. "Just being able to talk with other guys, and men, about it."

"About what?" I asked.

"Stuff like being abused. About having a drinking problem. I realized I wasn't the only person in the world with these issues. It took me about a year before I opened up. It was what I needed. Obviously I had trust issues with men [because of the boyfriend's physical abuse]. It was great to have a grown man listen to me and care about what's going on. It was awkward and scary but I liked it."

It may not sound like much: one or two hours, once a week, with a bunch of other boys plus one or two men. But it turned Louis's life around. After a year, he was ready to return to his old school, Mount Miguel.

"It was difficult" returning to his old school, Louis told me. "The kids hated me. Teachers hated me. But Anthony [one of the mentors at Boys to Men] told me that the best way is to succeed and prove them wrong. It took a year." Louis continued attending the Boys to Men meetings as well as the initiation rites at Palomar Mountain. He has now participated in more than ten of the mountain rites. I asked him to tell me about them. "We're not supposed to talk about it," he said. I didn't press.

"Does it have to be all men? Could a woman lead the session?" I asked.

"There are things that only men can teach men, that a woman can't," Louis said simply.

Louis is now a freshman at Grossmont College in El Cajon. He hopes to work in health and human services, maybe as a counselor.

Craig McClain, the Boys to Men cofounder, will sometimes hire one of the boys to do some work at the ranch on Palomar Mountain, where typically a boy can earn about $50 for a few hours' work. He recently hired a boy to come to the ranch to do various chores, including getting the nails out of a pile of old lumber. He showed the boy the stack of lumber and handed him a hammer.

"That whole job should have taken maybe 30 minutes," McClain told me. But when McClain returned 30 minutes later, the boy was sweating and frustrated. The boy had removed the nails from just one plank of lumber, in 30 minutes. The boy had been using *the blunt end* of the hammer. Nobody had ever shown him how to use the lever end of the hammer to pry the nails loose. He didn't know what the lever end was for. He had never asked.

McClain took the hammer from the boy and—in less than a minute—showed him how to use the correct end of the hammer to pry the nails free. McClain handed the hammer back to the boy, who finished the job.

This kind of story now is common. We assume that a teenage boy knows how to use a hammer to get nails out of an old piece of wood. But how should a boy know, if he has never been taught, if he has never seen a man use a hammer for that purpose?

McClain sees this story as a metaphor for the plight of many young men today. They have never been trained in the tools of traditional manhood. Then they come of age, angry and frustrated because the tools don't seem to work. Yet it is not the tools that have failed. The culture has failed. The culture has not provided a community of men to train the boys.

And the end result of that failure is an angry young man with a hammer in his hand.

CRAIG MCCLAIN'S BOYS TO MEN PROGRAM IS ONE KIND OF solution, where the focus is on creating bonds across generations: boys with men. It's not the only kind of solution. I have been just as impressed with another approach, which I observed in Burlington, Wisconsin. Parents there, working with the local school district, have created a community of parents who agree to abide by some basic rules to be observed in each household:

- No child or teenager will be allowed to consume drugs or alcohol in this house.
- A parent will always be present and involved whenever a party or other social gathering is taking place at this house.
- Parents will enforce a curfew of 10:30 p.m. on school nights and midnight on weekends.

The exact rules aren't so important. What's important is creating a community of parents who agree jointly and communally to share responsibility for safeguarding their children. And the category of "children" includes teenagers.

Teenagers want to do fun stuff. These parents in Burlington understand that. These parents provide healthy alternatives to the teen culture. They sponsor Ping-Pong tournaments, *Guitar Hero* tournaments, even dodgeball tournaments. If you don't appreciate the boy-friendly significance of a real dodgeball tournament, please reread chapter 2 of this book. Note that this parents' group does not sponsor *Halo* tournaments or *Grand Theft Auto* tournaments. *Guitar Hero* is fine. *Grand Theft Auto* is not. If you don't understand that distinction, please reread chapter 3. "It's good, clean fun," as one parent said to me. If such

opportunities sound unremarkable to you, then you don't realize how rare such opportunities have become throughout the
United States today.

These activities are sponsored by the parents and chaperoned
by the parents. One guideline the parents try to follow is to be *in*
the party but not *of* the party. You should not try to be the "cool
parent" who parties with the kids. But by the same token, you
should not be in your study upstairs with your door closed while
the kids are partying downstairs. You should be downstairs, making lots of excuses to walk through the room. "Put out lots of
bowls with potato chips, M&Ms, nuts, that sort of thing," one parent told me. "But make sure the bowls are small," she added. "That
gives you a good excuse to keep going in and out of the room, re-
filling each bowl. One bowl at a time."

The mere existence of this community, which is called Partners 2, has made a tangible difference in the lives of many young
people in Burlington. I spoke with one of them, a young man
named Kyle Krien. Kyle told me that before Partners 2 was
launched, he had the impression that all the kids at his high school
drank alcohol. It's easy for high school kids to get that impression, because kids who drink often boast about their drinking,
while kids who don't drink are more likely to stay silent. But
Partners 2 conducted a survey of the high school kids. They discovered that one-third of kids at the high school didn't drink and
didn't want to drink. And they made sure that all the kids knew it,
too. "That really made a difference," Kyle told me. It helped him to
know that he wasn't the only teen who had chosen not to drink.

Even more important is the contact information of participat-
ing parents. When parents sign up, they enter their telephone

numbers and their e-mail addresses into an online directory. So if your son announces that he's going over to Jason's house, you can ask, "Jason who?" Your son tells you his friend's name and address. You can check to see whether Jason's parents are listed in the online directory. They're listed. The fact that they have chosen to be listed means that they want to hear from you. They want to work with you to make sure that their child, and your child, stay safe. So you can feel comfortable calling them, because they've given you permission to call; in fact, they have invited you to call. You call up Jason's mom or dad and say, "My son is coming over to your son's house. Will you be around? Could you please make sure that my son is not playing any violent video games? I've told him he's not allowed to play any violent video games." And that parent is likely to agree to enforce your rules, because that parent—by virtue of signing up with Partners 2— has agreed to be part of the solution, part of the community that cares. That parent understands that parenting is most effective when there is a community of parents working together.

Kyle told me that one of the biggest benefits of Partners 2 for him was realizing that getting drunk or using drugs is not the only option. That's an important insight. It reminds me of another parents' group, founded by a father named Bill Oliver after he discovered that his 15-year-old daughter was a drug addict. His group identified three beliefs that they think characterize the "toxic culture" in which today's teenagers live. They are:

1.   The belief that getting drunk and using drugs is normal
2.   The belief that sex is sport
3.   The belief that violence and death are entertainment

You have to fight all three of these beliefs. Joining a community of like-minded parents is a good place to start.

Some parents are uneasy when I tell them that parents must assert their authority, individually and collectively. I wrote my book *The Collapse of Parenting* in part to empower those parents to find the courage to do their job. Some parents respond that parents should be less anxious and more laid back. One parent told me, "Kids have always done things that bother their parents. Today's kids are no different." I told that parent about the three beliefs of today's "toxic culture" listed above. Those three beliefs are pathological. They're sick. No healthy culture has ever endorsed such beliefs. Forty years ago, teenagers who subscribed to even one of those notions might well have been sent to a psychiatrist. Today, teenagers who don't subscribe to all three notions may be regarded by their peers as strange.

We are facing a challenge. Our boys and young men are growing up in a culture that increasingly regards academic achievement as unmasculine. Our girls and young women have to deal with a culture that focuses relentlessly on their personal appearance, a culture in which what really counts for girls is not what kind of person you are inside, but how many likes you got on Instagram for your selfie in a bikini.

We must, for the sake of our children, rebel against that culture. We must create a subversive counterculture that promotes such unfamiliar notions as:

1. Real men love to read.
2. What really counts is not how you *look* but who you *are.*
3. Achievement in the real world is more important than achievement in the virtual world.

I realize that teaching our children these and similar ideas in the context of 21st-century culture is no easy task. But we must accomplish this task, for the sake of our children.

A FTER I HAD FINISHED RESEARCHING AND WRITING MOST OF *BOYS* *Adrift*, I met with a group of parents in the auditorium of the Arlington Central Library in Arlington, Virginia. The parents listened as I described the five factors that I believe are causing boys to disengage from school—and in a broader sense, from life, from the real world of striving and achievement and loss. I outlined how we might turn the situation around, encouraging more boys to succeed or at least to try harder, without disadvantaging girls—because, after all, it's in the interest of young women as well as young men that we change course. Young women are looking for good men, reliable and hard-working men, not bullies or slacker dudes.

Now it was time for the questions, which I knew from experience are always more challenging than the formal part of the presentation.

"I'm persuaded by what you said about video games," a parent said. "But what about my son's friends? He goes over to their house and plays all the video games you've been warning us about."

"You can't do this by yourself," I said again. "Call up the parents of your son's friends. Ask what video games their boys are playing. Work with your school to create a community of parents who share your concerns about video games. Ask the parent-teacher association to host a forum to educate other parents about the hazards of video games. Get the word out."

"Dr. Sax, I have to admit I'm kinda freaked out by what you said about Adderall," one woman said. "My son was on Adderall for three years, when he was 10 until he was 13. We stopped the medication when he started 9th grade. But I'm nagging him so much now. I have to nag him to do his homework. I nag him to go outside and get some exercise. I even nag him to call his friends. If I didn't push him, I think he might just stay in his room all the time with his computer and his video games and his television. He's not motivated. Do you think the Adderall damaged his brain?"

"Let me share two thoughts with you," I answered. "First, consider moving his computer and his television out of his room and into a public area, like the kitchen or the dining room. When he's alone in his room with the door closed, surfing the Net, you really don't know what's going on. But if he's in a public place, then it's easier for you to keep an eye on what he's doing. Don't be coy. Tell him that you have a responsibility to know what he's doing all the time that he's online, and the easiest way for you to honor that responsibility is for him to be in a public area of the house. No screens of any kind in the bedroom. That includes the cell phone. Anything with Internet access should be used only in a public area, like the kitchen."

"But is my son's brain damaged forever because he took Adderall for three years?" the mother asked.

"OK, so that's the second point. There's a lot we don't know about the effects of Adderall and other stimulant medications on the brain. I have seen boys who were on these medications, went off the medications, reengaged in the real world, and turned out OK. We don't know how long a boy can take the medication before damage occurs. We don't know how easily the damage can be reversed after the boy stops the medication."

"That's not very reassuring," she said.

"But remember, Dr. Carlezon didn't try to rehabilitate those laboratory animals," I added, referring to the professor at Harvard who tested the effects of stimulant medications on juvenile animals (see chapter 4). "He didn't go bike riding with them, or take them on hikes in the mountains, or encourage them to read good books. The brain has more power to grow and to change than we previously imagined. Get your son away from the video games and get him outdoors. That's a good first step."

"He used to love mountain biking," she said. "My husband still goes mountain biking, but my son hasn't gone with him for a long time. Maybe he and his father could start doing that again."

I nodded.

"I was stunned by what you said about plastic bottles," another woman said. "I thought it was so healthy to drink bottled water. What am I supposed to do about that—for my children, and for me?"

"Find a grocery store, like Whole Foods or Wegmans, where the management understands this issue. It's getting easier to find stores like that in just about every American city and even in some small towns. You can find water in glass bottles. They've got almost every beverage you can imagine in glass bottles. The people who buy for the Whole Foods chain are well aware of these concerns and they've provided plenty of safe, environmentally friendly alternatives—not just beverages but also prepared foods, poultry, fish, meat, produce—everything that you eat or drink."

It was getting late. Many parents had to get home to relieve the babysitter and put their kids to bed. I stayed and chatted with a group of parents until the janitor came to kick us out after 10 p.m.

I'm encouraged. We don't have all the answers. But I think we're at least asking the right questions. Parents who are adopting these strategies are sending me success stories from every corner of the country, from every demographic group, involving young boys, tweens, teenagers, and young men. Many parents have already figured out one or more of these factors on their own, before they hear me speak, but they welcome the research. "I knew video games were bad for my son, but I couldn't convince anybody else. It's good to have these studies, hard data, to share with other parents," one father told me.

We have a lot of work to do. No one person is going to be able to do this alone. We parents have to work together. So please let's get in touch with one another. You can connect with me via my website, www.leonardsax.com.

You and I want the same thing: a healthy world for our children and grandchildren. We all realize that "healthy" means more than just having enough food to eat and clothes to wear. It means our daughters and our sons living lives that are meaningful and fulfilled. It means girls who grow up to be confident women and boys who grow up to be gentlemen.

Let's get to work.

Acknowledgments

M Y FIRST DEBT, OF COURSE, IS TO ALL THE BOYS AND YOUNG MEN who shared their stories with me. I am also grateful to all the parents who have spent so many hours talking with me about this topic, as well as to all the people who sent me thoughtful and provocative e-mails. Although I was able to use only a few of those e-mails, I read every message and I appreciate the time people took to write.

Christopher Wadsworth, former executive director of the International Boys' Schools Coalition (www.theibsc.org), was a faithful friend and adviser throughout the years that went into the writing of the first edition. Brad Adams, Chris's successor as head of the IBSC, was equally supportive.

Professor Judith Kleinfeld helped to ground the "boys' issue" in careful scholarship. In founding and directing the Boys' Project prior to her retirement, she worked to bring together scholars, educators, parents, and others from every corner of North America and even outside of North America. Her guidance and insight were invaluable. I am also grateful for her helpful suggestions regarding early drafts of some chapters.

Professor Craig Anderson reviewed a draft of chapter 3 and offered many helpful suggestions and additions. He was even more helpful to me in 2015, for the updated edition, providing many insights from his perspective as a researcher studying the effects of video games.

Dr. Shanna Swan was kind enough to review an early draft of chapter 5 and to suggest some important corrections and clarifications.

Professor David Gilmore was gracious in sharing his perspective as an anthropologist who has studied the transition from boyhood to manhood in many cultures. I appreciate his honesty, his candor, and his encouragement.

More recently, Warren Farrell has helped me to formulate my ideas about boyhood and manhood more clearly. Although Warren and I do not sing in unison, we do sing in harmony. Warren introduced me to Craig McClain, cofounder of Boys to Men. I would also like to thank Mr. McClain and Louis Castrejon for allowing me to share their stories here.

Regarding the trades—carpentry, plumbing, masonry, electrical work, and so on: because I know so little about these vocations, I am especially indebted to Neal Brown, Jeff Donohoe, and Myles Gladstone for their instruction. I also thank my father-in-law, Bill Kautz, retired excavator and all-around handyman, for teaching me the relevant vocabulary—and for fixing our shower.

If I had based this book only on my experience in my office, combined with my reading of the scholarly papers, this book would have been much narrower in its focus and probably would be less useful to people outside the Mid-Atlantic states. It has been a great privilege to visit schools not only in the United States but also Australia, Canada, England, New Zealand, and Scotland to meet with girls and boys and their teachers and parents. I am particularly indebted to the teachers and administrators at the following schools who have shared with me their strategies for motivating boys to become good men and/or for creating a school culture in which it's cool to be a gentleman (listed in alphabetical order):

- Avalon School, Gaithersburg, Maryland
- Avon Old Farms, Avon, Connecticut
- Barack Obama Male Leadership Academy, Dallas, Texas
- Brighton Grammar, Melbourne, Australia
- Camberwell Grammar, Melbourne, Australia
- Christ Church Grammar, Perth, Australia
- Clear Water Academy, Calgary, Alberta
- Cunningham School for Excellence, Waterloo, Iowa
- DeMatha Catholic High School, Hyattsville, Maryland
- Georgetown Preparatory School, Bethesda, Maryland
- Harrow School, Middlesex, England
- Haverford School, Haverford, Pennsylvania
- Lindisfarne College, Hawkes Bay, New Zealand
- Loughborough Grammar, Leicestershire, England
- Merchiston Castle School, Edinburgh, Scotland
- Newcastle School for Boys, Newcastle upon Tyne, England
- Phelps School, Malvern, Pennsylvania
- Presentation School, Sonoma, California
- Princeton Academy of the Sacred Heart, Princeton, New Jersey
- San Antonio Academy, San Antonio, Texas

- Shore, a.k.a. Sydney Church of England School, Sydney, Australia
- St. Andrew's College, Aurora, Ontario, Canada
- Stuart Hall for Boys, San Francisco, California
- Upper Canada College, Toronto, Ontario, Canada
- Winchester College, Winchester, England

I benefited greatly from the advice and good judgment of my agent, Felicia Eth, from the inception of this project. Jo Ann Miller, my editor at Basic Books for the first edition, provided a detailed critique of the first draft of this book, improving it immeasurably. Publisher Lara Heimert suggested the idea of a second edition and has supported the project throughout. Any flaws that remain are solely my responsibility.

Almost two centuries ago, an old poet wrote that "the eternal feminine draws us onward" (*"das Ewig-Weibliche zieht uns hinan"*). For me, the eternal feminine is my wife, Katie, and my daughter, Sarah. But they don't draw me onward. They draw me Home—for which I am eternally grateful.

Notes

Chapter 1: The Riddle

1. All stories in this book are factual. In many cases I have changed names and identifying details to protect the individual's privacy. E-mail addresses, where given, are provided with the express permission of the e-mail correspondent.

2. See, for example, Tamar Lewin's lengthy feature for the *New York Times*, "At College, Women Are Leaving Men in the Dust," July 9, 2006, pp. A1, A18, A19.

3. US Department of Education, Institute of Education Sciences, National Center for Education Statistics, *Higher Education: Gaps in Access and Persistence Study*, August 2012, online at http://nces.ed .gov/pubs2012/2012046.pdf.

4. According to data published May 30, 2015, by the US Department of Education, in 2013 there were 1,699,704 women pursuing postgraduate degrees at American universities, compared with 1,201,160 men pursuing postgraduate degrees: those numbers work out to 58.6 percent women, 41.4 percent men. The source is US Department of Education, Institute of Education Sciences, National Center for Education Statistics, *Digest of Education Statistics*, Table

303.60, "Total Fall Enrollment in Degree-Granting Postsecondary Institutions, by Level of Enrollment, Sex of Student, and Other Selected Characteristics, 2013," online at http://nces.ed.gov/programs /digest/d14/tables/dt14_303.60.asp.

5. These figures are derived from US Department of Education, Institute of Education Sciences, National Center for Education Statistics, *Digest of Education Statistics*, Table 303.70, "Total Undergraduate Fall Enrollment in Degree-Granting Postsecondary Institutions, by Attendance Status, Sex of Student, and Control and Level of Institution: Selected Years, 1970 Through 2024," online at http://nces.ed.gov/programs/digest/d14/tables/dt14_303.70.asp. The figures for 2014 are estimates.

6. Quoting from US Department of Education, Institute of Education Sciences, National Center for Education Statistics, *The Condition of Education 2015*, May 2015, p. xxxiv: "About 59 percent of students who began seeking a bachelor's degree in fall 2007 completed that degree within 6 years. The graduation rate for females (62 percent) was higher than the rate for males (56 percent)," online at http:// nces.ed.gov/pubs2015/2015144.pdf. In 1976–1977, 494,424 men earned bachelor's degrees at American universities, compared with just 423,476 American women: that works out to men earning 53.9 percent of all bachelor's degrees awarded, compared with 46.1 percent earned by women. In 2011–2012, 765,317 men earned bachelor's degrees, compared with 1,025,729 women: that works out to men earning 42.7 percent of all bachelor's degrees awarded, compared with 57.3 percent earned by women. The data for 1976–1977 comes from US Department of Education, Institute of Education Sciences, National Center for Education Statistics, *Digest of Education Statistics*, Table 262, "Bachelor's Degrees Conferred by Degree-Granting Institutions, by Racial/Ethnic Group and Sex of Student: Selected Years, 1976–77 to 2002–03," 2004, online at http://nces.ed.gov/programs /digest/d04/tables/dt04_262.asp. The data for 2011–2012 comes from US Department of Education, Institute of Education Sciences, National Center for Education Statistics, *Digest of Education Statistics*,

Table 301.10, "Enrollment, Staff, and Degrees/Certificates Conferred in Degree-Granting and Non-Degree-Granting Postsecondary Institutions, by Control and Level of Institution, Sex of Student, Type of Staff, and Level of Degree: Fall 2010, Fall 2011, and 2011–12," 2013, online at https://nces.ed.gov/programs/digest/d13/tables/dt13_301.10.asp.

7. Please see notes 3, 4, 5, and 6, above.

8. My paper was entitled "Reclaiming Kindergarten: Making Kindergarten Less Harmful to Boys," published in *Psychology of Men and Masculinity*, volume 2, pp. 3–12, 2001. You can read the full text at no charge at www.leonardsax.com. But you don't need to, because everything in that paper, and much more, is in this book.

Chapter 2: The First Factor: Changes at School

1. Jerry D. Weast, Superintendent of Schools for Montgomery County, Maryland, "Why We Need Rigorous, Full-Day Kindergarten," from the May 2001 issue of *Principal* magazine.

2. Hyo Jung Kang and 24 coauthors, from the United States, Croatia, England, Germany, and Portugal, published an astonishing account of sex differences in gene expression in the human brain from the prenatal period through infancy, childhood, adolescence, young adulthood, middle adulthood, and late adulthood. I call their account "astonishing" because the biggest sex differences in the human brain were seen in the prenatal period. The paper is "Spatiotemporal Transcriptome of the Human Brain," *Nature*, volume 478, pp. 483–489, 2011.

3. Jay Giedd and colleagues, "Review: Magnetic Resonance Imaging of Male/Female Differences in Human Adolescent Brain Anatomy," *Biology of Sex Differences*, volume 3, issue 19, 2012, full text online at www.biomedcentral.com/content/pdf/2042-6410-3-19.pdf.

4. Jennifer Bramen and colleagues, "Sex Matters During Adolescence: Testosterone-Related Cortical Thickness Maturation Differs Between Boys and Girls," *PLOS One*, March 29, 2012, DOI: 10.1371/journal.pone.0033850. See also Tuong-Vi Nguyen and colleagues,

"Testosterone-Related Cortical Maturation Across Childhood and Adolescence," *Cerebral Cortex*, volume 23, pp. 1424–1432, 2013.

5. Rhoshel Lenroot and colleagues (12 authors in total), "Sexual Dimorphism of Brain Developmental Trajectories During Childhood and Adolescence," *NeuroImage*, volume 36, pp. 1065–1073, 2007.

6. Madhura Ingalhalikar and colleagues, "Sex Differences in the Structural Connectome of the Human Brain," *Proceedings of the National Academy of Sciences*, volume 111, pp. 823–828, 2014. These authors say their "results establish that male brains are optimized for intrahemispheric and female brains for interhemispheric communication" (p. 823). See also Julia Sacher and colleagues, "Sexual Dimorphism in the Human Brain: Evidence from Neuroimaging," *Magnetic Resonance Imaging*, volume 31, pp. 366–375, 2013. These investigators find larger sex differences in older children compared to younger children. However, Vickie Yu and colleagues—using magnetoencephalography rather than MRI—report larger sex differences in young children, 4 to 9 years of age, compared to children age 10 and older. See their paper "Age-Related Sex Differences in Language Lateralization: A Magnetoencephalography Study in Children," *Developmental Psychology*, volume 50, pp. 2276–2284, 2014. Likewise, in a magnetoencephalographic study of children 6 to 17 years of age, Abhijeet Gummadavelli and colleagues found larger sex differences in children 6 to 13 years of age than among children 14 to 17 years of age. See their paper "Spatiotemporal and Frequency Signatures of Word Recognition in the Developing Brain: A Magnetoencephalographic Study," *Brain Research*, volume 1498, pp. 20–32, 2013.

Magnetoencephalograms measure electrical activity, whereas MRI scans show anatomy. One plausible interpretation of the difference between these studies is that sex differences in brain electrical activity are most pronounced in the early years; in later childhood and in adolescence, sex differences in connectivity and anatomy become more pronounced.

7. The comments in this section are based on my own longitudinal observations of more than 1,000 children in my practice in Montgomery County, Maryland, over 18 years (1990–2008), as well as a series of papers by Deborah Stipek and her associates. See:

- Deborah Stipek and colleagues, "Good Beginnings: What Difference Does the Program Make in Preparing Young Children for School?" in the *Journal of Applied Developmental Psychology*, volume 19, pp. 41–66, 1998.
- Deborah Stipek, "Pathways to Constructive Lives: The Importance of Early School Success," in the book *Constructive & Destructive Behavior: Implications for Family, School, & Society*, published by the American Psychological Association, pp. 291–315, 2001.
- Tricia Valeski and Deborah Stipek, "Young Children's Feelings About School," *Child Development*, volume 72, pp. 1198–1213, 2001. In this review, Valeski and Stipek observe that children who fail to do well in kindergarten develop "negative perceptions of competence," and those negative perceptions may be "difficult to reverse as children progress through school" (p. 1199).

8. These data are taken from Organisation for Economic Co-operation and Development (OECD), *PISA 2012 Results: What Students Know and Can Do: Student Performance in Mathematics, Reading, and Science*, 2014, www.oecd.org/pisa/keyfindings/pisa -2012-results-volume-i.htm, Figure 1.4.1, "Comparing Countries' and Economies' Performance in Reading."

9. I am not suggesting that waiting until age 7 to begin formal education is the only factor responsible for the success of Finnish education, although I do think that this factor does not get the attention it deserves. Another important factor is certainly the selection criteria for teacher candidates in Finland—comparable to the selectivity of medical students in the United States. For more on the reasons for the success of education in Finland, see Pasi Sahlberg's book *Finnish Lessons 2.0: What Can the World Learn from Educational Change in Finland?* (New York: Teachers College Press, 2014).

10. I obtained these data from US Department of Education, Institute of Education Sciences, National Center for Education Statistics, Program for International Student Assessment (PISA) Table S2, "Average Scores of 15-Year-Old Students on PISA Science Literacy Scale, by Education System: 2012," online at http://nces.ed.gov/surveys/pisa/pisa2012/pisa2012highlights_4a.asp. Shanghai, Hong Kong, Taipei, and Macao also outperformed the United States. The PISA data were for examination year 2012, the latest available when I accessed the site in November 2015.

11. See, for example, Daphna Bassok and Sean Reardon, "'Academic Redshirting' in Kindergarten: Prevalence, Patterns, and Implications," *Educational Evaluation and Policy Analysis*, volume 35, pp. 283–297, 2013.

12. The quotations from Betsy Newell and Dana Haddad both come from Elissa Gootman's front-page article for the *New York Times*, "Preschoolers Grow Older as Parents Seek an Edge," October 19, 2006.

13. See my paper "Reclaiming Kindergarten: Making Kindergarten Less Harmful to Boys," *Psychology of Men & Masculinity*, volume 2, pp. 3–12, 2001. You can read the full text of this article at no charge at www.leonardsax.com.

14. Elizabeth Lonsdorf, Lynn Eberly, and Anne Pusey, "Sex Differences in Learning in Chimpanzees," *Nature*, volume 428, pp. 715–716, 2004.

15. Elizabeth Lonsdorf and colleagues, "Boys Will Be Boys: Sex Differences in Wild Infant Chimpanzee Social Interactions," *Animal Behavior*, volume 88, pp. 79–83, 2014; and also Lonsdorf and colleagues, "Sex Differences in Wild Chimpanzee Behavior Emerge During Infancy," *PLOS One*, June 9, 2014, DOI: 10.1371/journal.pone.0099099.

16. Derek Wildman and colleagues, "Implications of Natural Selection in Shaping 99.4 Percent Nonsynonymous DNA Identity Between Humans and Chimpanzees," *Proceedings of the National Academy of Sciences*, volume 100, pp. 7181–7188, 2003.

17. For my analysis of sex differences in **vision** in humans and other primates, please see pp. 132–138 of my book *Girls on the Edge* (New York: Basic Books, 2010). See also the review by Robert Handa and Robert McGivern, "Steroid Hormones, Receptors, and Perceptual and Cognitive Sex Differences in the Visual System," *Current Eye Research*, volume 40, pp. 110–127, 2015. For my analysis of sex differences in **hearing**, see my article "Sex Differences in Hearing: Implications for Best Practice in the Classroom," *Advances in Gender and Education*, volume 2, pp. 13–21, 2010. For a review that looks across species and modalities (hearing, vision, and smell), see Joseph Schroeder's chapter "Sex and Gender in Sensation and Perception," pp. 235–257 in *Handbook of Gender Research in Psychology*, edited by J. C. Chrisler and D. R. McCreary (New York: Springer, 2010).

18. Gillian Brown and Alan Dixon, "The Development of Behavioural Sex Differences in Infant Rhesus Macaques," *Primates*, volume 41, pp. 63–77, 2000.

19. Primatologists don't use the word babysitting; they prefer the term *alloparenting*. When Mom needs to forage, she leaves her baby with her daughter, never her son. Our primate cousins commonly engage in alloparenting, but it's always the daughter, not the son, who watches baby. See David Watts and Anne Pusey, "Behavior of Juvenile and Adolescent Great Apes," pp. 148–167 in Michael Pereira and Lynn Fairbanks, *Juvenile Primates: Life History, Development, and Behavior* (New York: Oxford University Press, 2002).

20. Carolyn Pope Edwards, "Behavioral Sex Differences in Children of Diverse Cultures: The Case of Nurturance to Infants," chapter 22 in Pereira and Fairbanks, *Juvenile Primates*.

21. We teach all girls and all boys the rule that underage teens should not drink alcohol. One consequence of this phenomenon—whereby ignoring the rules raises your status in the eyes of the boys—is that girls attending coed high schools, and women who attend coed colleges, are more likely to get drunk or to have problems with alcohol compared with girls from the same communities who attend girls' schools or women who attend women's colleges. See

Avshalom Caspi and colleagues, "Unraveling Girls' Delinquency: Biological, Dispositional, and Contextual Contributions to Adolescent Misbehavior," *Developmental Psychology*, volume 29, pp. 19–30, 1993. Regarding women at women's colleges compared with women at comparable coed colleges, see George Dowdall, Mary Crawford, and Henry Wechsler, "Binge Drinking Among American College Women: A Comparison of Single-Sex and Coeducational Institutions," *Psychology of Women Quarterly*, volume 22, pp. 705–715, 1998. See also Miriam Curtin, "Smoking and Drinking Among 15–16-Year-Old Girls: Do Male Peers Have an Influence?" *Irish Journal of Medical Science*, volume 173, pp. 191–192, 2004.

22. Marianne Hurst, "Girls Seen to Help Avert Violence," *Education Week*, May 18, 2005, p. 12.

23. See, for example, Omar Yousaf, Elizabeth Grunfeld, and Myra Hunter, "A Systematic Review of the Factors Associated with Delays in Medical and Psychological Help-Seeking Among Men," *Health Psychology Review*, volume 9, pp. 264–276, 2015.

24. Although many researchers have noted the greater propensity of women to ask for directions, the author best known for highlighting this difference between the sexes is Deborah Tannen; see her book *You Just Don't Understand: Men and Women in Conversation*, revised edition (New York: HarperCollins, 2001).

25. Pereira and Fairbanks, *Juvenile Primates*, Part II, "Growing into Different Worlds," p. 75.

26. Russell Mittermeier and colleagues, "Primates in Peril: The World's 25 Most Endangered Primates, 2004–2006," *Primate Conservation*, volume 20, pp. 1–28, 2006.

27. Lisbeth B. Lindahl and Mikael Heimann, "Social Proximity in Early Mother-Infant Interactions: Implications for Gender Differences?" *Early Development and Parenting*, volume 6, pp. 83–88, 1997.

28. See Jianzhong Xu, "Gender and Homework Management Reported by High School Students," *Educational Psychology*, volume 26, pp. 73–91, 2006; and also Wei-Cheng Mau and Richard Lynn, "Gender Differences in Homework and Test Scores in Mathematics,

Reading and Science at Tenth and Twelfth Grade," *Psychology, Evolution, and Gender*, volume 2, pp. 119–125, 2000.

29. Lynne Rogers and Sue Hallam, "Gender Differences in Approaches to Studying for the GCSE Among High-Achieving Pupils," *Educational Studies*, volume 32, pp. 59–71, 2006.

30. Angela Lee Duckworth and Martin E. P. Seligman, "Self-Discipline Gives Girls the Edge: Gender in Self-Discipline, Grades, and Achievement Test Scores," *Journal of Educational Psychology*, volume 98, pp. 198–208, 2006.

31. Valeski and Stipek, "Young Children's Feelings About School," cited above.

32. Eva Pomerantz, Ellen Altermatt, and Jill Saxon, "Making the Grade but Feeling Distressed: Gender Differences in Academic Performance and Internal Distress," *Journal of Educational Psychology*, volume 94, pp. 396–404, 2002.

33. Duckworth and Seligman, "Self-Discipline Gives Girls the Edge."

34. René A. Spitz, "Hospitalism: An Enquiry into the Genesis of Psychiatric Conditions in Early Childhood," *Psychoanalytic Study of the Child*, volume 1, pp. 53–74, 1945.

35. Richard Louv, *Last Child in the Woods: Saving Our Children from Nature-Deficit Disorder* (Chapel Hill, NC: Algonquin Books, 2005).

36. Louv, *Last Child in the Woods*, p. 57.

37. Louv, *Last Child in the Woods*, pp. 63, 67.

38. Quoted in Louv, *Last Child in the Woods*, p. 66.

39. Quoted in Louv, *Last Child in the Woods*, p. 104.

40. See, for example, Andrea Faber Taylor and Frances E. Kuo, "Could Exposure to Everyday Green Spaces Help Treat ADHD? Evidence from Children's Play Settings," *Applied Psychology: Health and Well-Being*, volume 3, pp. 281–303, 2011.

41. For documentation of the rise in diagnosis of ADHD in the United States over the past three decades, and an exploration of the reasons underlying that rise, please see chapter 3 of my book *The Collapse of Parenting* (New York: Basic Books, 2015).

42. Quoted in Louv, *Last Child in the Woods*, p. 47.

43. This simple definition is drawn from Ulric Neisser's more elaborate definition. Neisser was the first to coin the term "cognitive psychology" (in 1967). Here is his definition of cognition from *Cognitive Psychology* (New York: Appleton-Century-Crofts, 1967), p. 4:

> The term "cognition" refers to all processes by which the sensory input is transformed, reduced, elaborated, stored, recovered, and used. It is concerned with these processes even when they operate in the absence of relevant stimulation, as in images and hallucinations. Given such a sweeping definition, it is apparent that cognition is involved in everything a human being might possibly do; that every psychological phenomenon is a cognitive phenomenon.

44. Gabrielle Weiss and Lily Hechtman, "The Hyperactive Child Syndrome," *Science*, volume 205, pp. 1348–1354, 1979.

45. Alan Schwarz and Sarah Cohen, "A.D.H.D. Seen in 11% of U.S. Children as Diagnoses Rise," *New York Times*, March 31, 2013.

46. Jay Mathews's article was entitled "Study Casts Doubt on the Boy Crisis: Improving Test Scores Cut into Girls' Lead," published on the front page of the *Washington Post*, June 26, 2006.

47. Judith Warner, "What Boy Crisis?," *New York Times*, July 3, 2006.

48. Judith Warner, "Is There Really a 'Boy Crisis'? Most Boys Are Doing Just Fine," March 21, 2013, http://ideas.time.com/2013/03/21 /the-boy-crisis-is-it-fictional.

49. David Von Drehle, "The Myth About Boys," *Time*, July 26, 2007.

50. For a discussion of the interaction between race, gender, and social class, see the conversation between Richard Whitmire and Susan McGee Bailey entitled "Gender Gap," Spring 2010, Education Next website, http://educationnext.org/gender-gap.

51. Professor Judith Kleinfeld presented this analysis of the NAEP data at the White House Conference on Helping America's Youth, June 6, 2006. You can read the full text of her analysis at www.singlesexschools.org/Kleinfeld.htm.

52. You can pull up all the NAEP data cited in this chapter by going to US Department of Education, Institute for Education Sciences, National Center for Education Statistics, National Assessment of Education Progress (NAEP), http://nces.ed.gov/nations reportcard/naepdata. Click on "Main NDE" (NDE stands for "NAEP Data Explorer"). The data are from the 2011 Writing assessment, which is the most recent available as of November 2015.

53. Judy Willis, "The Gully in the 'Brain Glitch' Theory," *Educational Leadership*, volume 64, pp. 68–73, 2007. The quotation comes from p. 72.

54. Mark Bauerlein and Sandra Stotsky, "Why Johnny Won't Read," *Washington Post*, January 25, 2005, p. A15.

55. See William Killgore, Mika Oki, and Deborah Yurgelun-Todd, "Sex-Specific Developmental Changes in Amygdala Responses to Affective Faces," *NeuroReport*, volume 12, pp. 427–433, 2001; William Killgore and Deborah Yurgelun-Todd, "Sex Differences in Amygdala Activation During the Perception of Facial Affect," *NeuroReport*, volume 12, pp. 2543–2547, 2001; and William Killgore and Deborah Yurgelun-Todd, "Sex-Related Developmental Differences in the Lateralized Activation of the Prefrontal Cortex and Amygdala During Perception of Facial Affect," *Perceptual and Motor Skills*, volume 99, pp. 371–391, 2004. Dr. Yurgelun-Todd has since moved to the University of Utah.

56. The rule is "Snow is to stay on the ground at all times." Variations of this policy are found across North America. For example, the Morning Glory Public School of the York Region District School Board in Ontario, Canada, reminds students that "Snow Must Stay Out Of Hands And On The Ground At All Times." This rule was stated in a newsletter from the Morning Glory school in December 2013 posted at www.yrdsb.ca/schools/morningglory.ps/NewsEvents/Documents/Dec%202013%20vol%201%20mgps.pdf.

57. See, for example, Stephanie Martinez, "A System Gone Berserk: How Are Zero-Tolerance Policies Really Affecting Schools?"

Preventing School Failure, volume 53, pp. 153–158, 2009; and also Russell Skiba and Kimberly Knesting, "Zero Tolerance, Zero Evidence: An Analysis of School Disciplinary Practice," *New Directions for Youth Development*, issue 92, pp. 17–43, 2001.

58. Margaret Shih, Todd Pittinsky, and Nalini Ambady, "Stereotype Susceptibility: Identity Salience and Shifts in Quantitative Performance," *Psychological Science*, volume 10, pp. 80–83, 1999.

59. Princeton psychologists Joel Cooper and Kimberlee Weaver, in their book *Gender and Computers: Understanding the Digital Divide* (Mahwah, NJ: Lawrence Erlbaum, 2003), describe many studies demonstrating that young girls and teenage girls underperform on tests of math and science ability particularly when they are reminded of the gender stereotype. See, especially, their chapter 3, "The Social Context of Computing," and chapter 5, "A Threat in the Air." These authors also describe studies showing how much better girls do, on average, in single-sex classrooms, perhaps in part because the stereotype threat is not present. See chapter 7, "Solutions: Single-Sex Schools and Classrooms?" I have written more about the potential of all-girls classrooms to break down gender stereotypes and broaden education in chapter 5 of my book *Girls on the Edge*.

60. Roy Baumeister and colleagues, "Does High Self-Esteem Cause Better Performance, Interpersonal Success, Happiness, or Healthier Lifestyles?" *Psychological Science in the Public Interest*, volume 4, pp. 1–44, 2003.

61. Martinez, "A System Gone Berserk"; Skiba and Knesting, "Zero Tolerance, Zero Evidence," both cited above.

62. The classic scholarly paper on this topic is "The Classroom Avenger," by Dr. James McGee and Dr. Caren DeBernardo, originally published in *The Forensic Examiner*, volume 8, May-June 1999.

63. Peter Langman, "School Shooters: The Warning Signs," *Forensic Digest*, Winter-Spring 2012.

64. All quotations in this paragraph come from Dave Cullen's *Columbine* (New York: Twelve, 2010), pp. 307–308.

65. Cullen, *Columbine*, p. 309.

66. "Court Found Cho Mentally Ill," *The Smoking Gun*, www
.thesmokinggun.com/file/court-found-cho-mentally-ill.

67. Michael Luo, "U.S. Rules Made Killer Ineligible to Purchase
Gun," *New York Times*, April 21, 2007.

68. All quotations in this paragraph come from the article by
Manny Fernandez and Marc Santora, "Gunman Showed Signs of
Anger," *New York Times*, April 18, 2007.

69. Both quotations in this paragraph come from Ian Urbina's article, "Virginia Tech Criticized for Actions in Shooting," *New York
Times*, August 30, 2007.

70. Liz Klimas, "10-Year-Old Suspended for an Imaginary
Weapon," *The Blaze*, December 9, 2013, www.theblaze.com/stories
/2013/12/09/10-year-old-suspended-for-shooting-imaginary-bow
-and-arrow.

71. Donna St. George, "Anne Arundel Officials Decline to Clear
Record of Second-Grader Who Made 'Pastry Gun,'" *Washington
Post*, May 15, 2013.

72. This example comes from the article "Zero Tolerance for Common Sense," by Paul Rosenzweig and Trent England, August 5, 2004,
Heritage Foundation, www.heritage.org/research/commentary/2004
/08/zero-tolerance-for-common-sense.

73. The original Latin is *Naturam expellas furca, tamen usque re-
curret*, from the *Epistles of Horace*, volume 1, §10, line 24.

Chapter 3: The Second Factor: Video Games

1. The global *Halo* competition I am referring to here took place in
May 2005. Although the organizers requested that participants be at
least 18 years of age, no serious mechanism was in place to ensure
compliance with this rule.

Video game competitions, now known as "e-sports," have come a
long way since 2005. In an article for the *New York Times*, "In
E-sports, Video Gamers Draw Real Crowds and Big Money," August
30, 2014, reporter Nick Wingfield described a Defense of the Ancients

(DOTA) tournament in which two teams of expert gamers competed for $11 million in prize money at a Seattle basketball arena in front of a live, paying audience of more than 11,000 spectators. Robert Morris University in Chicago now awards more than $500,000 in scholarships to gamers, just as it awards scholarships to athletes. And the Ivy League now offers intercollegiate gaming. Wingfield's article is online at www.nytimes.com/2014/08/31/technology/esports-explosion-brings-opportunity-riches-for-video-gamers.html.

2. John S. Watson, "Memory and 'Contingency Analysis' in Infant Learning," *Merrill-Palmer Quarterly*, volume 13, pp. 55–76, 1967.

3. Henry Gleitman, *Psychology* (New York: W. W. Norton, 1980), p. 147.

4. Nietzsche himself made this point most emphatically when he wrote that the free spirit—by which he meant the person motivated by the will to power, unconstrained by other considerations—is a person in whom "the manly instincts, the instincts for war and for victory, have mastery over the other instincts, for example over the instinct for 'happiness.' The person who has become free—and even more so the *spirit* who has become free—stomps on the contemptible sort of comfort which is dreamt of by small merchants, Christians, cows, women, Englishmen and other democrats." The translation is my own (emphasis in original). The original German reads: *"Freiheit bedeutet, daß die männlichen, die kriegs-und siegsfrohen Instinkte die Herrschaft haben über andre Instinkte, zum Beispiel über die des »Glücks." Der freigewordne Mensch, um wie viel mehr der freigewordne* **Geist**, *tritt mit Füßen auf die verächtliche Art von Wohlbefinden, von dem Krämer, Christen, Kühe, Weiber, Engländer und andre Demokraten träumen."* (From Nietzsche's 1889 book *Götzen-Dämmerung* [*Twilight of the Idols*], section 38, "Mein Begriff von Freiheit," widely available online, for example, at www.textlog.de /8119.html.)

5. This quotation is the closing line of section 349 of Nietzsche's *The Will to Power*, translated by Walter Kaufmann and R. J. Hollingdale (New York: Vintage Books, 1968), p. 191.

6. These examples come from Mike Musgrove's article for the *Washington Post*, "Family Game Night, Version 2.0," March 4, 2007, pp. F1, F4.

7. The simplest way to watch the commercial is to go to YouTube and enter "Greatness Awaits, PS4," in the search box.

8. Alan Castel, Jay Pratt, and Emily Drummond, "The Effects of Action Video Game Experience on the Time Course of Inhibition of Return and the Efficiency of Visual Search," *Acta Psychologica*, volume 119, pp. 217–230, 2005.

9. Edward Swing and colleagues, "Television and Video Game Exposure and the Development of Attention Problems," *Pediatrics*, volume 126, pp. 214–221, 2010. See also Douglas Gentile and colleagues, "Video Game Playing, Attention Problems, and Impulsiveness: Evidence of Bidirectional Causality," *Psychology of Popular Media Culture*, volume 1, pp. 62–70, 2012.

10. Jay Hull, Ana Draghici, and James Sargent, "A Longitudinal Study of Risk-Glorifying Video Games and Reckless Driving," *Psychology of Popular Media Culture*, volume 1, pp. 244–253, 2012.

11. Kathleen Beullens and Jan Van den Bulck, "Predicting Young Drivers' Car Crashes: Music Video Viewing and the Playing of Driving Games. Results from a Prospective Cohort Study," *Media Psychology*, volume 16, issue 1, 2013.

12. Stervo Mario and colleagues, "Frequent Video-Game Playing in Young Males is Associated with Central Adiposity and High-Sugar, Low-Fibre Dietary Consumption," *Eating and Weight Disorders*, volume 19, pp. 515–520, 2014. See also Catherine Berkey and colleagues, "Activity, Dietary Intake, and Weight Changes in a Longitudinal Study of Preadolescent and Adolescent Boys and Girls," *Pediatrics*, volume 105, pp. e56, 2000; and Elizabeth Vandewater and colleagues, "Linking Obesity and Activity Level with Children's Television and Video Game Use," *Journal of Adolescence*, volume 27, pp. 71–85, 2004.

13. Jean-Philippe Chaput and colleagues, "Video Game Playing Increases Food Intake in Adolescents: A Randomized Crossover Study,"

American Journal of Clinical Nutrition, volume 93, pp. 1196–1203, 2011.

14. Megan Mathers and colleagues, "Electronic Media Use and Adolescent Health and Well-Being: Cross-Sectional Community Study," *Academic Pediatrics*, volume 9, pp. 307–314, 2009.

15. Brock Bastian, Jolanda Jetten, and Helena Radke, "Cyber-Dehumanization: Violent Video Game Play Diminishes Our Humanity," *Journal of Experimental Social Psychology*, volume 48, pp. 486–491, 2012. See also Tobias Greitemeyer and Neil McLatchie, "Denying Humanness to Others: A Newly Discovered Mechanism by Which Violent Video Games Increase Aggressive Behavior," *Psychological Science*, volume 22, pp. 659–665, 2011.

16. Jay Hull and colleagues, "A Longitudinal Study of Risk-Glorifying Video Games and Behavioral Deviance," *Journal of Personality and Social Psychology*, volume 107, pp. 300–325, 2014.

17. Julia Fischer and colleagues, "The Delinquent Media Effect: Delinquency-Reinforcing Video Games Increase Players' Attitudinal and Behavioral Inclination Toward Delinquent Behavior," *Psychology of Popular Media Culture*, volume 1, pp. 201–205, 2012. See also Peter Holtz and Markus Appel, "Internet Use and Video Gaming Predict Problem Behavior in Early Adolescence," *Journal of Adolescence*, volume 34, pp. 49–58, 2011.

18. Alessandro Gabbiadini and colleagues, "Interactive Effect of Moral Disengagement and Violent Video Games on Self-Control, Cheating, and Aggression," *Social Psychological and Personality Science*, volume 5, pp. 451–458, 2014.

19. Mirko Pawlikowski and Matthias Brand, "Excessive Internet Gaming and Decision Making: Do Excessive World of Warcraft Players Have Problems in Decision Making Under Risky Conditions?" *Psychiatry Research*, volume 188, pp. 428–433, 2011.

20. Jih-Hsuan Lin, "Do Video Games Exert Stronger Effects on Aggression Than Film? The Role of Media Interactivity and Identification on the Association of Violent Content and Aggressive Outcomes," *Computers in Human Behavior*, volume 29, pp. 535–543, 2013.

21. Marc Sestir and Bruce Bartholow, "Violent and Nonviolent Video Games Produce Opposing Effects on Aggressive and Prosocial Outcomes," *Journal of Experimental Social Psychology*, volume 46, pp. 934–942, 2010. See also Muniba Saleem, Craig Anderson, and Douglas Gentile, "Effects of Prosocial, Neutral, and Violent Video Games on College Students' Affect," *Aggressive Behavior*, volume 38, pp. 263–271, 2012.

22. Bruce Bartholow and colleagues, "Chronic Violent Video Game Exposure and Desensitization to Violence: Behavioral and Event-Related Brain Potential Data," *Journal of Experimental Social Psychology*, volume 42, pp. 532–539, 2006. See also Tom Hummer and colleagues, "Short-Term Violent Video Game Play by Adolescents Alters Prefrontal Activity During Cognitive Inhibition," *Media Psychology*, volume 13, pp. 136–154, 2010.

23. Christopher Barlett and Christopher Rodeheffer, "Effects of Realism on Extended Violent and Nonviolent Video Game Play on Aggressive Thoughts, Feelings, and Physiological Arousal," *Aggressive Behavior*, volume 35, pp. 213–224, 2009.

24. Craig Anderson and colleagues, "Violent Video Game Effects on Aggression, Empathy, and Prosocial Behavior in Eastern and Western Countries: A Meta-Analytic Review," *Psychological Bulletin*, volume 136, pp. 151–173, 2010. For a thoughtful comment on this paper—observing that some doubters will never be persuaded, no matter how strong the evidence—see L. Rowell Huesmann, "Nailing the Coffin Shut on Doubts That Violent Video Games Stimulate Aggression: Comment on Anderson et al. 2010," *Psychological Bulletin*, volume 136, pp. 179–181, 2010.

25. See Craig Anderson, "Violent Video Games: Myths, Facts, and Unanswered Questions," *Psychological Science Agenda*, volume 16, October 2003.

26. The full text of Justice Alito's concurrence is online at US Supreme Court, www.supremecourt.gov/opinions/10pdf/08-1448.pdf. The quotations in this paragraph come from pp. 12 and 14 of Justice Alito's concurrence.

27. All quotations in this paragraph come from Patrick Welsh's article for the *Washington Post*, "It's No Contest; Boys Will Be Men, and They'll Still Choose Video Games," December 5, 2004, p. B1.

28. You can read Professor Anderson's guidelines in full at Iowa State University of Science and Technology, Department of Psychology, www.psychology.iastate.edu/faculty/caa/VG_recommendations .html.

29. Welsh, "It's No Contest," p. B1.

30. Tamar Lewin, "At Colleges, Women Are Leaving Men in the Dust," *New York Times*, July 9, 2006, pp. A1, A18, A19.

31. Lewin, "At Colleges," pp. A18, A19.

32. Craig Anderson, Douglas Gentile, and Katherine Buckley, *Violent Video Game Effects on Children and Adolescents* (New York: Oxford University Press, 2007), p. 66.

33. David Riley, "Average Time Spent Playing Games on Mobile Devices Has Increased 57 Percent Since 2012," January 27 2015, online at NPD Group, www.npd.com.

34. I have posted the AAP guidelines online at www.leonardsax .com/guidelines.pdf. The guidelines do not explicitly advise the use of monitoring software, but they do recommend against kids having unsupervised access to the Internet. Unless you are able to monitor everything your child is doing online, in person, the only way to prevent unsupervised use of the Internet is to install some kind of monitoring software along with parental controls.

Chapter 4: The Third Factor: Medications for ADHD

1. "National Institute of Mental Health Multimodal Treatment Study of ADHD Follow-up: Changes in Effectiveness and Growth After the End of Treatment," *Pediatrics*, volume 113, pp. 762–769, 2004. See also Stephen Faraone and colleagues, "Effects of Lisdexamfetamine Dimesylate [Vyvanse] Treatment for ADHD on Growth," *Journal of the American Academy of Child & Adolescent Psychiatry*, volume 49, pp. 24–32, 2010.

2. Dr. Peter Breggin is one writer who has argued that ADHD was invented by the pharmaceutical industry in order to sell drugs. See his books *Talking Back to Ritalin: What Doctors Aren't Telling You About Stimulants for Children* (Monroe, ME: Common Courage Press, 1998); and also *The Ritalin Fact Book: What Your Doctor Won't Tell You* (New York: Perseus, 2002).

3. American Psychiatric Association, *Diagnostic and Statistical Manual of Mental Disorders*, 5th edition (Washington, DC: APA, 2013), p. 59. (DSM-5 hereafter.)

4. As I pointed out in my book *The Collapse of Parenting* (New York: Basic Books, 2015), in 1979, only about 1.2 percent of American children, or 12 out of 1,000, had the condition we now call ADHD. It was then known as "hyperkinetic reaction of childhood." Boys outnumbered girls by 2 to 1 (or greater), so that we might estimate that the 1979 figures would be 1.6 percent of boys and 0.8 percent of girls (yielding an average rate of 1.2 percent). In 2013, the Centers for Disease Control and Prevention announced that 20 percent of American high school boys had been diagnosed with ADHD, representing a roughly tenfold increase between 1979 and 2013, from 1.6 percent or thereabouts to 20 percent. See *The Collapse of Parenting*, chapter 3.

5. The phrase "medicate young minds" is borrowed from Elizabeth Roberts's article, "A Rush to Medicate Young Minds," *Washington Post*, October 8, 2006, p. B7.

6. DSM-5's criteria for Oppositional-Defiant Disorder (313.81, p. 462) include, among others:
- often argues with adults.
- often actively defies or refuses to comply with requests from authority figures.
- often deliberately annoys others.

7. Jennifer Harris, *Psychotherapy Networker*, February 2006, quoted in Roberts's article, "A Rush to Medicate Young Minds."

8. Leonard Sax and Kathleen Kautz, "Who First Suggests the Diagnosis of Attention-Deficit Hyperactivity Disorder? A Survey of

Primary-Care Pediatricians, Family Physicians, and Child Psychia-
trists," *Annals of Family Medicine*, volume 1, pp. 171–174, 2003.

9. Dr. Gabrieli's presentation was entitled "Educating the Brain."
You can purchase the audio of the presentation by going to the website
of Fleetwood Onsite Conference Recording, www.fleetwoodonsite
.com, and entering "Gabrieli" in the search engine. There is a charge of
$15.00 for the CD.

10. Much of the substance of this section, particularly the text of the
endnotes, is drawn from my discussion of this topic in my book *The
Collapse of Parenting*, pp. 65–66 and the accompanying endnotes.

11. Here are three of the papers that Dr. Carlezon coauthored on
this topic:

• "Enduring Behavioral Effects of Early Exposure to Methylphenidate in Rats," *Biological Psychiatry*, volume 54, pp. 1330–
  1337, 2003.

• "Understanding the Neurobiological Consequences of Early
  Exposure to Psychotropic Drugs," *Neuropharmacology*, volume 47, Supplement 1, pp. 47–60, 2004.

• "Early Developmental Exposure to Methylphenidate Reduces
  Cocaine-Induced Potentiation of Brain Stimulation Reward in
  Rats," *Biological Psychiatry*, volume 57, pp. 120–125, 2005.

12. Many scholarly studies have now demonstrated that methylphenidate and amphetamine—the active ingredients in these medications—can cause lasting changes to those areas of the developing
brain where dopamine receptors are found. The disrupting effects
appear to be centered on the nucleus accumbens, which is not sur-
prising, because, as noted, the nucleus accumbens has a high density
of dopamine receptors. Terry Robinson and Bryan Kolb at the University of Michigan were among the first to demonstrate that low-
dose amphetamine leads to damage to neurons in the nucleus
accumbens. They first documented this finding in their paper "Persistent Structural Modifications in Nucleus Accumbens and Prefrontal Cortex Neurons Produced by Previous Experiences with
Amphetamine," *Journal of Neuroscience*, volume 17, 8491–8497, 1997.

They later reviewed this emerging field in their article "Structural Plasticity Associated with Exposure to Drugs of Abuse," *Neuropharmacology*, volume 47, pp. 33–46, 2004. See also Claire Advokat, "Literature Review: Update on Amphetamine Neurotoxicity and Its Relevance to the Treatment of ADHD," *Journal of Attention Disorders*, volume 11, pp. 8–16, 2007.

Other relevant articles include (in alphabetical order):

- Esther Gramage and colleagues, "Periadolescent Amphetamine Treatment Causes Transient Cognitive Disruptions and Long-Term Changes in Hippocampal LTP," *Addiction Biology*, volume 18, pp. 19–29, 2013.
- Rochellys D. Heijtz, Bryan Kolb, and Hans Forssberg, "Can a Therapeutic Dose of Amphetamine During Pre-adolescence Modify the Pattern of Synaptic Organization in the Brain?" *European Journal of Neuroscience*, volume 18, pp. 3394–3399, 2003.
- Yong Li and Julie Kauer, "Repeated Exposure to Amphetamine Disrupts Dopaminergic Modulation of Excitatory Synaptic Plasticity and Neurotransmission in Nucleus Accumbens," *Synapse*, volume 51, pp. 1–10, 2004.
- Manuel Mameli and Christian Lüscher, "Synaptic Plasticity and Addiction: Learning Mechanisms Gone Awry," *Neuropharmacology*, volume 61, pp. 1052–1059, 2011.
- Shao-Pii Onn and Anthony Grace, "Amphetamine Withdrawal Alters Bistable States and Cellular Coupling in Rat Prefrontal Cortex and Nucleus Accumbens Neurons Recorded in Vivo," *Journal of Neuroscience*, volume 20, pp. 2332–2345, 2000.
- Margery Pardey and colleagues, "Long-Term Effects of Chronic Oral Ritalin Administration on Cognitive and Neural Development in Adolescent Wistar Kyoto Rats," *Brain Sciences*, volume 2, pp. 375–404, 2012.
- Scott Russo and colleagues, "The Addicted Synapse: Mechanisms of Synaptic and Structural Plasticity in the Nucleus Accumbens," *Trends in Neuroscience*, volume 33, pp. 267–276, 2010.

• Louk J. Vanderschuren and colleagues, " A Single Exposure to
Amphetamine Is Sufficient to Induce Long-term Behavioral,
Neuroendocrine, and Neurochemical Sensitization in Rats,"
Journal of Neuroscience, volume 19, pp. 9579–9586, 1999.
For a review of the underlying neurochemistry, the similarities be-
tween the prescription stimulant medications and cocaine, and an
assessment of the long-term risks for people who take these medica-
tions, please see the review by Heinz Steiner and Vincent Van Waes,
"Addiction-Related Gene Regulation: Risks of Exposure to Cognitive
Enhancers vs. Other Psychostimulants," *Progress in Neurobiology*,
volume 100, pp. 60–80, 2013.

13. There is consensus that methylphenidate works by increasing
the action of dopamine in the synapse: see, for example, Nora Volkow
and colleagues, "Imaging the Effects of Methylphenidate on Brain Dopamine: New Model on Its Therapeutic Actions for Attention-Deficit
/ Hyperactivity Disorder," *Biological Psychiatry*, volume 57, pp. 1410–
1415, 2005. And it has long been recognized that amphetamine mimics the action of dopamine in the brain, and that the dopamine system
is key to ADHD. See, for example, James Swanson and colleagues,
"Dopamine and Glutamate in Attention Deficit Disorder," pp. 293–
315 in *Dopamine and Glutamate in Psychiatric Disorders*, edited by
Werner Schmidt and Maarten Reith (New York: Humana Press,
2005).

14. For more information on the central role of the nucleus accumbens in motivation, see Dr. Carlezon's paper, "Biological Sub-
strates of Reward and Aversion: A Nucleus Accumbens Activity
Hypothesis," *Neuropharmacology*, volume 56, Supplement 1, pp.
122–132, 2009.

15. See Elseline Hoekzema and colleagues, "Stimulant Drugs
Trigger Transient Volumetric Changes in the Human Ventral Stri-
atum," *Brain Structure and Function*, volume 219, pp. 23–34, 2013,
especially figures 2 and 3. See also Mónica Franco Emch, "Ventro-
Striatal / Nucleus Accumbens Alterations in Adult ADHD: Effects

of Pharmacological Treatment: A Neuroimaging Region of Interest Study," Universitat Pompeu Fabra, 2015, especially figure 2. The full text is online at http://repositori.upf.edu/bitstream/handle /10230/24651/Franco_2015.pdf.

16. See Scott Mackey and colleagues, "A Voxel-Based Morphometry Study of Young Occasional Users of Amphetamine-Type Stimulants and Cocaine," *Drug and Alcohol Dependence*, volume 135, pp. 104–111, 2014.

17. L. J. Seidman and colleagues, "Dorsolateral Prefrontal and Anterior Cingulate Cortex Volumetric Abnormalities in Adults with Attention Deficit / Hyperactivity Disorder Identified by Magnetic Resonance Imaging," *Biological Psychiatry*, volume 60, pp. 1071–1080, 2006. See also Hoekzema and colleagues, "Stimulant Drugs," and Emch, "Ventro-Striatal / Nucleus Accumbens Alterations," both cited above.

18. See Nicolas Carriere and colleagues, "Apathy in Parkinson's Disease Is Associated with Nucleus Accumbens Atrophy: A Magnetic Resonance Imaging Shape Analysis," *Movement Disorders*, volume 29, pp. 897–903, 2014. See also Robert Paul and colleagues, "Apathy Is Associated with Volume of the Nucleus Accumbens in Patients Infected with HIV," *Journal of Neuropsychiatry and Clinical Neuroscience*, volume 17, pp. 167–171, 2005.

19. Please see my paper "The Diagnosis and Treatment of ADHD in Women," *Female Patient*, volume 29, pp. 29–34, November 2004. See also Julia Rucklidge, "Gender Differences in Attention-Deficit / Hyperactivity Disorder," *Psychiatric Clinics of North America*, volume 33, pp. 357–373, 2010.

20. The book he recommended—and which I subsequently purchased and read—was *Unearthing Atlantis*, by Charles Pellegrino (New York: Random House, 1994).

21. Leonard Sax, "The Feminization of American Culture: How Modern Chemicals May Be Changing American Biology," *The World & I*, pp. 243–261, October 2001.

Chapter 5: The Fourth Factor: Endocrine Disruptors

1. David Fahrenthold, "Male Bass Across Region Found to Be Bearing Eggs: Pollution Concerns Arise in Drinking-Water Source," *Washington Post*, September 6, 2006, pp. A1, A8.

2. Fahrenthold, "Male Bass Across Region Found to Be Bearing Eggs."

3. See the paper that Dr. Blazer coauthored with Jo Ellen Hinck and other colleagues, "Widespread Occurrence of Intersex in Black Basses (*Micropterus* species) from US Rivers, 1995–2004," *Aquatic Toxicology*, volume 95, pp. 60–70, 2009. For an update on what's happening specifically in the Potomac River, see the paper by Dr. Blazer and colleagues "Reproductive Endocrine Disruption in Smallmouth Bass (*Micropterus dolomieu*) in the Potomac River Basin: Spatial and Temporal Comparisons of Biological Effects," *Environmental Monitoring and Assessment*, volume 184, pp. 4309–4334, 2012. These scholars note that there is a strong association between the severity of the intersex phenomena observed and the proximity to wastewater treatment plant runoff, agricultural runoff, and exposure to other manmade pesticides and other chemicals. But the exact identity of the compound or compounds responsible for the feminization of the males is still unclear.

4. Laura Sessions Stepp, "Cupid's Broken Arrow: Performance Anxiety and Substance Abuse Figure into the Increase in Reports of Impotence on Campus," *Washington Post*, May 7, 2006.

5. The quotations from Dr. Brodie and Dr. Pryor both come from Stepp, "Cupid's Broken Arrow," cited above.

6. For an overview of this topic, at least as it relates to the pesticide-related feminization of wildlife, see the article by Heinz-R. Köhler and Rita Triebskorn, "Wildlife Ecotoxicology of Pesticides: Can We Track Effects to the Population Level and Beyond?" *Science*, volume 341, pp. 759–765, 2013. Here are some of the specific cases to which I am referring:

- **Washington and Idaho:** James Nagler and his associates, examining the tributaries of the Columbia River in Washington and Idaho, discovered that many of the female-appearing fish they found were actually genetically male. These fish were completely feminized: they looked female, and they made eggs instead of sperm, but they were genetically male. See James Nagler and colleagues, "High Incidence of a Male-Specific Genetic Marker in Phenotypic Female Chinook Salmon from the Columbia River," *Environmental Health Perspectives*, volume 109, pp. 67–69, 2001.

- **Florida:** In central Florida, Dr. Louis Guillette and associates with the US Fish and Wildlife Service found male alligators with shriveled testicles. These alligators also have abnormally low male hormone levels and abnormally high female hormone levels. Likewise, male panthers living in the wildlife preserves around Lake Apopka, not far from Orlando, are going extinct, at least in part because the male panthers are no longer capable of making sperm. The emasculation of male panthers has been linked to plastic derivatives, such as various phthalates and bisphenol A, in the watershed. See Louis J. Guillette Jr. and colleagues, "Developmental Abnormalities of the Gonad and Abnormal Sex Hormone Concentrations in Juvenile Alligators from Contaminated and Control Lakes in Florida," *Environmental Health Perspectives*, volume 102, pp. 680–688, 1994. See also Charles F. Facemire, Timothy S. Gross, and Louis J. Guillette Jr., "Reproductive Impairment in the Florida Panther," *Environmental Health Perspectives*, volume 103, Supplement 4, pp. 79–86, 1995.
- **Great Lakes:** Theo Colborn, Frederick vom Saal, and Ana Soto, "Developmental Effects of Endocrine-Disrupting Chemicals in Wildlife and Humans," *Environmental Health Perspectives*, volume 101, pp. 378–384, 1993.
- **Alaska:** Kurunthachalam Kannan, Se Hun Yun, and Thomas J. Evans, "Chlorinated, Brominated, and Perfluorinated Contaminants in Livers of Polar Bears from Alaska," *Environmental Science and Technology*, volume 39, pp. 9057–9063, 2005.

- **England:** Susan Jobling and colleagues, "Widespread Sexual Disruption in Wild Fish," *Environmental Science and Technology*, volume 32, pp. 2498–2506, 1998.
- **Greenland:** Christian Sonne and colleagues, "Xenoendocrine Pollutants May Reduce Size of Sexual Organs in East Greenland Polar Bears (*Ursus maritimus*)," *Environmental Science and Technology*, volume 40, pp. 5668–5674, 2006.

7. Carmen Sáenz de Rodriguez, Alfred Bongiovanni, and Lillian Conde de Borrego, "An Epidemic of Precocious Development in Puerto Rican Children," *Journal of Pediatrics*, volume 107, pp. 393–396, 1985.

8. Lambertina Freni-Titulaer and colleagues, "Premature Thelarche in Puerto Rico: A Search for Environmental Factors," *Archives of Pediatrics & Adolescent Medicine* (now known as *JAMA Pediatrics*), volume 140, pp. 1263–1267, 1986.

9. See Guillette and colleagues, "Developmental Abnormalities of the Gonad and Abnormal Sex Hormone Concentrations," cited above. See also Charles F. Facemire and colleagues, "Reproductive Impairment in the Florida Panther," cited above.

10. Polyethylene terephthalate (PET) is chemically distinct from the phthalates; however, a bottle made from PET may leach phthalates from the bottle into the beverage. I helped to call scholarly attention to this concern back in 2010. See my article "Polyethylene Terephthalate May Yield Endocrine Disruptors," *Environmental Health Perspectives*, volume 118, pp. 445–448, 2010, full text online at www.leonardsax.com/pet.pdf. My article prompted an angry letter to the editor from Ralph Vasami, executive director of the PET Resin Association, the trade group representing manufacturers of PET. His letter and my reply, both entitled "Polyethylene Terephthalate and Endocrine Disruptors," were published in *Environmental Health Perspectives*, volume 118, pp. A196–A197, 2010. You can also read Mr. Vasami's letter and my reply at www.leonardsax.com/wordpress/wp-content/uploads/2015/01/PET-response.pdf. See also Chun Yang and colleagues, "Most Plastic Products Release Estrogenic Chemicals: A

Potential Health Problem That Can Be Solved," *Environmental Health Perspectives*, volume 119, pp. 989–996, 2011; Martin Wagner and Jörg Oehlmann, "Endocrine Disruptors in Bottled Mineral Water: Estrogenic Activity in the E-screen," *Journal of Steroid Biochemistry and Molecular Biology*, volume 127, pp. 128–135, 2011; and Syam Andra and colleagues, "Co-leaching of Brominated Compounds and Antimony from Bottled Water," *Environment International*, volume 38, pp. 45–53, 2012.

11. Ivelisse Colón and colleagues, "Identification of Phthalate Esters in the Serum of Young Puerto Rican Girls with Premature Breast Development," *Environmental Health Perspectives*, volume 108, pp. 895–900, 2000.

12. Danielle Bodicoat and colleagues, "Timing of Pubertal Stages and Breast Cancer Risk: The Breakthrough Generations Study," *Breast Cancer Research*, volume 16, 2014, online at www.breast-cancer -research.com/content/16/1/R18.

13. Paul Kaplowitz and Sharon Oberfield, "Reexamination of the Age Limit for Defining When Puberty Is Precocious in Girls in the United States: Implications for Evaluation and Treatment," *Pediatrics*, volume 104, pp. 936–941, 1999.

14. See, for example, Jonathan Roy and colleagues, "Estrogen-like Endocrine Disrupting Chemicals Affecting Puberty in Humans—A Review," *Medical Science Review*, volume 15, pp. 137–145, 2009. See also Samim Özen and Sükran Darcan, "Effects of Environmental Endocrine Disruptors on Pubertal Development," *Journal of Clinical Research in Pediatric Endocrinology*, volume 3, pp. 1–6, 2011.

15. Sandra Steingraber, *The Falling Age of Puberty in U.S. Girls: What We Know, What We Need to Know* (San Francisco: Breast Cancer Fund, 2007).

16. Regarding the effects of endosulfan on puberty, see Kate Ramsayer, "Slowing puberty? Pesticide may hinder development in boys," *Science News*, volume 164, p. 372, 2003. This article is based in part on a study published by Habibullah Saiyed and colleagues, "Effect of endosulfan on male reproductive development," *Environmental*

Health Perspectives, volume 111, pp. 1958–1962, 2003. See also R. Sebastian and S. C. Raghavan, "Exposure to endosulfan can result in male infertility due to testicular atrophy and reduced sperm count," *Cell Death Discovery*, 2015, full text online at http://www.nature.com /articles/cddiscovery201520.

Regarding production of endosulfan: According to a 2002 report from the US Environmental Protection Agency (EPA), the annual use of endosulfan in the United States at that time was 1.38 million pounds, and the crops with the highest sales were cotton, cantaloupe, tomatoes, and potatoes. These figures come from p. 1 of the report "Reregistration Eligibility Decision for Endosulfan," report EPA 738-R-02–013, published by the EPA in November 2002, full text online at http://archive.epa.gov/pesticides/reregistration/web /pdf/endosulfan_red.pdf.

17. See Marla Cone's article, "EPA Bans Pesticide Found on Cucumbers and Other Vegetables," originally published by the *Daily Green* on June 14, 2010. When the *Daily Green* was acquired by *Good Housekeeping* in 2013, most of the articles archived on the *Daily Green* were purged; they are not available at the relocated home of the *Daily Green*, www.goodhousekeeping.com/home/a19703/the -daily-green. I found Marla Cone's article at www.highstrangeness. tv/0–10346-epa-bans-pesticide-found-on-cucumbers-and-other -vegetables.html (accessed October 10, 2015).

18. Dale Kemery, "EPA Moves to Terminate All Uses of Insecticide Endosulfan to Protect Health of Farmworkers and Wildlife," June 9, 2010, online at US Environmental Protection Agency, http:// yosemite.epa.gov/opa/admpress.nsf/eeffe922a687433c85257359003 f5340/44c035d59d5e6d8f8525773c0072f26b!opendocument.

19. I first came across this research in the article "Chemical Used in Food Containers Disrupts Brain Development," no byline, *Science Daily*, December 3, 2005. This article was based on two articles published by Dr. Scott Belcher and his colleagues: (1) "Ontogeny of Rapid Estrogen-Mediated Extracellular Signal-Regulated Kinase Signaling in the Rat Cerebellar Cortex: Potent Nongenomic Agonist

and Endocrine Disrupting Activity of the Xenoestrogen Bisphenol A," *Endocrinology*, volume 146, pp. 5388–5396, 2005; and (2) "Rapid Estrogenic Regulation of Extracellular Signal-Regulated Kinase 1/2 Signaling in Cerebellar Granule Cells Involves a G Protein- and Protein Kinase A-dependent Mechanism and Intracellular Activation of Protein Phosphatase 2A," *Endocrinology*, volume 146, pp. 5397–5406, 2005.

20. Walter Adriani and colleagues, "Altered Profiles of Spontaneous Novelty Seeking, Impulsive Behavior, and Response to D-Amphetamine in Rats Perinatally Exposed to Bisphenol A," *Environmental Health Perspectives*, volume 111, pp. 395–401, 2003.

21. Yoshinori Masuo and Masami Ishido, "Neurotoxicity of Endocrine Disruptors: Possible Involvement in Brain Development and Neurodegeneration," *Journal of Toxicology and Environmental Health*, volume 14, pp. 346–369, 2011.

22. Paola Palanza and colleagues, "Effects of Developmental Exposure to Bisphenol A on Brain and Behavior in Mice," *Environmental Research*, volume 108, pp. 150–157, 2008.

23. For a review, see Beverly Rubin's article "Bisphenol A: An Endocrine Disruptor with Widespread Exposure and Multiple Effects," *Journal of Steroid Biochemistry and Molecular Biology*, volume 127, pp. 27–34, 2011.

24. George Bittner and colleagues, "Estrogenic Chemicals Often Leach from BPA-Free Plastic Products That Are Replacements for BPA-Containing Polycarbonate Products," *Environmental Health*, May 28, 2014, online at www.ehjournal.net/content/13/1/41. See also Chun Yang and colleagues, "Most Plastic Products Release Estrogenic Chemicals," cited above.

25. John Meeker, "Exposure to Environmental Endocrine Disruptors and Child Development," *JAMA Pediatrics*, volume 166, pp. 952–958, 2012. The estimate of 84,000 chemicals comes from this article.

26. This quotation comes from the article by Philippe Grandjean and Philip Landrigan, "Neurobehavioural Effects of Developmental Toxicity," *Lancet Neurology*, volume 13, pp. 330–338, 2014.

27. Yoshinori Masuo and colleagues, "Motor Hyperactivity Caused by a Deficit in Dopaminergic Neurons and the Effects of Endocrine Disruptors: A Study Inspired by the Physiological Roles of PACAP in the Brain," *Regulatory Peptides*, volume 123, pp. 225–234, 2004. See also Masami Ishido and colleagues, "Dicyclohexylphthalate Causes Hyperactivity in the Rat Concomitantly with Impairment of Tyrosine Hydroxylase Immunoreactivity," *Journal of Neurochemistry*, volume 91, pp. 69–76, 2004.

28. Bung-Nyun Kim and colleagues, "Phthalates Exposure and Attention-Deficit / Hyperactivity Disorder in School-Age Children," *Biological Psychiatry*, volume 66, pp. 958–963, 2009.

29. Stephanie Engel and colleagues, "Prenatal Phthalate Exposure Is Associated with Childhood Behavior and Executive Functioning," *Environmental Health Perspectives*, volume 118, pp. 565–571, 2010. See also Amir Miodovnik and colleagues, "Endocrine Disruptors and Childhood Social Impairment," *Neurotoxicology*, volume 32, pp. 261–267, 2011.

30. I discuss the association between exposure to endocrine disruptors and the subsequent risk of breast cancer in chapter 4 of my book *Girls on the Edge*. For a review of some of the literature linking endocrine disruptors to prostate cancer, see Gail Prins, "Endocrine Disruptors and Prostate Cancer Risk," *Endocrine-Related Cancer*, volume 15, pp. 649–656, 2008. For a balanced review of evidence that endocrine disruptors may be contributing to the rise in rates of testicular cancer, see Fabrizio Giannandrea and colleagues, "Effect of Endogenous and Exogenous Hormones on Testicular Cancer: The Epidemiological Evidence," *International Journal of Developmental Biology*, volume 57, pp. 255–263, 2013. For an alarming forecast of what may be in store if present trends continue, see Charlotte Le Cornet and colleagues, "Testicular Cancer Incidence to Rise by 25% by 2025 in Europe? Model-Based Predictions in 40 Countries Using Population-Based Registry Data," *European Journal of Cancer*, volume 50, pp. 831–839, 2014.

31. Laura Vandenberg and colleagues, "Hormones and Endocrine-Disrupting Chemicals: Low-Dose Effects and Nonmonotonic Dose

Responses," *Endocrine Reviews*, volume 33, pp. 378–455, 2012. See also Frederick vom Saal and Claude Hughes, "An Extensive New Literature Concerning Low-Dose Effects of Bisphenol A Shows the Need for a New Risk Assessment," *Environmental Health Perspectives*, volume 113, pp. 926–933, 2005.

32. These figures come from Cheryl Fryar and colleagues, "Prevalence of Obesity Among Children and Adolescents: United States, Trends 1963–1965 Through 2009–2010," published September 13, 2012, by the Centers for Disease Control and Prevention, full text online at www.cdc.gov/nchs/data/hestat/obesity_child_09_10/obesity_child_09_10.htm.

33. Yann Klimentidis and colleagues, "Canaries in the Coal Mine: A Cross-Species Analysis of the Plurality of Obesity Epidemics," *Proceedings of the Royal Society*, volume 278, pp. 1626–1632, 2011.

34. Jill Schneider and colleagues, "Our Stolen Figures: The Interface of Sexual Differentiation, Endocrine Disruptors, Maternal Programming, and Energy Balance," *Hormones and Behavior*, volume 66, pp. 104–119, 2014. See also Shane Regnier and Robert Sargis, "Adipocytes Under Assault: Environmental Disruption of Adipocyte Physiology," *Biochimica et Biophysica Acta—Molecular Basis of Disease*, volume 1842, pp. 520–533, 2014.

35. Nathaniel Mead, "Origins of Obesity: Chemical Exposures," *Environmental Health Perspectives*, volume 112, p. A344, 2004.

36. The quotation is from Mead, "Origins of Obesity," cited above. For a scholarly presentation of these findings, see Frederick vom Saal, "The Estrogenic Endocrine Disrupting Chemical Bisphenol A (BPA) and Obesity," *Molecular and Cellular Endocrinology*, volume 354, pp. 74–84, 2012.

37. Ines Sedlmeyer and Mark Palmert, "Delayed Puberty: Analysis of a Large Case Series from an Academic Center," *Journal of Clinical Endocrinology and Metabolism*, volume 87, pp. 1613–1620, 2002.

38. Antony Johansen and colleagues, "Fracture Incidence in England and Wales: A Study Based on the Population of Cardiff," *Injury*, volume 28, pp. 655–660, 1997.

39. A. Gulati and colleagues, "Pediatric Fractures: Temporal Trends and Cost Implications of Treatment Under General Anesthesia," *European Journal of Trauma and Emergency Surgery*, volume 38, pp. 59–64, 2012.

40. Juha-Jaakko Sinikumpu, *Forearm Shaft Fractures in Children* (Oulu, Finland: Oulu University Hospital, 2013), full text online at http://herkules.oulu.fi/isbn9789526203003/isbn9789526203003.pdf. A condensed version of this report was published under the title "The Changing Pattern of Pediatric Both-Bone Forearm Shaft Fractures Among 86,000 Children from 1997 to 2009," *European Journal of Pediatric Surgery*, volume 23, pp. 289–296, 2013. See also C. E. de Putter and colleagues, "Trends in Wrist Fractures in Children and Adolescents, 1997–2009," *Journal of Hand Surgery*, volume 36, pp. 1810–1815, 2011.

41. For more documentation of the shift away from milk toward soda over the past 40 years, see chapter 2 of my book *The Collapse of Parenting* (New York: Basic Books, 2015). For an overview of the literature demonstrating how cola beverages adversely affect bone mineralization in children, see my chapter "Dietary Phosphorus as a Nutritional Toxin: The Influence of Age and Sex," pp. 158–168 in *Annual Reviews in Food & Nutrition*, edited by Victor Preedy (London: Taylor and Francis, 2003).

42. E. M. Clark and colleagues, "Adipose Tissue Stimulates Bone Growth in Prepubertal Children," *Journal of Clinical Endocrinology & Metabolism*, volume 91, pp. 2534–2541, 2006.

43. Dimitrios Agas and colleagues, "Endocrine Disruptors and Bone Metabolism," *Archives of Toxicology*, volume 87, pp. 735–751, 2013.

44. See Mari Golub and colleagues, "Endocrine Disruption in Adolescence: Immunologic, Hematologic, and Bone Effects in Monkeys," *Toxicological Sciences*, volume 82, pp. 598–607, 2004; Monica Lind and colleagues, "Abnormal Bone Composition in Female Juvenile American Alligators from a Pesticide-Polluted Lake (Lake Apopka, Florida)," *Environmental Health Perspectives*, volume 112, pp. 359–362, 2004; and Christian Sonne and colleagues, "Is Bone Mineral Composition

Disrupted by Organochlorines in East Greenland Polar Bears (*Ursus maritimus*)?" *Environmental Health Perspectives*, volume 112, pp. 1711–1716, 2004.

45. In chapter 5 of my book *Girls on the Edge* (New York: Basic Books, 2010), I focused on research on the play behaviors of human children compared with monkeys. In our species, and in monkeys, juvenile males prefer to play with a dull gray truck—with wheels—rather than with a colorful plush doll without wheels. See, for example, Janice Hassett, Erin Siebert, and Kim Wallen, "Sex Differences in Rhesus Monkey Toy Preferences Parallel Those of Children," *Hormones and Behavior*, volume 54, pp. 359–364, 2008. Other researchers have reported similar sex differences in chimpanzees. See, for example, Sonya Kahlenberg and Richard Wrangham, "Sex Differences in Chimpanzees' Use of Sticks as Play Objects Resemble Those of Children," *Current Biology*, volume 20, pp. 1067–1068, 2010.

46. A. K. Hotchkiss and colleagues, "Androgens and Environmental Antiandrogens Affect Reproductive Development and Play Behavior in the Sprague-Dawley Rat," *Environmental Health Perspectives*, volume 110, Supplement 3, pp. 435–439, 2002.

47. See Beverly Rubin and colleagues, "Evidence of Altered Brain Sexual Differentiation in Mice Exposed Perinatally to Low, Environmentally Relevant Levels of Bisphenol A," *Endocrinology*, volume 147, pp. 3681–3691, 2006; and Frederick vom Saal, "Bisphenol A Eliminates Brain and Behavior Sex Dimorphisms in Mice: How Low Can You Go?" *Endocrinology*, volume 147, pp. 3679–3680, 2006.

48. See, for example, Ernie Hood's essay, "Are EDCs Blurring Issues of Gender?" *Environmental Health Perspectives*, volume 113, pp. A670–A677, 2005.

49. Leonard Paulozzi, "International Trends in Rates of Hypospadias and Cryptorchidism," *Environmental Health Perspectives*, volume 107, pp. 297–302, 1999. Paulozzi's dataset ends in the mid-1990s, but more recent data show that the rates of both hypospadias and cryptorchidism continue to climb. See the International Clearinghouse for Birth Defects Surveillance and Research Annual Report

2012, online at www.icbdsr.org/filebank/documents/ar2005
/Report2012.pdf. According to this report, the rate of hypospadias
more than quintupled in Atlanta, Georgia, between 1974–1980 and
2006–2010 (p. 235). See also C. L. Acerini and colleagues, "The De-
scriptive Epidemiology of Congenital and Acquired Cryptorchidism
in a UK Infant Cohort," *Archives of Diseases in Childhood*, volume 94,
pp. 868–872, 2009. These researchers document a phenomenon that
they call "ascending testis," a.k.a. *acquired* cryptorchidism, in which a
baby is born with normally descended testicles, but one or both testicles subsequently climbs back up into the inguinal canal.

50. Thomas Travison and colleagues, "A Population-Level Decline
in Serum Testosterone Levels in American Men," *Journal of Clinical
Endocrinology and Metabolism*, volume 92, pp. 196–202, 2007. A
similar decline has been documented in Europe. See Anna-Maria
Andersson and colleagues, "Secular Decline in Male Testosterone
and Sex Hormone Binding Globulin Serum Levels in Danish Population Surveys," *Journal of Clinical Endocrinology and Metabolism*, volume 92, pp. 4696–4705, 2007.

51. See, for example, Tina Lassen and colleagues, "Trends in Male
Reproductive Health and Decreasing Fertility: Possible Influence of
Endocrine Disruptors," *International Studies in Population*, volume
11, pp. 117–135, 2014. See also Julia Barrett, "Fertile Grounds for
Inquiry: Environmental Effects on Human Reproduction," *Environ-
mental Health Perspectives*, volume 114, pp. A644–A649, 2006.

52. Nils Skakkebæk, E. Rajpert-De Meyts, and Katharina Main,
"Testicular Dysgenesis Syndrome: An Increasingly Common Developmental Disorder with Environmental Aspects," *Human Reproduction*, volume 16, pp. 972–978, 2001. The quotations are from p. 977.

53. Shanna H. Swan and colleagues, "Decrease in Anogenital
Distance Among Male Infants with Prenatal Phthalate Exposure,"
Environmental Health Perspectives, volume 113, pp. 1056–1061,
2005. For a more recent update on this research, see Dr. Swan's
paper (with six colleagues), "First Trimester Phthalate Exposure
and Anogenital Distance in Newborns," *Human Reproduction*,

volume 30, pp. 963–972, 2015. See also L. P. Bustamante-Montes and colleagues, "Prenatal Exposure to Phthalates Is Associated with Decreased Anogenital Distance and Penile Size in Male Newborns," *Journal of Developmental Origins of Health and Disease*, volume 4, pp. 300–306, 2013.

54. This exact phrase comes from Dr. Swan's e-mail to me, February 7, 2007.

55. See, for example, Norman Barlow and colleagues, "Male Reproductive Tract Lesions at Six, Twelve, and Eighteen Months of Age Following In Utero Exposure to Di(n-butyl) Phthalate," *Toxicology and Pathology*, volume 32, pp. 79–90, 2004; and Makato Ema and Emiko Miyawaki, "Adverse Effects on Development of the Reproductive System in Male Offspring of Rats Given Monobutyl Phthalate, a Metabolite of Dibutyl Phthalate, During Late Pregnancy," *Reproductive Toxicology*, volume 15, pp. 189–194, 2001.

56. Shanna Swan, E. P. Elkin, and L. Fenster, "The Question of Declining Sperm Density Revisited: An Analysis of 101 Studies Published 1934–1996," *Environmental Health Perspectives*, volume 108, pp. 961–966, 2000.

57. See Loa Nordkap and colleagues, "Regional Differences and Temporal Trends in Male Reproductive Health Disorders: Semen Quality May Be a Sensitive Marker of Environmental Exposures," *Molecular and Cellular Endocrinology*, volume 355, pp. 221–230, 2012; M. Rolland and colleagues, "Decline in Semen Concentration and Morphology in a Sample of 26,609 Men Close to General Population Between 1989 and 2005 in France," *Human Reproduction*, volume 28, pp. 462–470, 2013; Jaime Mendiola, "Sperm Counts May Have Declined in Young University Students in Southern Spain," *Andrology*, volume 1, pp. 408–413, 2013; Helena Virtanen and colleagues, "Finland Is Following the Trend—Sperm Quality in Finnish Men," *Asian Journal of Andrology*, volume 15, pp. 162–164, 2013; Edson Borges and colleagues, "Decline in Semen Quality Among Infertile Men in Brazil During the Past 10 Years," *International Brazilian Journal of Urology*, volume 41, pp. 757–763, 2015.

This finding has been replicated not only in humans in developed countries around the world but also in cattle. See Tomaz Snoj and colleagues, "Retrospective Study of Bull Semen Quality—Possible Correlation with Pesticide Use?" *Acta Veterinaria Hungarica*, volume 61, pp. 495–504, 2013.

58. Shanna Swan and colleagues, "Geographic Differences in Semen Quality of Fertile U.S. Males," *Environmental Health Perspectives*, volume 111, pp. 414–420, 2003. For a more recent review, see Sheena Martenies and Melissa Perry, "Environmental and Occupational Pesticide Exposure and Human Sperm Parameters: A Systematic Review," *Toxicology*, volume 307, pp. 66–73, 2013.

59. Susan Duty and colleagues, "Phthalate Exposure and Human Semen Parameters," *Epidemiology*, volume 14, pp. 269–277, 2003. See also Richard Grady and Sheela Sathyanarayana, "An Update on Phthalates and Male Reproductive Development and Function," *Pediatric Urology*, volume 13, pp. 307–310, 2012. There is also evidence that exposure to phthalates decreases male hormone levels. See, for example, John Meeker and Kelly Ferguson, "Urinary Phthalate Metabolites Are Associated with Decreased Serum Testosterone in Men, Women, and Children from NHANES 2011–2012," *Journal of Clinical Endocrinology and Metabolism*, volume 99, pp. 4346–4352, 2014; and Jaime Mendiola and colleagues, "Urinary Concentrations of Di(2-ethylhexyl) Phthalate Metabolites and Serum Reproductive Hormones: Pooled Analysis of Fertile and Infertile Men," *Journal of Andrology*, volume 33, pp. 488–498, 2012.

60. Jane Fisher, "Environmental Anti-Androgens and Male Reproductive Health: Focus on Phthalates and Testicular Dysgenesis Syndrome," *Reproduction*, volume 127, pp. 305–315, 2004. See also Lise Aksglaede and colleagues, "The Sensitivity of the Child to Sex Steroids: Possible Impact of Exogenous Estrogens," *Human Reproduction Update*, volume 12, pp. 341–349, 2006.

61. This paragraph summarizes a large body of work. More than 100 studies over the past 30 years have demonstrated the association between testosterone and "drive" in men and the relative lack of such

association in women. Here are some representative studies, in chronological order:

- Alan Booth and colleagues, "Testosterone and Winning and Losing in Human Competition," *Hormones and Behavior*, volume 23, pp. 556–571, 1989.
- B. Gladue, M. Boechler, and K. McCaul, "Hormonal Response to Competition in Human Males," *Aggressive Behavior*, volume 15, pp. 409–422, 1989.
- K. D. McCaul, B. Gladue, and M. Joppa, "Winning, Losing, Mood, and Testosterone," *Hormones and Behavior*, volume 26, pp. 486–504, 1992.
- A. Mazur, E. J. Susman, and S. Edelbrock, "Sex Differences in Testosterone Response to a Video Game Contest," *Evolution and Human Behavior*, volume 18, pp. 317–326, 1997.
- A. Mazur and Alan Booth, "Testosterone and Dominance in Men," *Behavioral and Brain Sciences*, volume 21, pp. 353–363, 1998.
- E. Cashdan, "Are Men More Competitive Than Women?" *British Journal of Social Psychology*, volume 34, pp. 213–229, 1998.
- David Geary and M. V. Flinn, "Sex Differences in Behavioral and Hormonal Response to Social Threat," *Psychological Review*, volume 109, pp. 745–750, 2002.
- H. S. Bateup and colleagues, "Testosterone, Cortisol, and Women's Competition," *Evolution and Human Behavior*, volume 23, pp. 181–192, 2002.
- Katie Kivlighan, Douglas Granger, and Alan Booth, "Gender Differences in Testosterone and Cortisol Response to Competition," *Psychoneuroendocrinology*, volume 30, pp. 58–71, 2005.
- Gonçalo Oliveira and colleagues, "Testosterone Response to Competition in Males Is Unrelated to Opponent Familiarity or Threat Appraisal," *Frontiers in Psychology*, volume 5, article 1240, pp. 1–7, 2014.

62. These recommendations are derived in part from Dr. Swan's article, "Parents Needn't Wait for Legislation to Shield Kids from Toxins in Products," *San Francisco Chronicle*, January 9, 2006.

Chapter 6: End Result: Failure to Launch

1. I am indebted to Walt Prichard for this anecdote—which he insists is a true story.

2. I hosted a symposium at the annual convention of the American Psychological Association in August 2005 on the topic of sex differences in hearing, vision, and smell. Among the presenters at my symposium was Dr. Pamela Dalton of the Monell Chemical Senses Center in Philadelphia. Dr. Dalton has conducted research showing that for many odors, a woman's sense of smell can become 100,000 times more sensitive than any man's. She and her colleagues have published two articles on this topic: Pamela Dalton and colleagues, "Gender-Specific Induction of Enhanced Sensitivity to Odors," *Nature Neuroscience*, volume 5, pp. 199–200, March 2002; and Jeanmarie Diamond, Pamela Dalton, and colleagues "Gender-Specific Olfactory Sensitization: Hormonal and Cognitive Influences," *Chemical Senses*, volume 30, Supplement 1, pp. 224–225, 2005. More recent research has provided evidence of substantial hardwired male/female differences in the olfactory bulb, the organ of smell. See, for example, Ana Oliveira-Pinto and colleagues, "Sexual Dimorphism in the Human Olfactory Bulb: Females Have More Neurons and Glial Cells Than Males," *PLOS One*, November 2014, online at http://journals.plos.org/plosone/article?id=10.1371/journal.pone.0111733.

3. Charles Murray, "What's Wrong with Vocational School?" *Wall Street Journal*, January 17, 2007.

4. All quotations in this paragraph come from Murray, "What's Wrong with Vocational School?"

5. E-mail from Professor Judith Kleinfeld, January 19, 2007.

6. The analysis was "The State of American Manhood," by Tom Mortenson, writing for the September 2006 edition of *Postsecondary Education Opportunity*, www.postsecondary.org.

7. Louis Uchitelle, David Leonhardt, and Amanda Cox, "Men Not Working, and Not Wanting Just Any Job," *New York Times*, July 31, 2006, pp. A1, A18, A19.

8. Steven Hipple, "People Who Are Not in the Labor Force: Why Aren't They Working?" Bureau of Labor Statistics, *Beyond the Numbers*, volume 4, number 15, December 2015, Table 2, "Men Aged 25 to 54 Years Who Did Not Work or Look for Work in 2004 and 2014," www.bls.gov/opub/btn/volume-4/pdf/people-who-are-not -in-the-labor-force-why-arent-they-working.pdf.

9. Laura Sessions Stepp, *Unhooked: How Young Women Pursue Sex, Delay Love and Lose at Both* (New York: Riverhead/Penguin, 2007), p. 9. Stepp hired an independent research group, Child Trends, to conduct this study, www.childtrends.org.

10. As of November 2015, the latest report from the US Census Bureau on this topic is by Jonathan Vespa and colleagues, "America's Families and Living Arrangements: 2012," published by the bureau in 2013, available online at www.census.gov/prod/2013pubs/p20 -570.pdf. These numbers are taken from the Introduction to this publication.

11. These figures come from the graph "Share of Men Never Married, by Cohort," in the Pew Report *Record Share of Americans Have Never Married*, by Wendy Wang and Kim Parker, published September 24, 2014, available online at www.pewsocialtrends.org/2014/09/24 /record-share-of-americans-have-never-married.

12. All quotations in this paragraph are from Blaine Harden's article "Numbers Drop for the Married with Children," *Washington Post*, March 4, 2007.

13. Eduardo Porter and Michelle O'Donnell, "Facing Middle Age with No Degree, and No Wife," *New York Times*, August 6, 2006, p. A18.

14. US Census Bureau, *Families and Living Arrangements*, "Living Arrangements of Adults," Table AD-1, "Young Adults Living at Home," www.census.gov/hhes/families/data/adults.html, accessed October 19, 2015.

15. Centers for Disease Control and Prevention, National Center for Health Statistics, "Data Brief 162: Recent Declines in Nonmarital Childbearing in the United States. Data Table for Figure 1: Number, Percentage, and Rate of Births to Unmarried Women: United States, 1940–2013," online at www.cdc.gov/nchs/data/databriefs/db162 _table.pdf, accessed October 23, 2015.

16. Sam Roberts and colleagues, "51 Percent of Women Are Now Living Without Spouse," *New York Times*, January 16, 2007.

17. US Census, "Families and Living Arrangements: Living Arrangements of Adults," Table UC-1, "Unmarried Couples of the Opposite Sex," www.census.gov/hhes/families/data/adults.html, accessed January 6, 2016.

18. Cynthia Robbins and colleagues, "Prevalence, Frequency, and Associations of Masturbation with Partnered Sexual Behaviors Among US Adolescents," *JAMA Pediatrics*, volume 165, pp. 1087–1093, 2011.

19. See, for example, Jennifer Schneider's paper, "A Qualitative Study of Cybersex Participants: Gender Differences, Recovery Issues, and Implications for Therapists," *Sexual Addiction and Compulsivity*, volume 7, pp. 249–278, 2000. Schneider found many men who had experienced an "escalating pattern of compulsive cybersex use after they discovered Internet sex."

20. Martin Kafka and John Hennen, "The Paraphilia-Related Disorders: An Empirical Investigation of Nonparaphilic Hypersexuality Disorders in Outpatient Males," *Journal of Sex and Marital Therapy*, volume 25, pp. 305–319, 1999.

21. Najah S. Musacchio, Molly Hartrich, and Robert Garofalo, "Erectile Dysfunction and Viagra Use: What's Up with College-Age Males?" *Journal of Adolescent Health*, volume 39, pp. 452–454, 2006. These authors surveyed sexually active males from 18 to 25 years of

age. The abstract is confusing: in the abstract, the authors state that "13% reported ED . . . [and] 25% reported ED occurring with condom use." In the full text, the authors explain that 29 out of 234 of the men reported erectile dysfunction, while 58 men reported erectile dysfunction occurring primarily when putting on a condom: the penis became soft as the man attempted to put on the condom. Twenty men had both erectile dysfunction and erectile dysfunction with condom use. A total of 78 men therefore had some form of erectile dysfunction (either with or without condom use). If you do the math (divide 78 by 234), you get 0.333, or 33.3 percent: one out of three.

22. Amado Bechara and colleagues, "Recreational Use of Phosphodiesterase Type 5 Inhibitors by Healthy Young Men," *Journal of Sexual Medicine*, volume 7, pp. 3736–3742, 2010.

23. The article I wrote, "What's Happening to Boys?," was published in the *Washington Post*, March 31, 2006. The e-mail I quoted was written not directly in response to the article, but in follow-up to the online real-time chat hosted by the *Washington Post*, based on my article.

24. The monograph in question is *net.seXXX: Readings on Sex, Pornography, and the Internet*, edited by Dennis Waskul (New York: Peter Lang Publishing, 2004). The quotation is from Andreas Philaretou's review of this monograph, which appeared in the *Journal of Sex Research* under the title "Sexuality and the Internet," volume 42, pp. 180–181, 2005.

25. Andreas Philaretou, "Sexuality and the Internet."

26. See, for example, Gail Gines, *Pornland: How Porn Has Hijacked Our Sexuality* (Boston: Beacon Press, 2011). See also Ariel Levy, *Female Chauvinist Pigs: Women and the Rise of Raunch Culture* (New York: Free Press, 2005).

27. Erik Hedegaard, "The Dirty Mind and Lonely Heart of John Mayer," *Rolling Stone* (cover story), February 4, 2010.

28. You can read the full text of John Mayer's interview with *Playboy* (without the photos), at this link: http://dbeaumonte.com/2010/02/10/what-did-john-mayer-say-read-full-playboy-article-here.

29. The full transcript of the online conversation appears at *Washington Post*, www.washingtonpost.com/wp-dyn/content/discussion/2006/03/30/DI2006033001398.html.

30. For the streaming audio of the program (42 minutes), see "Failure to Launch," WBUR, *On Point with Tom Ashbrook*, April 4, 2006, http://onpoint.wbur.org/2006/04/04/failure-to-launch.

31. See, for example, "Mammoni: The 'Mama's Boys' of Italy," CBS News, March 4, 2001, www.cbsnews.com/videos/mammoni-the-mamas-boys-of-italy.

32. For more about the *hikikomori*, see Michael Zielenziger's book *Shutting Out the Sun: How Japan Created Its Own Lost Generation* (New York: Nan A. Talese, 2006).

Chapter 7: The Fifth Factor: The Revenge of the Forsaken Gods

1. I am grateful to my former patient Anders Eklof for suggesting this title.

2. J. R. Moehringer, *The Tender Bar* (New York: Hyperion, 2005), p. 39.

3. David Brooks, "Virtues and Victims," *New York Times*, April 9, 2006.

4. David Gilmore, *Manhood in the Making: Cultural Concepts of Masculinity* (New Haven, CT: Yale University Press, 1990), pp. 14–15.

5. Gilmore, *Manhood in the Making*, p. 25.

6. Elisabeth Griffith, PhD, personal communication, November 6, 2003.

7. Gary Leupp, *Male Colors: The Construction of Homosexuality in Tokugawa Japan* (Berkeley: University of California Press, 1996).

8. Thorkil Vanggaard, *Phallos: A Symbol and Its History in the Male World* (New York: International Universities Press, 1972). For more about the status of homosexuality among the Spartans and other ancient Greeks, see chapter 3 of Vanggaard's book, "Phallic Worship in Ancient Greece," pp. 59–70.

9. Actually there have been two cultures on record that have broken these rules: two cultures in which brave men were not esteemed above cowards, and in which hardworking men were not celebrated: Tahiti and Semai. The Semai are found today only in the remotest parts of central Malaysia. This culture has no tradition of masculinity, no competitions, no private ownership of land, and no notion of protecting women from other men. "Without any conception of male honor or paternal rights to inspire them, the Semai men make no effort to resist," Gilmore writes in *Manhood in the Making* (p. 212). "In short, the Semai men do not worry about honor, paternity, or social boundaries." There is little gender differentiation in the adult life of the Semai. All possessions are held in common. The Semai have "not even the remotest notion of 'protecting your own,' as the concept 'your own' has no meaning to them" (p. 214). If you want to study the Semai, you'd better buy your tickets soon. This culture is vanishing with astonishing speed: it appears to be completely unable to survive even incidental contact with other cultures.

The second case was the indigenous culture of Tahiti—a culture that is now extinct. Gilmore concludes that the native Tahitian culture was perhaps the most gender-blind society of which we have detailed knowledge. Even today, the Tahitian language has no terms that specify male or female. Adult roles in traditional Tahiti were also as nearly gender-blind as human physiology can allow. Men shared roughly equally with women in childrearing, cooking, and keeping house.

What factors enabled Tahiti to create such a gender-neutral culture? The first is, most likely, plentiful resources. Gilmore observes that resources are abundant on Tahiti and the surrounding islands. Food is easily obtained without much effort or risk. Most human communities have to deal with scarcity and limited resources. The anomaly of Tahiti, with its seemingly inexhaustible abundance, creates a unique situation that cannot be generalized to almost any other place on earth. Gilmore himself, in his conclusion (p. 224), writes that "the harsher the environment and the scarcer the resources, the more manhood is stressed as inspiration and goal."

The second factor that explains the uniqueness of Tahiti's native culture—and very likely the culture of Semai as well—is the lack of contact with other cultures. Gilmore argues that one of the chief functions of "real men" in most human communities is to manage encounters with other communities: either to subordinate those cultures through violent conflict, or to negotiate peaceful relations with them. Tahitians had no meaningful or sustained contact with other cultures until the arrival of European colonists in the early 1800s. Barely 60 years elapsed from the arrival of the first missionaries in 1815 to the complete collapse of native Tahitian culture following the death of Queen Pomare IV in 1877. "Within a generation, traditional [Tahitian] culture had been all but obliterated," according to Jean-Bernard Carillet, in *Tahiti and French Polynesia* (Melbourne, Australia: LP Publications, 2000), p. 13. The Semai, as I have already observed, are practically extinct as well, except in the most remote enclaves.

Neither of these cultures could survive contact with outside cultures even for the span of a single lifetime. I assert that the rapid collapse of these cultures suggests that enduring cultures need to have "real men" in order for the culture to survive contact with other cultures. Gender-blind cultures do not endure.

10. I am referring, of course, to the Kinaaldá ceremony. For a lightweight but wonderfully photographed introduction to this ceremony, I recommend Monty Roessel's photographic essay *Kinaaldá: A Navajo Girl Grows Up* (Minneapolis: Lerner, 1993).

11. Peggy Drexler, *Raising Boys Without Men: How Maverick Moms Are Creating the Next Generation of Exceptional Men* (Emmaus, PA: Rodale, 2006), p. 92.

12. My comment about "rappers who boast of being, or who pretend to be, convicted felons" is a reference to Lil Wayne and Akon, respectively. Lil Wayne was convicted of felony firearms offenses, and he reminds the listener of that fact in, for example, his song "Paint Tha Town."

But at least Lil Wayne is telling the truth about his criminal past: Lil Wayne actually *is* a convicted felon who has done time behind bars for his crime. Akon, a.k.a. Aliaume Thiam, is one of the most successful hip-hop artists of the 21st century, with more than ten songs certified as platinum. He boasted of being the mastermind behind a car theft ring that specialized in stealing Porsches and Lamborghinis, claiming to have been convicted of grand theft auto and to have served three years, from 1999 to 2002, in the Georgia state penitentiary. All those claims turn out to be false. He was never convicted of grand theft auto and has never been inside the Georgia state penitentiary (although he was held in the DeKalb County Jail, on charges of possession of stolen property, before charges were dropped). According to a story on The Smoking Gun, "Akon has overdubbed his biography with the kind of grit and menace that he apparently believes music consumers desire from their hip-hop stars. Akon's invented tales appear to be part of a cynical marketing plan. Akon repeats the phrase 'notorious car theft operation' so frequently it seems like he is reading it from a sheet of talking points." See "Akon's Con Job," The Smoking Gun, April 16, 2008, www.thesmokinggun.com/documents/crime/akons-con-job, accessed October 30, 2015.

13. Gilmore, *Manhood in the Making*, p. 11.

14. Gilmore, *Manhood in the Making*, p. 150.

15. Gilmore, *Manhood in the Making*, p. 95.

16. Jeffrey P. Hantover, "The Boy Scouts and the Validation of Masculinity," *Journal of Social Issues*, volume 34, pp. 184–195, 1978. See also Julia Grant's article "A 'Real Boy' and Not a Sissy: Gender, Childhood, and Masculinity, 1890–1940," *Journal of Social History*, volume 37, pp. 829–851, Summer 2004.

17. Alfred Habegger, *Gender, Fantasy, and Realism in American Literature* (New York: Columbia University Press, 1982), pp. 199–200.

18. Gilmore, *Manhood in the Making*, p. 108.

19. Gilmore, *Manhood in the Making*, p. 136.

20. Gilmore, *Manhood in the Making*, p. 141.

21. Gilmore, *Manhood in the Making*, p. 145.

22. Gilmore, *Manhood in the Making*, p. 39.

23. Here are some citations demonstrating that girls whose families have recently immigrated to the United States are less likely to be anxious or depressed compared with girls born and raised in the United States:

- Margarita Alegria and colleagues, "Prevalence of Mental Illness in Immigrant and Non-immigrant Latino Groups," *American Journal of Psychiatry*, volume 165, pp. 359–369, 2008, full text online at no charge at National Center for Biotechnology Information, US National Library of Medicine, National Institutes of Health (NIH), www.ncbi.nlm.nih.gov /pmc/articles/PMC2712949.
- Huong Nguyen, "Asians and the Immigrant Paradox," pp. 1–22 in *Asian American and Pacific Islander Children and Mental Health*, volume 1, edited by Frederick Leong and Linda Juang (New York: Praeger, 2011).
- Liza Suárez and colleagues, "Prevalence and Correlates of Childhood-Onset Anxiety Disorders Among Latinos and Non-Latino Whites in the United States," *Psicologia Conductual / Behavioral Psychology*, volume 17, pp. 89–109, 2009, full text available online at no charge at National Center for Biotechnology Information, US National Library of Medicine, NIH, www.ncbi.nlm.nih.gov/pmc/articles/PMC2800359.
- David Takeuchi and colleagues, "Immigration and Mental Health: Diverse Findings in Asian, Black, and Latino Populations," *American Journal of Public Health*, volume 97, pp. 11– 12, 2007. This article is an introduction to a special issue of the *American Journal of Public Health* (*AJPH*) devoted to documenting and understanding the interaction between immigration status and mental health in the United States. Full text online at National Center for Biotechnology Information, US National Library of Medicine, NIH, www.ncbi.nlm.nih.gov /pmc/articles/PMC1716240. From that special issue of *AJPH*,

see, for example, "Immigration-Related Factors and Mental Disorders Among Asian Americans," *American Journal of Public Health*, volume 97, pp. 84–90, full text at *AJPH*, http:// ajph.aphapublications.org/doi/abs/10.2105/AJPH.2006.088401. This article documents a peculiar gender quirk in the immigrant paradox: while the immigrant-paradox effect was generally stronger for females than for males (i.e., being born outside of the United States was more protective for females than for males), English-language proficiency was a greater risk factor for males than for females. If you are male, and you were born in Asia, and you move to the United States, then mastering English puts you at greater risk of mental disorder; but that's not true if you are female. Go figure.

Here is some of the evidence that girls whose families have recently immigrated to the United States are less likely than American-born girls to engage in binge drinking or other forms of alcohol and/or substance abuse:

- Michele Allen and colleagues, "The Relationship Between Spanish Language Use and Substance Use Behaviors Among Latino Youth," *Journal of Adolescent Health*, volume 43, pp. 372–379, 2008.
- Donald Hernandez and colleagues, "Children in Immigrant Families: Demography, Policy, and Evidence for the Immigrant Paradox," in *The Immigrant Paradox in Children and Adolescents: Is Becoming American a Developmental Risk?* edited by Cynthia García Coll and Amy Kerivan Marks (Washington, DC: American Psychological Association, 2011).
- Guillermo Prado and colleagues, "What Accounts for Differences in Substance Use Among U.S.-Born and Immigrant Hispanic Adolescents? Results from a Longitudinal Prospective Cohort Study," *Journal of Adolescent Health*, volume 45, pp. 118–125, 2009. Prado and his colleagues document that foreign-born Hispanic adolescents are significantly less likely to engage in drug abuse than similarly situated US-born

Hispanic adolescents. They conclude that the key difference is that the US-born Hispanic teens are looking to their same-age peers for guidance, while the foreign-born Hispanic teens are looking to their parents and to other adults for guidance.

- William Armando Vega and colleagues, "Illicit Drug Use Among Mexicans and Mexican Americans in California: The Effects of Gender and Acculturation," *Addiction*, volume 93, pp. 1839–1850, 1998.

    For more documentation of the immigrant paradox with regard to adolescent sexuality, particularly intercourse before 15 years of age, see Marcela Raffaelli, Hyeyoung Kang, and Tristan Guarini, "Exploring the Immigrant Paradox in Adolescent Sexuality: An Ecological Perspective," chapter 5 in Coll and Marks, editors, *The Immigrant Paradox in Children and Adolescents*, cited above. See also Tristan Guarini and colleagues, "The Immigrant Paradox in Sexual Risk Behavior Among Latino Adolescents: Impact of Immigrant Generation and Gender," *Applied Developmental Science*, volume 15, pp. 201–209, 2011.

24. For studies demonstrating that boys born in the United States are at higher risk of psychiatric disorders compared with boys born outside the United States, see the previous note. Here are some citations demonstrating that boys who are first-generation immigrants are less likely than US-born boys to engage in delinquent behaviors such as street racing or criminal violence:

- Xi Chen and Hua Zhong, "Delinquency and Crime Among Immigrant Youth—An Integrative Review of Theoretical Explanations," *Laws*, volume 2, pp. 210–232, 2013.
- Donald Hernandez and colleagues, "Children in Immigrant Families: Demography, Policy, and Evidence for the Immigrant Paradox," in Coll and Marks, editors, *The Immigrant Paradox in Children and Adolescents*, cited above. These researchers find that "the immigrant paradox holds true regarding delinquency, both before and after controlling for

[socioeconomic status], for most groups across the first and second generations but not across the second and third generations. The first generation of nearly all groups is less likely than Whites in native-born families [in the USA] to have engaged in delinquent behaviors."

- John MacDonald and Jessica Saunders, "Are Immigrant Youth Less Violent? Specifying the Reasons and Mechanisms," *Annals of the American Academy of Political and Social Science*, volume 641, pp. 125–147, 2012.

The boy who says "School is a stupid waste of time" is a boy who is not *academically engaged*. Here are some of the studies demonstrating that boys born in the United States are less academically engaged compared with boys who have immigrated to the United States:

- Emily Greenman, "Educational Attitudes, School Peer Context, and the Immigrant Paradox in Education," *Social Science Research*, volume 42, pp. 698–714, 2013.
- Lingin Hao and Yingyi Ma, "Immigrant Youth in Postsecondary Education," chapter 12 in Coll and Marks, editors, *The Immigrant Paradox in Children and Adolescents*, cited above.
- Carola Suárez-Orozco and colleagues, "Unraveling the Immigrant Paradox: Academic Engagement and Disengagement Among Recently Arrived Immigrant Youth," *Youth and Society*, volume 41, pp. 151–185, 2009.
- Vivian Tseng, "Family Interdependence and Academic Adjustment in College: Youth from Immigrant and U.S.-Born Families," *Child Development*, volume 75, pp. 966–983, 2004. Tseng finds that the key factor explaining the immigrant paradox in her study of 998 youth with Asian Pacific, Latino, African / Afro-Caribbean, and European backgrounds was the sense of "family obligation" that many of the immigrant youths felt, but that many of the US-born youths did *not* feel.

25. For a sympathetic treatment of this topic and an exploration of the barriers to assimilation facing immigrants prior to 1960, see

328   Notes to Chapter 8

Milton Gordon's monograph *Assimilation in American Life: The Role of Race, Religion, and National Origins* (New York: Oxford University Press, 1964).

26. Coll and Marks, editors, *The Immigrant Paradox in Children and Adolescents*, cited above.

27. See notes 23 and 24 above.

28. Sherry Benton and associates, "Changes in counseling center client problems across 13 years," *Professional Psychology: Research and Practice*, volume 34, p. 69, 2003.

29. The experts convened at Dartmouth wrote a monograph entitled *Hardwired to Connect: The New Scientific Case for Authoritative Communities* (New York: Broadway, 2003). This quotation is from p. 10 of that monograph.

30. Alison Cooper, "One Mazda, Two Mishaps, and a Couple of Lessons in Parenting," *Washington Post*, November 19, 2006, p. B8, www.washingtonpost.com/wp-dyn/content/article/2006/11/17/AR2006111701421.html.

31. *Hardwired to Connect*, pp. 23, 24.

32. Harvey Mansfield, *Manliness* (New Haven, CT: Yale University Press, 2006), p. 17.

33. Mansfield, *Manliness*, p. 23.

34. Mansfield, *Manliness*, p. 20.

35. Mansfield, *Manliness*, p. 20.

Chapter 8: Detox

1. Rhea Borja, "Nebraska Tangles with U.S. over Testing," *Education Week*, February 21, 2007.

2. Rhea Borja, "Nebraska Swims Hard Against Testing's Tides," *Education Week*, February 21, 2007, pp. 32, 33, 34.

3. Betsy Stahler and Jill Renn spoke at the National Association for Single Sex Public Education (NASSPE) Midwest Regional Conference in Lisle, Illinois, on October 14, 2006.

4. Roland Gorges, "Der Waldkindergarten," *Unsere Jugend*, Spring 2000, pp. 275–281. See also Amanda Kane and Judy Kane, "Waldkindergarten in Germany," *Green Teacher*, volume 94, pp. 16–19, 2011.

5. The statement about more than 1,500 Waldkindergärten, as well as the quotation from Schulte-Ostermann, come from Rupert Neate's English-language article for the international website of *Der Spiegel*, "Campfire Kids: Going Back to Nature with Forest Kindergartens," November 22, 2013, www.spiegel.de/international /zeitgeist/forest-kindergartens-could-be-the-next-big-export-from -germany-a-935165.html.

6. A handful of American schools now offer a *Waldkindergarten* experience. See Kathy Boccella, "Into the Woods: At Chesco School, the Emphasis Is on Outdoors," *Philadelphia Inquirer*, November 8, 2015, pp. B1, B2. See also Ruth Wilson's article "Teaching Among the Trees," *American Forests*, Winter 2012, www.americanforests.org/ magazine/article/teaching-among-the-trees.

7. Ernesto Londoño and Ruben Castaneda, "Driver Who Hit Race Crowd Tried to Stop, Uncle Says," *Washington Post*, February 19, 2008.

8. All quotations in these two paragraphs come from George P. Blumberg's article for the *New York Times*, "Full Throttle and Fully Legal," September 17, 2004.

9. Bill Center, "RaceLegal Praised for Contributing to Decline in Street Racing," *San Diego Union-Tribune*, December 22, 2005.

10. See my op-ed article "Teens Will Speed: Let's Watch Them Do It," *Washington Post*, November 28, 2004, p. B8.

11. Charles Moore, "Give Car Racers a Chance," *Halifax Daily News* (Nova Scotia), August 13, 2007, p. 11.

12. Valerie Kalfrin, "Police Offer Racers Chance to Beat Heat," *Tampa Tribune*, December 18, 2006, Metro, p. 1.

13. Moore, "Give Car Racers a Chance," p. 11.

14. The five racing options in this sentence are drawn from the list of ten posted at Guyspeed, http://guyspeed.com/10-wild-places-to -legally-race-your-car/, accessed November 2, 2015.

15. Elizabeth Roberts, "A Rush to Medicate Young Minds," *Washington Post*, October 8, 2006, p. B7.

16. Dr. Kathleen Salyer, personal communication, November 3, 2015.

17. Rhoda Miel, "With 1 Billion Pounds of PLA Sold, Nature-Works Sees Rapid Growth to 2 Billion," *Plastics News*, March 6, 2014.

18. Amanda Datnow, Lea Hubbard, and Elisabeth Woody, *Is Single Gender Schooling Viable in the Public Sector?* Ford Foundation, 2001, p. 51. Full text available at http://files.eric.ed.gov/fulltext /ED471051.pdf, accessed November 20, 2015.

19. Datnow and colleagues, *Is Single Gender Schooling Viable in the Public Sector?* (cited above), p. 7.

20. Centers for Disease Control and Prevention, National Center for Health Statistics, "Data Brief 162: Recent Declines in Nonmarital Childbearing in the United States. Data Table for Figure 1: Number, Percentage, and Rate of Births to Unmarried Women: United States, 1940–2013," online at www.cdc.gov/nchs/data/databriefs/db162 _table.pdf, accessed October 23, 2015.

21. As of November 2015, the latest report from the US Census Bureau on this topic is by Jonathan Vespa and colleagues, "America's Families and Living Arrangements: 2012," published by the bureau in 2013, available online at www.census.gov/prod/2013pubs /p20-570.pdf. These figures are taken from the Introduction to this publication.

22. All quotations in these two paragraphs come from Lonnae O'Neal Parker's article for the *Washington Post*, "The Old Kinship Team 33 Laments Disintegration of Traditional Values, Ties," December 29, 2006, pp. A1, A10.

23. Actually, in 2015, two women were ordained as *rabbot* in Jerusalem. But the standard rule in Orthodox Judaism remains: no female rabbis. See the article by Rabbi Yehoshua Looks, "Why Orthodox Jews in Israel Can Ordain Women as Rabbis, but Those in the Diaspora Won't," *Haaretz*, June 18, 2015.

24. For an introduction to Campbell's ideas, you might start with the book he coauthored with Bill Moyers, based on the PBS television series they did together, *The Power of Myth* (New York: Anchor, 1991).

25. These biographical details are based on Alice Rains Trulock's biography, *In the Hands of Providence: Joshua L. Chamberlain and the American Civil War* (Chapel Hill: University of North Carolina Press, 1992). See also Edward Longacre's *Joshua Chamberlain: The Soldier and the Man*, reprint edition (New York: Da Capo Press, 2003).

26. Glenn LaFantasie has challenged the conventional view regarding the strategic significance of the events on Little Round Top, in particular with regard to the bayonet charge. He asserts that the 15th Alabama was not preparing a sixth charge up the hill and may in fact have been preparing to retreat—which might explain their hasty surrender in response to the bayonet charge. See his book *Twilight at Little Round Top: July 2, 1863—The Tide Turns at Gettysburg* (Hoboken, NJ: John Wiley and Sons, 2005). For the more traditional view, see, for example, Michael Shaara's Pulitzer Prize–winning *The Killer Angels* (New York: Ballantine, 1974), on which the movie *Gettysburg* was based. Shaara made Chamberlain a major character in his account of the battle, which is drawn from letters and diary entries of the combatants. See also Stephen W. Sears, *Gettysburg* (New York: Houghton Mifflin, 2003).

27. LaFantasie, *Twilight at Little Round Top*, p. 172.

28. LaFantasie, *Twilight at Little Round Top*, p. 189.

29. Sears, *Gettysburg*, p. 296.

30. Innumerable eyewitness records document this account and historians agree on its veracity. See, for example, Trulock, *In the Hands of Providence*, cited above, pp. 304–306.

Index

ADHD (Attention-Deficit
Hyperactivity Disorder)
coed *vs.* single-sex schools,
123–125, 240
description and prevalence,
109–111
diagnosis, 38, 111–113,
114–115, 120–121, 238–
245, 247–249
and endocrine disruptors,
138–139, 142–143
and hate for school, 246–247
medication, 106–108, 110–111,
113–122, 124–125, 245–246,
272–273
and motivation, 41–42, 108,
116–117, 126
and nature, 37–38
overcoming of side effects,
119–125

parental assessment guide,
240–244
parents' stories, 103–108
side effects of medication,
107–108, 115–120, 122,
272–273
The Adventures of Tom Sawyer
(Twain), 109–110
African Americans, NAEP
scores, 45, 46–47
age to begin school, 23–25, 106
Alaskan Native way of life,
159–162
Alito, Justice Samuel, 84–85
*All I Really Need to Know I
Learned in Kindergarten*
(Fulghum), 18
alligators, feminization, 131–132
American Civil Liberties Union
(ACLU), 84

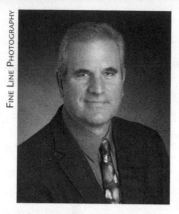

LEONARD SAX, MD, PhD, is a practicing family physician, psychologist, and author of *The Collapse of Parenting, Girls on the Edge*, and *Why Gender Matters*. He lives near Exton, Pennsylvania.